SECOND EDITION

Television
CRITICISM

I dedicate this book to the memory of
my beloved son Christopher, who died on September 12, 2011.

Dear Chris,

The leaves on the Aspen trees in Montana will soon turn gold.

When the wind blows, the leaves whisper.

I will try to hear your voice there and feel your strong spirit.

You will live in my broken heart forever.

SECOND EDITION

Television
CRITICISM

Victoria O'Donnell
Montana State University

SAGE

Los Angeles | London | New Delhi
Singapore | Washington DC

Los Angeles | London | New Delhi
Singapore | Washington DC

FOR INFORMATION:

SAGE Publications, Inc.
2455 Teller Road
Thousand Oaks, California 91320
E-mail: order@sagepub.com

SAGE Publications Ltd.
1 Oliver's Yard
55 City Road
London EC1Y 1SP
United Kingdom

SAGE Publications India Pvt. Ltd.
B 1/I 1 Mohan Cooperative Industrial Area
Mathura Road, New Delhi 110 044
India

SAGE Publications Asia-Pacific Pte. Ltd.
33 Pekin Street #02-01
Far East Square
Singapore 048763

Acquisitions Editor: Matthew Byrnie
Editorial Assistant: Elizabeth Borders
Production Editor: Catherine M. Chilton
Copy Editor: Terri Lee Paulsen
Typesetter: C&M Digitals (P) Ltd.
Proofreader: Annette R. Van Deusen
Indexer: Marilyn Augst
Cover Designer: Anupama Krishnan
Marketing Manager: Liz Thornton
Permissions Editor: Karen Ehrmann

Printed in the United States of America

Library of Congress Cataloging-in-Publication Data

O'Donnell, Victoria.

Television criticism / Victoria O'Donnell. — 2nd ed.

p. cm.
Includes bibliographical references and index.

ISBN 978-1-4129-9105-6 (pbk.)

1. Television criticism. 2. Television criticism—United States. I. Title.

PN1992.8.C7O33 2013
791.45—dc23
2011033243

This book is printed on acid-free paper.

SUSTAINABLE FORESTRY INITIATIVE

Certified Chain of Custody
Promoting Sustainable Forestry
www.sfiprogram.org
SFI-01268

SFI label applies to text stock

12 13 14 15 16 10 9 8 7 6 5 4 3 2 1

Brief Contents

Detailed Contents

PART III: THEORETICAL APPROACHES TO TELEVISION CRITICISM 123

6 Rhetoric and Culture 125

7 Representation and Its Audience 149

8 Postmodernism   165

PART IV: CRITICAL APPLICATIONS   179

9 Guidelines for Television Criticism   181

Preface

*T*elevision Criticism was written to help students become serious watchers of television with critical acumen. Students will determine what questions to ask of a television program, learn how to choose or develop a methodology to answer the questions, and develop informed judgment. *Television Criticism* was designed to enable its readers to understand the various elements of a television program from script to performance in order to analyze, through critical methodology, how the elements make a program what it is; to interpret the sundry meanings that the program may have by understanding the nuances of the culture in which it appears and the multiple meanings it may have for different audiences; to pass judgment on the quality of the program; and to communicate that judgment to others. The goal of the book is to not only produce quality criticism but also to give students going into television careers a foundation for making creative choices.

In addition to having an academic background rich in critical methodologies, I interviewed prominent television directors, producers, writers, and camera operators. I attended rehearsals and tapings of major television shows. I also observed, in person, on tape, or on the Web, many seminars put on by the Academy of Television Arts and Sciences that featured writers, producers, directors, and actors from television series. Consequently, I gained valuable insights into the realities of the television industry.

Television Criticism would be an appropriate text in departments of mass communication, film and television, television studies, and communication. Additionally, it could be used as a text in rhetorical criticism and cultural studies courses.

MAJOR FEATURES

Television Criticism focuses on developing quality criticism using theory-based critical guidelines. Because television production is a business, there are restrictions and limitations; therefore, an explanation of demographics and ratings is included. Also, because television production is a creative endeavor, television style must be understood. Good criticism is based on appropriate theoretical background; therefore there are several chapters on various theories, written in clear and concise language.

Television Criticism is divided into four parts:

- Part I, Orientation: "The Work of the Critic" and "Demystifying the Business of Television"
- Part II, Formal Aspects of Television: "Television Style"; "Television, the Nation's Storyteller"; and "Television Genres"

- Part III, Theoretical Approaches to Television Criticism: "Rhetoric and Culture," "Representation and Its Audience," and "Postmodernism"
- Part IV, Critical Applications: "Guidelines for Television Criticism" and "Sample Criticism of a Television Program: *Parenthood.*"

The ninth chapter transforms the contents of the previous eight chapters into eight categories of questions for analysis and criticism. Students are given a template from which to develop critical methodology designed to address their questions about a specific television program and to write a distinctive critique. The final chapter is a detailed criticism that demonstrates how to use the material in the book to understand and criticize the complexities of a television program.

PEDAGOGICAL AIDS

At the end of each chapter there are exercises for students to apply the concepts they have learned. There are also additional readings listed at the end of each chapter. Boxes containing salient information can be found throughout the book. Examples from contemporary television programs are used throughout the book to illustrate critical techniques. A complete and detailed critical analysis constitutes the last chapter in the book. A glossary of terms is included.

NEW TO THIS EDITION

Internet and digital devices have changed the ways we watch television and some of the ways programs and commercials are produced. Correspondingly, ratings systems have adapted to the new delivery systems. Social media have had an impact on television watching. Television viewers are more active via blogging and have opportunities for interactivity by voting and reacting to programs. All of these changes are included in this new edition. Furthermore, there are many references in the book to ways in which the Internet enhances television criticism. New language terms, such as *digital convergence* (the coming together of media technologies as the result of digitalization and offering alternative ways of viewing television) and *time-shifting*, reflect changes as well.

The book is significantly updated with examples from recent television channels, programs, and techniques. All but one of the photos is new, and there are new boxes and exercises as well. There are more references to statements from directors, art directors, directors of photography, and writers. The sections on rhetoric, culture, representation, and postmodernism have been updated. A glossary has been added, and the sample criticism in the last chapter is new.

Acknowledgments

Sara Miller McCune, former president of Sage Publications, originally encouraged me to write this book. Todd Armstrong, former editor at Sage, made helpful suggestions for the first edition and encouraged me to write a second edition. Matthew Byrnie, the current editor at Sage, saw me through the second edition with support and encouragement. Elizabeth Borders, editorial assistant, tirelessly assisted me in acquiring screenshots and preparing the book for production. Terri Lee Paulsen did a masterful job of copyediting this edition. Many thanks are in order for the outstanding work done by my production editor, Catherine Chilton.

Five reviewers of the first edition—Annette M. Holba, Plymouth State University; Bill Huntzicker, St. Cloud State University; Lynn C. Spangler, State University of New York at New Paltz; John G. Cooper, Eastern Michigan University; and Jenny Nelson, Ohio University—and Erika Johnson-Lewis, who joined them in reviewing this new edition—offered many valuable suggestions, which I hope I have incorporated to their satisfaction.

This book could not have been written without the hundreds of students who took my film and television classes and who wrote graduate theses and dissertations about film and television under my direction. They have been a joy to teach and to join in discussions about films and television programs. It pleases me so much that many of them still stay in touch with me.

I also wish to thank my friends Patricia Hill, camera operator for *M*A*S*H, Cheers, Frasier, Caroline in the City, The New Adventures of Old Christine,* and *S#*! My Dad Says,* and Jeff Meyer, director for *Coach, Everybody Loves Raymond, Yes, Dear,* and *Mad Love,* for introducing me to their writers, directors, and producers, and for letting me sit in on television program run-throughs and taping. They also provided very useful information about the television business.

I also wish to acknowledge Paul Monaco's valuable contribution to this book. He co-authored Chapter 3, "Television Style," which reflects his personal experiences as a film and video creator and educator, and made helpful suggestions to the manuscript.

Introduction

Television presents the new American Dream.

—Ron Howard on *Today,* March 24, 1999

Years ago, when my youngest son came home from a day at the Montessori kindergarten, he watched late-afternoon television shows. I discussed this with his teacher, who said not to worry. "He does stimulating activities in school, so when he comes home, he just wants to relax by watching television," she said. Of course, we all use television to relax. Many people who tire after a day of working at computers, talking and texting on cell phones, and using all kinds of digital gadgets, just want to sit in a comfortable chair to watch television and relax. We laugh at the comedies and watch crimes get solved. Even shows that would not seem to be relaxing, such as the grisly *CSI: Crime Scene Investigation* or *Criminal Minds,* comfort us because we see good triumphing over evil. We can enjoy vicarious experiences by watching reality shows, see how other people live on the talk shows, find out what is news, check the weather, keep up with sports on the news shows and channels, stay informed through public affairs programs, and get new recipes on the food channels. When a national or world crisis occurs, we are more likely to turn on the television. A survey conducted by the Pew Research Center's Internet & American Life Project and *Federal Computer Week* magazine one year after the September 11, 2001, attacks on the World Trade Center in New York City found that 57% of Americans said they would go to their television sets to get information first (Associated Press, 2003, p. A7). Another survey conducted four days after 9/11 found that Americans watched an average of 8.1 hours of television coverage of the disaster (Vedantam, 2001). Television is not only a very important part of our lives, but also it has the power to change our lives. Haynes Johnson, a Pulitzer Prize–winning journalist for *The Washington Post,* said in a speech at the Annenberg School of the University of Pennsylvania in 1993:

> From the fall of the Soviet Union to Tiananmen Square, the umbilical cord of
> television, those electronic impulses, actually moved and changed history. It was
> no one person who led it. It was no Genghis Khan, no Caesar, no Roman Legion,
> but television that really propelled all those events. ("Haynes Johnson Delivers the
> Annenberg Lecture," 1994, p. 5)

Most of you who read this book have never known a life without television. Television sets are turned on for several hours in more than one room in our homes, and they are turned on all day long in malls, fitness clubs, university student unions, bars, restaurants, airports, schools, department stores, appliance stores, and gasoline pumps. We receive television on our iPhones, iPods, iPads, wristwatches, and computers. Television producers shoot more close-ups to accommodate the various small screens. The Fox network developed **"mobisodes,"** customized mini-programs for cell phones to promote television series (McDowell & Ressner, 2006). Shows such as *The Office* and *Battlestar Galactica* can be viewed on *"webisodes,"* specifically designed to be watched online. Video images are featured in rock concerts and fashion shows. Banks have television sets turned on for customers waiting in line to see a teller; hotels put television sets in bathrooms and elevators; dentists are using high-tech headsets that let patients tune to a channel while having their teeth drilled; doctors have the Better Health Network playing in waiting rooms; veterinarians have Animal Planet turned on for clients in the waiting rooms; and many public schools start the day with Channel One, a teen news network with an abundance of athletic shoe and food commercials. Television sets in airports have a special "drown-out" volume control. If people sitting near the set are talking, the volume automatically rises. If you miss a program or forget to record it, you can watch it later on YouTube, Hulu.com, Joost, Google TV Web Browser, and other network sites. Paul Farhi wrote in the *Washington Post,* "Like an invisible gas, television's flickering light . . . has seeped into nooks and crannies that once were blissfully TV-free" (Farhi, 1997, p. 21).

In 1971, when there were three broadcast networks and cable and satellite television were less widespread, the average American household had the set on for slightly more than 6 hours a day (Farhi, 1997). With multiple television sets in households and hundreds of channels to choose from, different family members may be watching preferred programs individually rather than together. The more choices we have, the more likely we are to diverge in our preferences. On the other hand, we may gather together to watch a program while talking to each other about it. This is especially so when we watch a game show such as *Jeopardy* or *Dancing With the Stars.* It is also commonplace to communicate with "friends" on Facebook or Twitter about a show while watching it. James Poniewozik (2010), television critic for *Time,* said "Social media enhance rather than replace [television]. . . . Social media have turned the world into one big living room" (p. 21).

Cable television and satellite transmission deliver hundreds of channels to viewers. Between 2010 and 2011, the number of television channels doubled. Remote control devices make rapid channel switching, known as **"surfing"** or "grazing," a norm for many viewers whose desire for television images cannot be satisfied by one channel at a time. Some television sets have additional windows to allow a viewer to watch a drama while keeping up with a football game. High-definition television (**HDTV**) provides images so sharp that watching the television screen is like looking out a window and is capable of showing up to eight different channels on equal-sized windows on one screen. The Internet enables us to watch television news, programs, features, and sports events on our laptop computers and other devices. Connected television streams specialized programming, movies, and information services from the Internet directly to a television set, bypassing cable and satellite providers. Interactive television via the Internet enables us to vote for contestants on various shows. In addition, the public watches more movies than ever before on rented and purchased DVDs.

Technological advancement has perpetuated the mass production of television images. Historian Asa Briggs said that this basic technological revolution is comparable to the

Industrial Revolution and to other times of radical change in human history "that involved the mind as well as the body" (Haigh, Gerbner, & Byrne, 1981, p. 208). With the information highways of the 21st century and audiovisual innovations for digital convergence, Briggs's analogy seems even more compelling today than when he wrote it in 1981. Let us stop to consider what concerned Briggs when he wrote: "In a world of pictures, we have not learned the simple ABCs of interpretation and criticism" (Haigh et al., 1981, p. 208).

Television images are mediated by television production techniques, by the medium itself, and by the constraints of programming decisions. As Nick Browne said, "Television must be studied in terms of the institution that provides it, the advertising that drives it, and the audience that consumes it" (1994, p. 69). Pay-per-view and DVD rentals and purchases, and the Internet, of course, give us the opportunity to watch recent and older television series and films on our own time. DVD recorders and DVRs (digital video recorders) allow us to record our favorite programs when we are not at home and to fast-forward through the commercials. These devices have changed the way people watch television—formerly, most people were passive *viewers,* but now they have become active *users* (Bellamy & Walker, 1996). They can control what, when, and how they watch. Because people can encounter a variety of programs, watch more than one program at a time, and avoid content they do not want to see, such as commercials, advertisers have been encouraged to try adaptation and corrective strategies to assure their clients that their products are seen. For example, there has been an increase in the 15-second spot, based on the assumption that a shorter commercial would not allow the viewer enough time to zap it. Another strategy incorporated into the shorter spot attempts to simulate grazing or surfing by placing plentiful images and rapid editing of the commercials. Product placement (common in motion pictures), infomercials, and integration of the product and program are other strategies. Because so many network and cable shows could be viewed on the Internet for free, in October 2010, broadcasters turned off access to full episodes when accessed from Google TV Web Browser. This sent the message that broadcasters are demanding to be paid for shows wherever they are seen. Google spokespersons said, "It is ultimately the content owners' choice to restrict users from accessing their content" (Nakashima, 2010, p. D2). Networks like NBC have websites (NBC.com) where entire programs can be watched after they have been aired on television.

The word "television" literally means seeing at a distance. As Joshua Meyrowitz (1985) reminded us, we respond to media images as if we were seeing something firsthand. Physical presence no longer seems required for firsthand experience. The obsessively repeated images of the two airplanes flying into the Twin Towers of the World Trade Center, the explosion of the space shuttle *Challenger,* the earthquake and tsunami in Japan, and the announcement that Osama Bin Laden was killed in Pakistan are examples that provoked "firsthand" reactions from a shocked public in a manner similar to the firsthand reactions of a shocked and grieving public to the assassination of President John F. Kennedy on November 22, 1963. Billions of people around the world watched the televised wedding of Prince William and Kate Middleton in London on April 29, 2011. Each of these instances was not fictional, yet they were mediated with camera work and editing decisions as fictional representation is on television.

Yet the quantity of television programs and varying opportunities in the ways we watch them does not make us better viewers. With more to choose from, it would seem that we could use some help to become more discriminating viewers. This book has been written to help you become a serious watcher of television, for as Alexander Nehamas (1990) wrote in *The South Atlantic Quarterly:* "Television rewards serious watching." A serious television watcher with critical acumen recognizes that criticism employs theoretical and critical standards, and that television is a business that employs talented professionals, who also take television seriously.

Figure 1.1 represents my model of the elements of television that critics should consider.

The **United States Federal Communications Commission (FCC)**—created by an act of Congress on June 19, 1934—regulates broadcasting. The Telecommunications Act of 1996 impels the FCC to promote competition and diversity in the media and to facilitate the transition to digital modes of delivery. While the FCC has many duties, its most controversial mandate is to fine television (and radio) programs on public airways for violating decency standards during the hours between 6 a.m. and 10 p.m. local time when children are likely to be in the audience. The FCC can revoke a license and deny a renewal application. In 2004, when Janet Jackson had a "wardrobe malfunction" during the Super Bowl half-time show, the FCC imposed a $550,000 fine on CBS, which was overturned by the 3rd U.S. Circuit Court in Philadelphia. Since 2006, this and other litigation have raised questions about the Commission's indecency authority, causing the FCC to defer action on most indecency cases, although the Commission continues to review and process cases. The indecency standards apply to over-the-air broadcasters but not to cable and satellite programming.

Figure I.1 O'Donnell Model of the Elements of Television

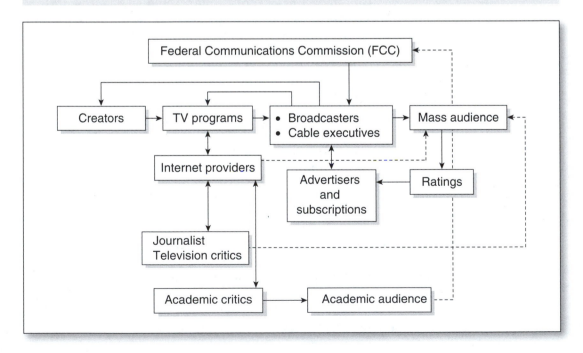

> Legal experts indicate that the Constitution protects free speech on the air. A statement on the FCC Web site refers to this as follows: "The Commission does not take action on indecent material aired between 10 p.m. and 6 a.m. In this way, constitutionally protected free speech rights of adults are balanced with the need to protect children from harmful content." (Federal Communications Commission [2011, March 1]. Regulation of obscenity, indecency, and profanity. Retrieved April 16, 2011, from http://www.fcc.gov/eb/oip)

The *creators* are the writers, producers, artistic directors, directors, costumers, actors, editors, camera operators, sound and music directors, animators, and special effects staff who develop the *television programs,* the finished products. Their creative work and the ways in which a television show is initiated and produced are discussed in Chapter 2, "Demystifying the Business of Television," and in Chapter 3, "Television Style." The producers pitch their programs to the **broadcast and cable channel executives.** The broadcast and cable channel executives are the administrators of the television networks and cable companies, both at the national and local levels. They are very powerful and determine what goes on and stays on the air and on what days and at which times a program is aired. *Advertising* pays for the broadcast channels, while viewer *subscriptions* support cable and satellite programming. The *mass audience* is numbered in the millions and is measured by *ratings,* which, in turn, determine whether a program is successful or not. This is discussed in Chapter 2. *Internet providers* are the multitude of websites sponsored by networks and various companies, such as Hulu.com and Google. **Journalist television critics** write for newspapers and the Internet. They tend to give plot summaries and discuss the pros and cons of story, visual style, and acting. *Academic critics,* which is what you will become, write for an *academic audience* utilizing the theoretical and critical standards discussed in this book. Chapter 1, "The Work of the Critic," discusses the nature of criticism, both journalistic and academic. It offers a critical orientation that will help you determine what and how you will criticize.

This book is divided into four parts: Part I orients you to the work of the critic and the business of television. Part II is about the formal aspects of television—its style, its position as the nation's storyteller, and the classification system known as television genre. Part III will introduce you to the major theoretical approaches to television criticism, rhetoric, cultural studies, representation, and postmodernism. Part IV includes the critical applications, with guidelines for television criticism and a sample criticism of a television show, *Parenthood*. Words that appear in bold in the text can also be found in the Glossary at the end of the book.

SUMMARY

Whether we watch television programs on television sets or computers or on various digital devices, we are still watching television. Whether we watch television programs in real time or through time-shifting via a recording device or on the Internet, we are still watching television. New technology enables us to watch more television when, where, and how we want to watch it. Furthermore, the Internet provides information about programs that is very helpful to the television critic. We can read interviews with the creators and actors, read summaries of forthcoming programs, and watch programs we have missed. Because the Internet is interactive, we can engage with other viewers. It is an exciting time to be a television critic. This book will help you be a better one.

SUGGESTED READINGS

Federal Communications Commission (FCC). Visit its website at http://www.fcc.gov for details of the FCC's responsibilities.

Murphy, Sheila. (2011). *How Television Invented New Media*. New Brunswick, NJ: Rutgers University Press.

Spigel, Lynn, & Olsson, Jan (Eds.). (2004). *Television After TV: Essays on a Medium in Transition*. Durham, NC: Duke University Press.

PART I

Orientation

The Work of the Critic

Oh, gentle lady, do not put me to't. For I am nothing if not critical.

—Iago to Desdemona
(Shakespeare, *Othello*, Act 2, Scene I)

INTRODUCTION

What is the advantage of knowing how to perform television criticism if you are not going to be a professional television critic? The advantage to you as a television viewer is that you will not only be able to make informed judgment about the television programs you watch, but also you will better understand your reaction and the reactions of others who share the experience of watching. Critical acuity enables you to move from casual enjoyment of a television program to a fuller and richer understanding. A viewer who does not possess critical viewing skills may enjoy watching a television program and experience various responses to it, such as laughter, relief, fright, shock, tension, or relaxation. These are fundamental sensations that people may get from watching television, and, for the most part, viewers who are not critics remain at this level. Critical awareness, however, enables you to move to a higher level that illuminates production practices and enhances your understanding of **culture,** human nature, and interpretation.

Students studying television production with ambitions to write, direct, edit, produce, and/or become camera operators will find knowledge of television criticism necessary and useful as well. Television criticism is about the evaluation of content, its context, organization, story and characterization, style, **genre,** and audience desire. Knowledge of these concepts is the foundation of successful production.

THE ENDS OF CRITICISM

Just as critics of books evaluate works of fiction and nonfiction by holding them to established standards, television critics utilize methodology and theory to comprehend, analyze, interpret, and evaluate television programs. As a critic, you can gain greater understanding and appreciation about television programming, as well as about your own culture and the social forces within it. You may also be able to demystify the meaning of a television program and create new perceptions for other viewers by communicating the criticism to them. As a critic, you become a "transformer" capable of generating new understanding and new awareness in the minds of other television viewers. Your comprehension of the importance of producing, writing, directing, camera work, sound, sets, costumes, and other production values opens up your understanding and appreciation of the aesthetic pleasures of good television and provides specific reasons for the displeasure caused by what some regard as poor television. As a critic, you will engage with the essential organization of television programs, context, time-space manipulation, the use of images and language, conventions and variations of genre, narrative patterns, character development, and the episodic nature of television. You will appreciate the recurrence of enduring myths, legends, and character types as they re-appear both in fiction and reality programs. You will also examine social and cultural values, ideology, possible meanings, codes, and the representation of gender, race, sexuality, age, ethnicity, employment, and nationality. As a critic, you must also understand the nature of the business of television and the viewing audience, its expectations, desires, participation, and satisfaction. Criticism also goes beyond understanding of the program itself and asks what conceptual or theoretical implications have resulted.

JOURNALISTIC TELEVISION CRITICISM

Journalists began writing television criticism in 1946, when Jack Gould of *The New York Times* and John Crosby of the *New York Herald Tribune* began reviewing television program content. From that time and into the 1950s, television critics had to wait to see the programs when they were aired in order to write about them because television was broadcast live. After more television programs were made on film, beginning with *I Love Lucy,* critics could preview the shows and have their columns published before the shows were on the air. The critics' reviews were influential because television executives and producers monitored their evaluations of programs; thus the importance of professional television criticism increased. Yet, the programs that the critics praised—e.g., *Studio One,* which broadcast modern plays and adaptations of Shakespeare, and *Playhouse 90,* a televised anthology of 90-minute original and adapted plays—were often not as well liked by the public, which appeared to prefer the classic sitcoms, such as *The Honeymooners* with Jackie Gleason, Art Carney, Audrey Meadows, and Joyce Randolph, and *I Love Lucy* with Lucille Ball and Desi Arnaz. In later years, print television criticism became less important as an influence on program decision making, although government agency personnel read television criticism in trade publications in order to examine responses to possible government policies.

Today there is a decline in newspaper readership, and revenue-starved newspapers have let their television reviewers go or have given them other assignments. Consequently, many former newspaper critics have turned to the Web to continue their work. David Bianculli, former critic for New York's *Daily News,* founded *TV Worth Watching* (http://www.david bianculli.com), where he posts his daily reviews. The site has several contributors, some of whom post lengthy critiques of various programs. There is also a list of other websites for episodes, segments, and information. Another website (http://www.metacritic.com) lists television shows by title with links to TV critic reviews. The critics rate programs with scores on a hundred-point scale. Viewers also enter their ratings on a 10-point scale. Journalist "criticisms" typically range from mere listings of current programs and their broadcast times to descriptive vignettes of upcoming programs. However, critics such as Tom Shales of *The Washington Post,* Robert Bianco of *USA Today,* and Howard Rosenberg of the *Los Angeles Times* write about television's style and taste. The Television Critics Association (**TCA**) represents more than 200 journalists who write about television for print and online outlets in the United States and Canada. There are links to them on the TCA website (http://tvcritics.org). Many newspapers now rely on copy supplied by wire services, such as the Associated Press. As James A. Brown explains in Newcomb's *Encyclopedia of Television,* journalistic television criticism is part of the publisher's larger purpose to gain readers for the newspaper or magazine, thus it

> puts a premium on relevance, clarity, brevity, cleverness, and attractive style. The TV column is meant to attract readers primarily by entertaining them, while also informing them about how the system works. . . . The critic serves as a guide, offering standards of criteria for judgment along with factual data, so readers can make up their own minds. . . . The critic-reviewer's role grows in usefulness as video channels proliferate; viewers inundated by dozens of cable and over-air channels can ensure optimum use of leisure viewing time by following critics' tips about what is worth tuning in and what to avoid. (Brown in Newcomb, 1997, p. 1643)

Brown lists the criteria for good journalistic television criticism as "sensitivity and reasoned judgment, a renaissance knowledge coupled with exposure to a broad range of art, culture, technology, business, law, economics, ethics, and social studies all fused with an incisive writing style causing commentary to leap off the page into the reader's consciousness" (Brown in Newcomb, 1997, pp. 1643–1644). These criteria would serve the academic television critic well, but they are general and have no specific reference to standards of judgment and methodology.

THE CRITICAL STANCE

The word "criticism" tends to have a negative connotation because we often associate it with finding something wrong with objects and people. If a person finds fault with something or someone, we are likely to say, "He or she is too critical." If your parents do not like your hairstyle or the way you dress, you might say, "Don't criticize me so much." We see the judges on *American Idol* or *Dancing With the Stars* criticizing the contestants, usually by drawing attention to positive and negative attributes of the performances.

Yet we define criticism differently when we check the newspaper or a website to find out what a television or film critic wrote about a television show or film before deciding what to watch. In this context, the critic usually writes about the quality of a television show or film—the story, the acting, the visual and sound aspects, and special effects. A critic may praise or pan a television program or film, thus telling the reader what is good and/or bad about it. For several years, I wrote film criticism in the local newspaper for the Bozeman Film Festival that featured independent and international films. If I thought a film had good qualities, I would urge my readers to be sure to see it. Sometimes filmgoers would disagree with my judgment, telling me, "I did not like the film. It was too long and moved too slowly." Others would thank me for alerting them about a film they might not otherwise have gone to see had they not read my review. This illustrates two points: (1) criticism is subjective, and (2) criticism can be persuasive.

Criticism is subjective. We bring to criticism our life experiences, our beliefs, attitudes, and values. Thus, we observe the critical object through our own perceptual filters. Perception is the process of extracting information from the world outside us as well as from within ourselves. Each individual has a perceptual field that is unique to that person and shaped by many influences, and this field forms the filters through which we perceive (O'Donnell & Kable, 1982). Our perceptions are based on our values, beliefs, attitudes, and experiences. Thus, as a critic, you are likely to have a perspective that includes biases and past experiences. You are also apt to select certain parts of a program to criticize. Thus, in addition to being subjective, criticism is also partial. Because most dramas and comedies on television are episodic, it is not likely that you would take on an entire season of a series to criticize unless you were writing a doctoral dissertation or a book about a series. The usual selection is a single episode, although you are advised to be aware of the other episodes in a series. A television program is not a reality that can be examined or proven in a completely objective manner. Therefore, you should not be concerned with finding the single correct interpretation, for there may be many possible ones. There may be a dominant meaning inscribed within the script, but different viewers can give alternative or multiple meanings to the same script. Many of my students like *The Bachelor* because they think it is glamorous and suspenseful, whereas I think it is banal and artificial. Some academics have criticized its representation as too "White." A television performance is potentially open to alternative interpretations. However, a competent critic who applies systematic analysis based on sound principles is not only more likely to evaluate fairly but also to illuminate. Readers of good criticism may have their appreciation of the critical object enhanced and thus may be moved to watch it.

Criticism can be persuasive. A television critic often functions as an advocate on behalf of a program or even a network, urging viewers to tune in to it. Further, a critic may construct a persuasive argument, offering good reasons and evidence to support the evaluation of a program. Criticism is capable not only of affecting our choices to watch a television program, but, more important, it can alter our perceptions, enabling us to see and hear more details, to anticipate certain moments, to ponder certain questions, and to recognize special qualities. Most students who take film and television criticism courses tell me that they see so much more than they did before taking the course and, furthermore, they are eager to talk about what they see. On the other hand, their friends, who have not studied critical methodologies, report that they do not like to watch films or television with their critic friends because they interpret too much and then talk about it during the screening.

Since television is so pervasive and—together with the Internet—is the most significant form of communication in the world, it is important to be sensitive to and understand what is communicated. Television is a cultural mirror, but it is also a two-way mirror in that it not only reflects our culture but also illuminates and influences how we see ourselves and others. Social science researchers have produced hundreds of studies regarding the influence of television on viewers. Whether viewers' behavior and/or attitudes are changed is not the primary concern of the television critic; however, the critic is an important observer of the content of television programs who can help us understand why such influence may occur.

Cultivation studies claim that people who watch television view the world as more violent than it actually is, causing them to be fearful, insecure, and dependent on authority as the result of seeing violence on television. The researchers concluded after their long-range study of heavy television viewing that "one correlate of television viewing is a heightened and unequal sense of danger and risk in a mean and selfish world" (Gerbner, Gross, Signorellli, Morgan, & Jackson-Beeck, 1979, p. 191). A television critic may note that, while physical violence is depicted in some television programming, notably historical dramas like *Game of Thrones* and vampire shows like *True Blood*, characters dealing with the consequences of violence are a more recent trend on shows such as *NCIS, NCIS: Los Angeles, CSI: Crime Scene Investigation, Criminal Minds*, and *Hawaii Five-0*.

Fashions, body image, and hairstyles are also copied from actors on television. Critics can note that imitations occur from show to show or appear in magazines and other publications. Subtle attitudes toward gender, race, ethnicity, age, sexual preference, and occupation as represented on television may or may not shape or reshape viewers' perceptions of reality, but you as a critic can observe changes in television programming itself. Cultural studies researchers use audience-response studies, wherein viewers are interviewed in depth to determine how television programs affect viewers (Morley, 1988). Television situation comedies, such as *The Cosby Show* and *Will & Grace,* appear to have made programs with African Americans or gays in leading roles more acceptable to the viewing public, but they probably did not resolve the actual tensions experienced by the general public concerning racial issues or homosexuality (Dow, 2001). Television viewers tend to make what they watch fit their own lives and experiences; therefore, the television critic can note other aspects of these programs. For example, according to John Marcus, writer for *The Cosby Show,* Bill Cosby insisted that the parents on the show be smarter than their children and that the characters' behavior be true to real-life behavior. The viewers would therefore comfortably identify with Cosby as a parent but not necessarily with his race. Since audience **identification** with television characters is a major key to audience enjoyment, approval or disapproval of controversial issues may not be the most important factor.

CRITICISM AND CULTURE

Television programs reflect a society's values, norms, and practices as well as its fads, interests, and trends. Because of this, your awareness and understanding of your own society give you insight into the meanings generated in television's fictional stories, coverage of real-life stories, **reality shows,** and other types of programming. Here you must use your own interpretative resources to make inferences about social relationships and configurations of value. Television programming, its structure, timing, and commercialism appropriate the structure and priorities of society, the distribution of goods and **power,** values and motives for behavior, and systems of reward and punishment. Its focus is tempocentric; that is, the time we live in is the most important time. Although television programs reflect the nation's cultural pluralism and may present a multiplicity of meanings, television programming, in general, reflects majority preferences because its commerce needs to appeal to the largest possible target audience. This is especially true for network television, but also for cable and satellite programs with their specialized target audiences. One can even say that television not only reflects culture, but that it also creates culture. As David Marc pointed out:

> Culture today is produced and distributed by a very few corporations, which, through their many divisions and subsidiaries, make decisions about what culture all members of society will consume, from the top of the social ladder to the bottom. . . . The success of the system is dependent on its ability to persuade the public to collaborate with it in the creation of a social product. (Marc, 1995, pp. 53, 56)

While the networks such as ABC, CBS, Fox, and NBC try to appeal to viewers between 18 and 49 years old, cable stations such as MTV, Lifetime, ESPN, E1, Food Network, Disney, Discovery, Animal Planet, History Channel, Home Shopping Network, SOAPnet, and Syfy appeal to very specific interests. This is known as "**brand identity**" because specific channels appeal to target audiences. For example, Lifetime appeals to adult women with stories featuring strong women and their relationships, while FX has introduced charismatic but deeply flawed men in various professions (plastic surgery, firefighting, law enforcement). This specificity, too, may be a reflection of culture in that it suggests that we live in an era of individualized culture, what Walt Whitman characterized as an America of "contradictory multitudes." We have so many choices—and we have television sets in different rooms as well as television reception on computers and telephones—that each member of a family can watch selected channels according to individual interests.

Because television programming is a reasonably good mirror of American culture, television criticism can go beyond description and evaluation of a television program or series to a level of deeper cultural diagnosis.

NARRATIVE AND CONTEXTUAL REALITY

Several television programs represent actual news events in fictional stories. In this way, television echoes real-life drama and reinforces its credibility by presenting familiar and true-to-life stories that appeal to viewers' interests. Three months after the mine explosion that killed 29 miners at the Upper Big Branch mine in West Virginia, *Leverage,* a TNT show about a team of three men and two women who expose corruption and take revenge on perpetrators, aired an episode in which the team infiltrated a mine in West Virginia to expose safety violations after a deadly explosion. One month later, an episode of *Leverage* featured the team going after a pharmaceutical CEO who wanted to release under a new name a dangerous drug capable of killing thousands of people. The story mirrored numerous newspaper releases about diet drugs that were recalled after several people died from taking them. The premise of the critically acclaimed show, *The Good Wife,* built on recent scandals involving prominent married, elected officials who were exposed in relationships with prostitutes. *Army Wives* on Lifetime has many fans among actual army wives because it is about the spouses and parents of military personnel who are deployed in Iraq and Afghanistan. Scenes often depict these soldiers fighting battles, getting wounded, or killed, but they also feature the mutual support that military spouses receive from one another. An article in *The Washington Post* revealed how this dramatic series offers an outlet to lessen stress on military spouses (Honan, 2010). The most specific reference to a major news story was on a former FX show that is now on a DirecTV channel, *Damages,* in which a high-powered lawyer, Patty Hewes, played by Glenn Close, attempts to recover billions of dollars for her clients from the family of a Wall Street financial advisor who was convicted for running a major Ponzi scheme. This was a direct allusion to Bernard Madoff, who was imprisoned for securities fraud, a Ponzi scheme that moved $65 billion out of investors' accounts. The investors sued to recover their money, mostly without success. *Law & Order,* a popular series that was cancelled in 2010 after 20 seasons, coined the phrase "Ripped from the Headlines" to introduce episodes about familiar events. Robert Thompson, director of Syracuse University's Center for Popular Television, said of these stories that reflect the news: "It's gripping and disturbing. Television is kind of the way that the entire collective subconscious of our culture plays out these issues" (Reuters, 2001).

CSI: Crime Scene Investigation and *CSI: Miami* utilize actual forensic science as the basis for their programs. Because both fictional and real-life crime scene investigators work for the state and must testify in court, they have to produce provable evidence based on scientific procedures. Jerry Bruckheimer, the producer of both shows, said, "On *CSI* I told them to use the correct terminology even if the audience doesn't know it, because even if they don't understand it, they'll know it's real" (Stein, 2003, p. 71). Consultants for the *CSI* shows include a forensic pathologist and a former crime scene analyst (CSA) as well as science researchers.

After the September 11, 2001, terrorist attacks on the Twin Towers of the World Trade Center in New York City, the Pentagon in Washington, D.C., and United Flight 93, television responded with shows about 9/11. *Rescue Me,* an FX summer series that concluded in September 2011, had a long-term commitment to story lines about the fallen firefighters of 9/11—stories about memories and grief. The lead character, Tommy Gavin, played by Denis Leary, lost his cousin and many friends in the Twin Towers. The 2010 season had a firefighter character who became seriously ill with cancer, apparently caused by his work at ground zero. Leary, one of the producer-writers, uses anecdotes he hears from real-life firefighters in the scripts. Other series have alluded to the unsettling fear of terrorism in the world with shows about strange deaths and unexpected phenomena *(The Event, Battlestar Galactica,* and *Falling Skies).*

Of course, not all cultural context plots are so tragic or serious. Comedy series also draw from real life for their humor. Through comic situations at home or at work, we

Photo 1.1   *Rescue Me*'s brave firefighters, Black Shawn and Sean, depicted as a tribute to the real New York City firefighters of 9/11.

can recognize our own fallibility and laugh at it. In contextualized situations, we experience the fictional comedy more intensely because it takes place in a real setting. Sometimes the decision to film in an actual setting is driven by production decisions. On March 3, 2004, *Yes, Dear* featured the former governor of California, Gray Davis, in a scene at a Los Angeles Lakers basketball game. Tim Conway, who played the lead actor's visiting father, got into a scripted argument with Davis in the team owner's special box. Conway made a joke that criticized Davis's handling of the state's budget and threw a glass of water in his face. Davis then chased Conway out of the owner's box, through the bleachers, and onto the floor during halftime—in front of the game's real spectators, who were unaware that a television show was being filmed. Jeff Meyer, the director of that *Yes, Dear* episode, said in a personal interview that the choice to film at an actual game was made because they wanted to have a live basketball audience in the show (O'Donnell, 2004). *Yes, Dear,* like most sitcoms, was normally filmed before live studio audiences in order to enhance the actors' sense of performing. To film the episode at a real basketball game was worth it to the producers of the show even though they needed to obtain complicated permissions from the NBA and the Lakers organization. Later, when Alan Kirschenbaum, *Yes, Dear*'s co-creator and executive producer, returned to his seat in the stands after filming, he overheard the man next to him saying to his friend who had just returned with their drinks: "You won't believe it, Joe, but Tim Conway was just chasing the former governor, Gray Davis, around the court," to which Joe replied: "No way, man!"

CRITICAL CATEGORIES AND CRITICAL CHOICES

The narrative of the aforementioned television shows, the remarks of Thompson, and the real-life context behind the programs are just a few of the items that a television critic would consider. Television shows are rich with issues; cultural values; legal information; courtroom ritual; psychological subtexts; controversy; family norms; gender, racial, age, and employment representation; and ideological hegemony or dominant cultural beliefs. Each has a distinctive style, a signature look, ensemble acting, realistic sets, and musical themes. Viewing audiences are expected to be informed, thinking, and feeling audiences that actively participate in the program by responding to and grappling with the issues. Critics may choose to deal with one or some of these categories, utilizing theoretical background and methodological analysis to appreciate, understand, and evaluate their observations.

How then do you, as a television critic, differ from other television viewers? You will analyze a television program in order to understand how it works and the choices its creators and producers made. You take television seriously and evaluate its expression of ideas, values, and conflicts, which give you and your readers deeper insight into our culture. You may make observations about what seems to be lacking in a program—but subsequently, you need to know what possible alternatives there are. As a competent critic, you know that different viewers derive different meanings from the same television program; therefore, you can interpret several possible meanings and their importance to those who might determine them. Further, you will go beyond the program itself and ask what conceptual or theoretical implications may have resulted. Finally, you will communicate to others the results of the critical observations in ways that can enrich their understanding. These critical observations are based on your informed judgment. Different academic television critics do not necessarily agree on what are the best critical methods and theories through which to criticize television, but as Horace Newcomb pointed out in the sixth edition of *Television: The Critical View,* their works are

> good faith attempts to recognize and understand how social life, now dependent on mass media, on popular forms of expression and entertainment, on the far-reaching lines of information afforded by new technologies, can best be taught and understood, learned and used by all citizens. (Newcomb, 2000, p. 6)

In order to do the work of a television critic, you have to (1) choose a television program to criticize, (2) submit yourself to the program and stay alert, (3) determine what questions to ask as you watch the program, and (4) choose or develop a methodology to answer the questions. Thus, your work as a television critic is to *understand* the various elements of a television program from script to performance in order to *analyze,* through *critical methodology,* how the elements make a program what it is; to *interpret* the sundry meanings that the program may have by understanding the nuances of the culture in which it appears and the multiple meanings it may have for different audiences; to pass *judgment* on the quality of the program; and, finally, to *communicate* that judgment to an audience. The chapters that follow will help you decide what questions to ask by presenting both theories and methods for analysis, as well as necessary information regarding the phenomena that make up a television program. It is also essential to understand that television production and distribution is a business dependent on profits.

THE BUSINESS OF TELEVISION

Because television production is a business that depends on public support measured by the ratings systems and paid subscriptions to cable channels, the programming norms tend to appeal to what the public prefers. From a business perspective, television programming is a product that is funded by advertising and/or subscription to cable and satellite services and used by the viewing public. The motive of television executives whose networks and cable channels are funded by advertising is simple: to deliver viewers to advertisers and advertising to viewers. Television commercials cause audiences to be the true medium of exchange. What sells products is what supports television programming. Therefore, the product culture largely determines what cultural models go on the air. Advertising is maintained if viewing levels and profiles support it; it is a matter of supply and demand. In other words, programming is determined by the interests and profits of the institution that produces and backs it. Network decisions also reflect the tastes and political ideologies of the controlling executives and the advertising sponsors. Chris Carter, creator of the successful television series *The X-Files,* told an audience at Montana State University that every script for his show had to be approved by the Fox network executives and "censors." In the second season of the show there was a script about a necrophiliac, a person who likes to have sex with corpses. The script was finally approved when the word "necrophiliac" was changed to "death fetishist." Another script for *The X-Files* that featured a story about incest and inbreeding was originally vetoed, but then, Carter said, it was allowed during "Sweeps Week," the times in January, May, September, and November when ratings companies measure viewing statistics for local television stations in each television market nationwide to set advertising rates (C. Carter, 2001). This latter example underscores the priority of the need for mass audience support. Television executives and producers try to figure out what it is that audiences desire and then satisfy that desire in order to maintain an audience following. Once the formula of desire/satisfaction is embodied in a television program, the show is then marketed to the consumers, the viewing public. Unhindered by advertising and the FCC,[1] HBO and Showtime cable subscription networks, have taken risks by developing programs that depict nudity, violence, and the use of obscene and sexually explicit language. *Boardwalk Empire, Deadwood, True Blood, Big Love, Game of Thrones,* and other HBO programs have attracted discriminating audiences and have won many awards. FX, a basic cable channel owned by Fox, has included shows that have violence, sex, foul language, and drug use in popular series such as *Sons of Anarchy, Rescue Me,* and *Justified.*

Knowledge of the critical methodology for analysis of television, together with an understanding of the business of television, enables you to realistically evaluate what you view. A competent television critic also knows his or her own culture and recognizes its representation in a television program.

---

[1]Because access to HBO is by subscription only, it is considered a private contractual agreement between viewers and HBO and not bound by FCC rules.

THE FAMILIAR AND THE UNFAMILIAR IN TELEVISION

Technological developments—satellite transmitters, DVD recorders, the DVR, cable and digital systems, HDTV, 3-D television, the Internet, and the development of interrelationships between and among different media—have given viewers an array of choices and enlarged awareness of the world and its people. Television today allows us to view programs from unfamiliar communities and countries, sometimes in other languages, giving us the experience of hearing and seeing different narrative forms and representations of cultural norms other than our own. These exposures and the choices they give us also provide opportunities to compare the familiar with the unfamiliar, and this requires knowledge of the familiar. Critical methodologies enable us to enhance our knowledge of the familiar and equip us to confront the unfamiliar. It is also important to recognize that the institutions of United States television are the dominant television industries in the world, and that American programming has become popular around the globe. While visiting the Tate Gallery in London, I noticed that the woman at the information desk had a picture of George Clooney as the screensaver on her computer. She told me that *ER* is her favorite television show, although now it can only be seen in syndication, DVD box sets, and on NBC.com. American programming has, in many cases, been adopted as a model for programming in other countries. A few years ago, my husband and I checked into a small hotel in Milan. The desk clerk was watching Italy's version of *The Dating Game,* a game show in which men and women choose a date by asking questions of several candidates. Except for the language difference, the show was nearly identical to America's *The Dating Game.* Of course, it works both ways. England's *Who Wants to Be a Millionaire*, *The Office*, and *Life on Mars* were the prototypes for America's versions of these shows. *Ugly Betty* was modeled after a telenovela from Colombia.

This chapter started off with the notion that critical acuity would give you a fuller and richer appreciation for a television program, as well as a better understanding of viewer response to it. Each of the chapters of this book is designed to help you become a critic who not only knows how to evaluate a television program but who also can construct a persuasive argument to support that judgment. To get started, you may be asking some very basic questions, such as, "How do I choose a television program to criticize?" and "How do I know what methods to use to criticize it?" So let us examine some basic, critical orientation concepts.

CRITICAL ORIENTATION

First, it is perfectly acceptable to choose one of your favorite television programs to criticize. Your familiarity with the show will enable you to select critical questions more easily, and your resulting critique will help you gain a deeper understanding of why you like it. For example, I like *The Good Wife,* and I often watch it for pure enjoyment as opposed to criticizing it. If I were to do a critique of *The Good Wife,* my job would be somewhat easier because I am familiar with the format and style of the show; I know most of the characters' names and their fictional histories; I have read articles about the show and watched an Academy of Television Arts and Sciences seminar (online) with the actors and writer-producers, who discussed the characters, the plot, and the production ("An Evening with *The Good Wife,*" 2011).

Second, you may select a television program that grapples with issues that interest you. What interests me about *The Good Wife* are the strong, professional women in the show. Each one has a different and complex personality, but they work as a team together with the male lawyers. Each episode has one court case, and I enjoy the way they uncover evidence, cross-examine witnesses, and interact with the judges. Perhaps there are issues that you would like to be involved in, and therefore you may select a television program about the law, medicine, crime, children, teenagers, reality, music, dance, science, animals, sports, or politics. Perhaps you are interested in how television presents information about disease or the environment. You may wish to observe how certain occupations are portrayed on television or how gender, age, race, and ethnicity are represented. Perhaps you would like to compare and contrast the ways in which the news is presented by different networks or by different anchors, or you may want to trace the human values that underlie the format and presentation of news stories. You may wish to examine certain sports coverage or look at the role of celebrities on television **talk shows.** You may be especially interested in a certain type of television program or a genre, whether it is a miniseries or reality-based television.

Third, you may want to attempt the application of a methodology to see what you can learn by applying it. You can examine how a narrative is shaped and structured, examine the conventions of genre, look for the various codes of television and try to extrapolate meaning from them, examine the characteristics of "families" and family values, look for evidence of the **postmodern** phenomena, and/or observe and evaluate the "look" and style of a television program. The following chapters present ways of observing, analyzing, and evaluating television programs. Chapter 9 consolidates those that precede it into a set of critical questions to ask of a television program.

Fourth, you may be interested in the making of a television show. Television programs are the result of the work of the creators, the executive producers, producers, writers, directors, actors, set designers, costumers, music directors, visual and sound editors, camera operators, and other staff, who may or may not be an independent production company. You can enjoy the convenience of the vast amount of information on a program's website. You can usually access character back-stories and interviews with the actors, producers, and other staff. Their creative work and the ways in which a television show is initiated and produced is the subject of Chapter 2, "Demystifying the Business of Television."

SUMMARY

Criticism is the practice of informed judgment through which a person understands, evaluates, and communicates to others the what, how, and why something is considered to be of quality. The result can illuminate, enlighten, and bring about appreciation for that which is criticized. Television criticism can bring about a fuller and richer understanding of people's reactions to a television program. Because television is ubiquitous in society, it is important to practice sound television criticism. Not only will the television critic gain deeper understanding of the production process, aesthetics, and genre standards, but also the critic can develop insight into cultural contexts and cultural norms inherent in the narrative and action of programs.

Television critics choose a program to criticize, watch the program in an alert state, determine what questions to ask, and choose or develop a methodology to answer the questions. The subsequent analysis and evaluation are then communicated to an audience.

Television criticism is subjective in that it subjects a program to interpretation through the critic's perceptual filters. Television criticism can also be persuasive in that it can alter the perceptions of viewers.

Television production and distribution is a business dependent upon advertising and subscriptions as well as audience support. Television production develops a "look," a visual style that should enhance the narrative as well. Mainstream representations of race, gender, sexuality, age, and occupation reflect societal changes and new norms. Narratives on fiction and nonfiction television reinforce cultural values. Television programs and their scheduling are bound by genres. These aspects, all of which you should be familiar with as a television critic, are explored in each of the parts of this book.

EXERCISES

1. Think of a time in your life when you received personal and constructive criticism. How did it help you in a positive way? Did it change you in any way?

2. Make a list of what you can gain from being an informed television critic.

3. What does it mean to be a "transformer" when you are a television critic?

4. Read an example of television criticism online or in a newspaper like *The New York Times,* the *Los Angeles Times, USA Today,* or any other major newspaper, or go to http://www.tvcritics.org and find the list of critics. Read a few critiques. What does the journalistic television criticism tell you? Do you think it is objective? Does it persuade you to watch a particular show?

5. What does it mean to say that television criticism is subjective? What does it mean to say that television criticism is persuasive?

6. Watch both a fiction and a nonfiction television program of your choice. Analyze your own perceptions of the content. Does this reveal your own biases and past experiences?

7. Have you ever been influenced by someone else to watch a particular television program? If so, did you continue watching the same program?

8. Have you ever been persuaded to adopt a hairstyle, a type of clothing, or an attitude because you observed it in a television program?

9. Can you name the "brand identity" of the television cable station that you watch on a regular basis? How do you regard yourself in terms of that brand?

10. Watch a television show such as *Leverage, Damages, Army Wives, NCIS,* or any of the episodic dramas. Can you identify true-to-life events in the story?

11. How do you, as a television viewer, participate when you watch? Do you fill in the blanks or predict what will happen?

12. Why is it important for a television critic to take television seriously?

13. What does the desire/satisfaction formula mean from a television business perspective?

14. What should you consider when you select a television show to criticize?

SUGGESTED READINGS

Archive of American Television. Half-hour interviews with television actors, producers, writers, casting directors, and other production staff. http://www.emmys.tv/foundation/archive. Also http://www.tvinterviewsarchive.blogspot.com for access and links to the newest interviews.

Marc, David. (1995). *Bonfire of the Humanities: Television, Subliteracy, and Long-Term Memory.* Syracuse, NY: Syracuse University Press.

Nehamas, Alexander. (Winter 1990). Serious watching. *South Atlantic Quarterly, 89*(1), 157–180.

Newcomb, Horace (Ed.). (1997). *Encyclopedia of Television* (3 vols.). Chicago, IL: Fitzroy Dearborn.

Demystifying the Business of Television

There's no business like show business.

—Irving Berlin (*Annie Get Your Gun*)

INTRODUCTION

This chapter focuses on what you need to know about the business of television. It is divided into two parts that cover essential information about (1) the role of advertising, the influence of ratings, the making of daily schedules, and the impact of the Internet; and (2) how a television show is produced and the roles of the producers, writers, and directors. The section on writing is longer than the other parts regarding production because an overwhelming majority of people in the television industry regard writing as the most important aspect of production.

Knowledge of each of these areas will help you understand why the final outcome is what it is. Because the creative process that goes into the making of a television program or series is dependent on the business of television production and delivery, restraints, institutional controls, and public tastes—and the subsequent popularity of television programs—the end product may not live up to critical demands. As an effective critic, you will use high standards and will be free to make suggestions for improvement, but you must also recognize the restrictions and limitations of the medium and judge how good or bad a program is accordingly. This chapter is not intended to provide a complete understanding of the television industry, but rather it will enable you to understand enough about the business of television to place it in that context when evaluating a program or series.

THE ROLE OF ADVERTISING, RATINGS, AND SCHEDULES

Advertising

The common wisdom in television is that its primary role is to deliver consumers to advertisers. Advertising income is what pays for television programs that are broadcast on commercial networks and on websites. The networks derive 100% of their revenues from advertising and **product placement.** With the exception of premium subscription channels such as HBO and Showtime, cable and satellite television include advertising and develop special programming or promotions and also offer local advertising. In the business of television, the goal is to sell as many commercials as possible and to charge as much as advertisers are willing to pay. In the business of advertising, the goal is to buy time in television programs watched by an audience who fits the demographic characteristics that advertisers market products to and to buy these audiences as efficiently as possible. In other words, television sells audiences to advertisers for billions of dollars.

A good illustration that the television audience is the commodity that networks and individual stations sell to advertisers is the description of the audience in terms of "costs per thousand." In other words, the cost to purchase air time for a commercial is divided by the number of people in thousands. For example, if the cost for a commercial is $300,000 and the audience for a program is 40 million women 18 to 49 years old, then the cost-per-thousand is $300,000 divided by 40,000 = $7.50. The advertiser is spending $7.50 for every 1,000 women 18 to 49 years old who watch the program in which the commercial is placed. How is such a description derived? Audience research provides the estimates of the size and demographics of the audience. Certain audience characteristics desired by advertisers are also incorporated into programming choices and their exposure to audiences.

Source: Lometti (1997).

After experimenting with free, advertising-supported viewing of their shows on various websites, ABC, CBS, FOX, and NBC began holding back full episodes of programming in disputes over getting paid. The broadcasters demanded to be paid for their shows wherever they are seen. HBO and other cable channels limit access to their shows for free online. Access requires passwords tied to cable and satellite subscriptions. Research analyst Rich Greenfield wrote on his blog, "Consumers must be made to realize that nothing is free anymore" (Nakashima, 2010, p. D2).

Ratings

Television revenues are determined by data derived from a quantitative measurement of the size and composition of the audience that are established by ratings and **shares** measured by a media market research firm known as the A. C. Nielsen Company. The Nielsen Company measures and compiles statistics on television and Internet audiences and sells these data to advertisers, advertising agencies, program syndicators, television networks, local stations, websites, and cable and satellite program and system operators.

Webster, Phalen, and Lichty (2000) define ratings as "a body of data on people's exposure to electronic media" (p. 10). Ratings are derived from a formula that calculates the percentage of the nationwide audience with television sets who are watching a particular program—in other words, how many people out of the total possible audience are watching at that time. The networks base their advertising rates on the regular weekly data that Nielsen produces, while stations in smaller markets—because they cannot afford Nielsen's research year-round—rely on **Sweeps** four times a year for all their important ratings numbers. Webster et al. describe ratings as follows: "Ratings are the tools used by advertisers and broadcasters to buy and sell audiences; the report cards that lead programmers to cancel some shows and clone others. Ratings are road maps to patterns of media consumption. . . . They are objects of fear and loathing" (p. 12).

With the expansion of television viewing in different venues, the Nielsen Company has subsequently expanded its research to include television outside of the home and television online. Nielson has announced that it is pursuing on-device measurement devices on mobile equipment.

Television Measurement

Using electronic metering technology known as TV meters and Local People Meters, Nielsen captures information on what is being viewed and when in the major markets in the United States. This information includes who and how many are watching programs. In addition, viewers in smaller markets keep paper diaries for a 7-day period during the four Sweeps months of January, May, September, and November. The Sweeps last for one month, thus diaries are mailed to different homes each week. These data are then delivered to local stations.

> My household was selected to keep paper diaries during the week of February 24-March 2, 2011. We were given a paper diary for each television set and a new $1 bill as a token of appreciation. We wrote down what, when, and who watched on each television set. If we watched a program that was recorded on the DVR, we indicated what, when, and who watched that too. Our viewing began on a Thursday, and on Saturday evening, I got a call from a Nielsen representative. He wanted to make sure we were recording in the diaries and to see if we had any questions. Each diary was mailed back separately.

Television that is digitally recorded on **DVRs** is measured using codes that are embedded in television programs that tell when something that has been recorded is actually watched. Nielsen compiles and sends clients six streams of data: live viewing, live viewing plus same-day DVR playback, live plus DVR playback after 1 day, 2 days, 3 days, and 7 days. Nielsen can even tell when people fast-forward through the commercials. Alan Wurtzel, NBC's head of research said, "We now know that 40 to 50 percent of the 7 percent who time-shift do see some commercials. Advertisers projected last year that everybody who watches shows in playback fast-forwards through the commercials. The reality is that they don't" (Block, 2007, p. 185). Networks want advertisers to pay for those who **time-shift** and watch some commercials, but advertisers still accept only live viewing or DVR viewing over the first 3 days after a show was broadcast, a model known as "commercial plus three" (C3) ratings. Nielsen has shown that a show might have low ratings on the night it was broadcast, but the ratings and number of viewers jump to much higher numbers by the time a week's worth of recorded playback is included. Wurtzel said, "You'd be foolish not to look at the DVR performance as a measure of the potential a program has" (B. Carter, 2011, April 24, p. 1). The reason that advertisers will not pay for commercials viewed well after a show has first aired is that some ads are designed to drive sales the very next day or that weekend, for example, a movie company's commercial that airs on the Thursday before a film's Friday opening. The C3 measure was a compromise between the networks who want all time-shifting counted and advertisers who prefer that only the first day be counted.

You can go on Nielsen's website (http://www.nielsen.com) to see the weekly lists of ratings for the top television programs broken down by broadcast television, cable television, and syndication. Ratings are also reported in various newspapers and industry magazines. *USA Today* began reporting the **Nielsen ratings** by total viewers rather than households in 2002. *USA Today* also reports the Nielsen breakdown of prime-time ratings by networks, cable, syndicated channels, and by age groups 18 to 49.

Television Measurement Outside the Home

Nielsen issues a Fourth Screen Network Audience Report on a quarterly basis that measures audience exposures by video networks in out-of-the-home locations such as restaurants, retail stores, bars, airports, gas stations, and other places. In addition to the number of participants who view in these venues, gender and age are also measured. CNN in airports, for example, accounted for 17.8 million viewers in one quarter in 2011.

> NBC's out-of-home unit expanded to 600 gas stations, with monitors embedded in 6,000 pumps in key markets. Local weather reports are popular as well as late-night talk shows and car shows. Because lifting the gas pump activates a continuous loop on the screen, Mark French, vice president of NBC Everywhere, said, "We know exactly how many people are seeing our content and ads, and for what duration."
>
> *Source:* Hendrickson (2010, p. 28).

Television Measurement Online

Nielsen uses people panels selected on a random basis. More than 200,000 Internet users across more than 30,000 sites are measured using Nielsen tags that are placed on participating sites to provide data to the panels. For television shows to be included in the rankings, the online versions must have the same content and national advertising as the regular television versions. Tables that rank the top Web companies (Google, Facebook, YouTube, etc.) in the United States and abroad are listed on the Nielsen website.

Categories of Ratings

There are several categories of ratings for television: the Nielsen Television Index (NTI), an estimate of how many people with certain demographic characteristics view each program based on a sample of 4,000 homes; the National Audience Demographics (NAD), a report that provides demographic information on network programs for both household and on a per-person basis; the Nielsen Station Index (NSI), a quarterly measurement of each local television station in each nationwide market; the Designated Market Areas (DMA), diaries in which separate samples of people record their viewing habits; Nielsen Syndicated Service (NSS), a service for syndicated television shows; and the Nielsen Homevideo Index (NHI), a service for cable networks, superstations, and home video. Other special reports are also produced for videocassette and DVD usage, sports programming, and political elections.

Demographics

Demographics is the practice of describing groups of people according to gender, age, ethnicity, income, educational level, and other information. Demographic information identifies target audiences for advertisers and commercial broadcasters. Advertisers believe that pinpointed messages aimed at their best prospects will be most successful; therefore, while age, gender, and occupation are considered important, they are also interested in whether individuals share a certain set of values (Buzzard, 1990). Thus, they may target the Generation X audience—with its perceived emphasis on material goods and action activities—for one ad, and Baby Boomers—who are concerned with health and security—for another.

The 18- to 49-year-old demographic group, called "the demo" by television executives, is favored by advertisers. For example, *Grey's Anatomy* at one time drew a 9.4 Nielsen rating, meaning that almost one in 10 potential viewers in the 18–49 age group tuned into it. Measured another way, *Grey's Anatomy* drew about 23% of the 18- to 49-year-old viewers who are watching television at that hour on Thursdays. When DVR ratings are factored in, increased ratings result for shows that previously had lower ratings among this age group. For example, audiences who want to watch live sports events may go back to watch a DVR recording later. For example, *The Event* had a 2.4 rating in its third week on the air, but when the DVR numbers were factored in, the rating climbed to 3.3 (Powers, 2010). Younger viewers are reported to watch more shows in time-shifts or online. The median age of network television viewers has increased to 50, a fact that advertisers note with interest. Newer hit shows tend to start out with a young audience, but as David Poltrack, chief research officer of CBS, notes, the median age goes up with each passing season: "Once a show is a big hit, it's not likely to get an influx of young, new viewers. They tend to move on to the next new thing" (Garron, 2008, p. 18). Other demographic groups that are important are African Americans, Asian Americans, and Hispanic Americans. Nielsen ratings indicate that African Americans aged 18 to 49 watched 2 hours more television per day on the average than the national average of 5 hours and 11 minutes. Asian Americans in the same age group watched about 2 hours less than the national average. Certain Hispanic American populations in places like Harlingen, Texas, and Los Angeles, California, watch predominantly Spanish-language television programs (Mindlin, 2011).

Public Television and Ratings

Public broadcasters usually do not use commercial advertisements, but they do have financial support from viewers and government. *Masterpiece Classic, Masterpiece Mystery,* and *Masterpiece Contemporary* are supported in part by the Masterpiece Trust that includes wealthy donors. In 1984, the Federal Communications Commission (**FCC**) relaxed the rules, allowing about 360 public broadcasting stations to air commercial messages as long as they did not ask for a sale or make price or quality comparisons and were not aired during local, 2.5-minute program breaks. The public broadcasters had requested the right to advertise after their federal funding was cut back by 30%, but not all public stations air advertisements (Wells, Burnett, & Moriarty, 2002). Many public broadcasting station managers subscribe to Nielsen ratings or use research consultants to analyze their data. The Public Broadcasting Service (PBS) subscribes to national ratings in order to evaluate the appeal of its programming. For example, Nielsen found that the PBS audience for the first episode of the April 2011 *Upstairs, Downstairs,* a three-part series on *Masterpiece Classic,* was 6.4 million viewers, an increase of 45% over 2010 viewership (PBS *Masterpiece* Viewership, 2011). Public broadcasting also has pledge drives during which programs are interrupted to appeal to prospective donors. Ratings help the public broadcasters learn when the largest number of viewers is available for their programs, and they can thus make adjustments to their program schedules and their pledge drives (Webster et al., 2000). I served as the "talent" for some of the pledge drives for Montana Public Television. We found that we got the most pledges on Saturday night, especially during *The Lawrence Welk Show,* even though they were reruns since the show's host, Lawrence Welk, had died many years before.

Ratings and the Cost of Advertising

Ratings are used as references for negotiations for the price of advertising time as well as for the salaries of the actors, the news anchors, and other on-screen personnel, decisions about syndicating programs, and other vital issues. Because ratings determine how much the advertisers pay for commercials, the larger the desired audience, the higher the cost of commercials.

> Although the desired audience for advertising tends to be 18- to 49-year-old consumers with disposable income, the lead characters in many television programs tend to be 20 to 30 years old because the shows are designed to appeal to a younger segment of the population, aged 18 to 34, to compensate for an audience that presumably watches little television except online. Reality programs such as *Survivor* and *Jersey Shore* are designed to court young adults, whom the advertisers hope will develop strong brand loyalty to their sponsors. The Baby Boomer generation, ages 55–64, now comprise a third of the population, and they watch more television, yet ad buyers, rather than courting them, are expanding their definition of family to include them.
>
> *Source:* Garron (2011, p. 19)

After a great deal of media hype, 52.2 million people watched the final episode of *Friends* on May 6, 2004, driving up the price of a beer commercial that evening to $2 million (B. Carter, 2004). Typically the Super Bowl broadcast, because of its huge audience, has the highest-priced commercials. In the year 1984, Apple Computer aired its *1984* commercial, a mini-epic about Big Brother propagandizing on a big screen in front of colorless, automaton humans when suddenly an athletic woman in red shorts, outrunning the "thought police," hurls a sledgehammer at the screen, which explodes in a flash of light. Ridley Scott made this commercial that ended with the announcer saying, "On January 24th, Apple Computer will introduce Macintosh. And you'll see why 1984 won't be like *1984.*" The next day, 200,000 consumers went to Apple dealers to view the new Macintosh computer, and 72,000 bought one in the next 100 days. The tremendous success of this ad ushered in a new era for advertising on the Super Bowl. As Jerry Della Femina, chairman of Della Femina Rothschild Jeary Advertising, wrote in *The Wall Street Journal,* "In my world—advertising—the Super Bowl is judgment day. If politicians have Election Day and Hollywood has the Oscars, advertising has the Super Bowl" (2001, p. A14). Television commercials for the February 6, 2011, Super Bowl cost $3 million for a 30-second spot, and the broadcast reached about 106 million Americans. Len Short, executive vice president for brand marketing at America Online (AOL), said "It gets to be more of a cultural phenomenon every year . . . a great place to launch something" (Associated Press, 2004, p. C4).

The Sweeps

Ratings Sweeps (the name is taken from the practice of sweeping all local markets four times a year) are the month-long periods in January, May, September, and November (the sweeps months vary from year to year) during which ratings set the advertising rates for the next 3 months for local stations, ranging from small towns to large cities. Sweeps do not set rates for all advertisers, just local ones. Nielsen introduced these Sweeps periods in the 1960s, and they have been big business ever since. Television programs are promoted, news specials are publicized, blockbuster miniseries and made-for-TV movies are aired, and series finales, often with cliffhanger situations, are shown in May. This is why many reruns are shown the month before the Sweeps because networks wait until the Sweeps months to air new scripts. Competition among channels is keen during the Sweeps, with newspapers and electronic trade journals reporting the winners. Ratings are reported first with shares second. The **share** is a mathematical formula that calculates the percentage of the nationwide audience with sets turned on and tuned into a particular program during a given time. This is a measure of the actual possible audience, known as Households Using Television (HUT). Shares enable station and network executives to learn how well their programs are doing compared with their competition. A good example is given in the *Encyclopedia of Television:*

> For example, station WXXX airs *Jeopardy!* at 7 p.m. Sample data estimate that 10,000 or 10 percent of the city's 100,000 TV households are viewing that program. Some 40,000 households are viewing other programs, but another 50,000 are not using their TV sets. Since 10,000 of the 50,000 active viewers (20%) are watching *Jeopardy!,* that program has a share of 20 even though its rating (the percentage of TV households) is only 10. (Newcomb, 1997, p. 1482)

If all households with television sets had people watching television during a given time period, the rating and the share would be equal, but this never happens; thus, the share for a program is always greater than its rating. The gap is greatest during periods of light viewing. Because new technologies can track viewing habits by the minute any time during the year, the Sweeps may no longer be necessary, yet they prevail perhaps to keep viewers interested.

Why Television Shows Get Renewed or Canceled

Ratings and shares are what determine whether programs get canceled or continued. The 2010 fall season had an unusual number of new shows, many of which were cancelled after a few weeks due to poor ratings and shares. Viewers who committed to watching those series were bitterly disappointed, however; if remaining episodes were available, they were put on the networks' websites for only a few weeks. *Law & Order* was cancelled in May 2010 after 456 episodes over 20 years because it had averaged a 1.8 rating among viewers aged 18 to 49 (Stelter & Carter, 2010, p. 2) Although it is a rare phenomenon, viewer reaction may sometimes "save" a television program. The first time this occurred was in 1968, when—despite a low number of viewers—NBC renewed *Star Trek* for a third season due to a massive letter-writing campaign that was secretly started by the show's creator, Gene Roddenberry (Cavanaugh, 2006). In 1984, the CBS program *Cagney & Lacey* was canceled because it had finished 55th among 99 prime-time series. Viewer outrage expressed in "an avalanche of mail," favorable press attention, and Tyne Daly's Emmy for her portrayal of one of two policewomen convinced CBS executives to restore the show. Also, according to David Poltrack, who was the vice president for research at CBS, "*Cagney & Lacey* had enthusiastic advertisers, despite the mediocre ratings. Its core audience, women 25 to 54, is the most saleable demographic segment" ("Viewer Reaction Saves *Cagney & Lacey,*" 1984, p. C11). *Hill Street Blues* finished 89th in the ratings during its first half season, but its small audience was demographically made up of POMs—an acronym for professionals, operatives, and managers—a clearly defined target audience with disposable income, and the show thus escaped cancellation (Marc & Thompson, 1995). A senior executive from a television production studio, speaking anonymously because of the need to sell shows to network program heads, said, "They will read the numbers and then they will secretly try to find the justification to renew the shows they love and cancel the ones they don't" (B. Carter, 2011, April 24, p. 4).

Ratings in the Summer

At one time, summer television was nothing but rerun programs, but that has changed in recent years. To acquire more viewers during the summer months, many new television programs have been developed. The award-winning *Mad Men* has been a summer series, as were *Leverage*, *Rescue Me*, *Men of a Certain Age,* and HBO's popular *True Blood*.

Yet, ratings make little difference in the summer because advertising rates have already been set for the fall. For example, in the summer of 2004, the quiz show *Jeopardy!* had a record-breaking winner with Ken Jennings, who won 38 games and $1,321,660. His long run boosted *Jeopardy!*'s ratings. According to an Associated Press release, *Jeopardy!* producers were probably annoyed that this happened during the summer when higher ratings don't mean as much financially. Michael Davies, executive producer of *Who Wants to be a Millionaire,* said that when the syndicated *Millionaire* had two big winners on shows taped to air in the summer, he delayed them to the fall ("'Jeopardy!' Star Jennings Gives Show a Boost," 2004).

Photo 2.1   Sookie, a human with psychic abilities who may also be a fairy, and Bill, her vampire lover, in *True Blood*.

THE STRATEGIES OF TELEVISION ADVERTISING

Typically, the basic formula for ads on television is 8 minutes of ads for a half-hour show; however, because air time is so expensive, advertisers tend to run shorter commercials, resulting in more ads per minute. Marketing communications company Young & Rubicam uses the **AQRI** rule—"arouse quick related interest" to relate to viewers' lives or experiences (Bellamy & Walker, 1996). In addition to ads for products, promotions for other television shows and films frequent the airwaves during the breaks of a show. Movie studios advertise heavily on Thursday nights to reach young adults before the weekend's new movie releases ("The Thursday Factor," 2005, p. 10). Advertisers prefer sponsoring shows that put viewers in a mood to buy. *The Day After,* a 1983 made-for-television movie about a nuclear holocaust, posted some of the highest ratings in the history of television. Yet some sponsors were afraid to run ads during the show because its message might make the audience feel bad and would not put the viewers in a mood to buy their products (Stark, 1997).

Sometimes advertising is directly linked to a show. Lowe's, a sponsor for *Parenthood,* features the series' art director, Steven Jordan, in its ads, in which he demonstrates how he dresses and lights the sets using Lowe's merchandise.

Advertising often functions as entertainment to hook the viewers. In the 1990s, Taster's Choice began running serialized commercials created by the McCann-Erickson ad agency that followed the romantic encounters of a man and woman who shared a fondness for this coffee. The commercials presented a soap opera environment in each episode that ended with ambiguous dialogue to create in the viewers a desire to tune in to see whether these people would become a couple. The commercials were so successful that they were given credit for a 10% increase in product sales soon after they were aired. Talking babies and animals have become commonplace in advertising for viewer entertainment.

Companies other than Nielsen have begun to track the effectiveness of advertising. IAG Research, an ad-effectiveness company with clients that include GM, Proctor & Gamble, American Express, Verizon, and major broadcast networks such as CBS, ABC, NBC, Fox, Turner, and ESPN, emails 20 questions to 5,000-6,000 viewers. Modest prizes (fast food and movie coupons) are awarded if the viewers answer ten questions correctly. The questions are about the content to insure that people actually watched the shows and the commercials. If a viewer gets 18-19 correct, it is assumed that the show has been carefully watched. If a viewer gets 1-3 correct, attention is questionable.

Another company, Marketing Evaluations, measures performers' familiarity and appeal. It also surveys how much viewers are loyal to brands and shows.

Source: Block (2007, pp. 183, 185).

---

comScore Video Metrix measures how over 170 million Internet users in the United States view video content on Google, Hulu, and others. In March 2011, for example, Americans viewed 3.8 billion streaming video advertisements with Hulu.com. Video ads reached 42 percent of the U.S. population, an average of 30 times during the month. Video ads accounted for 12.4 percent of all videos viewed and 1.2 percent of all minutes spent viewing video online.

Source: comScore Releases March 2011 U.S. Search Engine Rankings (Retrieved April 13, 2011, from http://www.comscore.com).

Because television is available 24 hours every day and because there are hundreds of channels to choose from, the television audience has become increasingly fragmented. With the enormous success of HBO and other cable channels such as MTV, CNN, and ESPN, there has been erosion in the viewership of the broadcasting networks ABC, CBS, NBC, and Fox. There is major competition for audiences, and strategies are planned to acquire them, especially in the 18- to 49-year-old range. One such strategy is "**narrowcasting**" or reaching for target audiences. CNN and CNN Headline News keep viewers informed of the latest developments in news. Lifetime and Oxygen attempt to attract women viewers by featuring numerous made-for-TV "weepies" and talk shows with emphasis on female issues. The various Fox sports channels and ESPN appeal to sports devotees alongside specific sports channels such as Golf and NFL Network; Animal Planet (APL) engages animal lovers; Court TV attracts people who like to watch trials and reruns of crime shows; the Food Channel interests people who like to cook; and the Syfy channel entertains **science fiction** and horror fans. As a result of narrowcasting, advertising is calculated to feature products that its target audience needs or desires. Lifetime programs, for example, feature ads for hair color, body wash, laundry detergent, toothpaste, yogurt, diapers, coffee cream, toilet paper, puppy food, and Lifetime movies.

Every spring the television industry hosts "upfront" meetings for prospective advertisers and the press. The name indicates that the purpose of the meetings is to allow marketers to buy commercial air time "up front," several months before the next television season begins. The networks announce their fall schedules, which are being "picked up"; thus they are called "**pickups**." The meeting is an extravaganza with clips from new series, entertainment, appearances by stars, and gifts.

PRODUCT PROMOTION WITHIN TELEVISION PROGRAMS

The Project for Excellence in Journalism reported a study of the content of the ABC, CBS, and NBC morning shows, calling them "a kind of sophisticated infomercial" because they tended to promote the products of their parent companies. The report said that one-third of the content on these morning shows essentially sold something—a book, a compact disc, a movie, or another television program. Twenty-seven percent of the products promoted on *The Early Show* are owned by Viacom, the parent company of CBS; 21% of the *Good Morning America* promotions are owned by the Walt Disney Company, which owns ABC; 12% of the products promoted on *Today* are owned by General Electric, which owns 80% of NBC (Associated Press, 2001). The remaining 20% is now owned by Vivendi Universal.

Likewise, game shows announce the brand names of the prizes they offer, such as automobiles, furniture, and appliances, and the names of airlines, hotels, and resorts that serve as prizes. Of course, in the process of covering the action of most athletic contests, televised sports also show the stadium billboards that promote specific products. An increasing number of sports arenas are named for their corporate and business sponsors, thus the sponsors' names are openly mentioned in the television coverage.

PRODUCT PLACEMENT

Product placement (brand names purposely placed within the context of a program) is another source of income for television programs. Although television product placement is not exactly new, it has become a widespread strategy in the 21st century due to escalating costs of television production. Erik Barnouw (1978) pointed out in *Sponsor* that in the 1940s, in the early days of television, there were *sub rosa* sponsors. Writers and directors were told that if they could put a certain brand of potato chips in a televised party scene, a publicity agent would send a $100 check. On a documentary program about skiing, the skiers would end with a social hour and be shown drinking Old Crow whiskey. Product placement has been used in films for a long time. When Reese's Pieces candy was shown in the 1982 film *ET,* sales of the candy increased by 65%.

Sometimes brand names of products are part of television's narrative. Steven Antin, producer of the WB show *The Young Americans* signed a deal with Coca-Cola in 2000 for $25 million, promising that the cast would be seen drinking Coca-Cola in every episode (Longworth, 2002). Jennifer Lopez, Stephen Tyler, and Randy Jackson, the judges on *American Idol,* sip Coca-Cola from glasses inscribed with the Coke logo. When Ryan Seacrest stands beside a contestant in center stage, a huge red and white screen flashes "Coca-Cola" in the background. The designers and models in *Project Runway* get sent to the Garnier Fructis (manufacturer of hair products) salon each week for hair and makeup styling for the runway show, and the winning team on *Survivor* gets cans of Mountain Dew. *Extreme Makeover: Home Edition* refurbishes houses with Sears tools and Pella windows. An episode of *The Big Bang Theory* featured the character Sheldon adopting several cats after the breakup with Amy. In one scene Sheldon is in the kitchen with a stack of Fancy Feast cat food. As he dishes some out of the can, he sniffs it and says, "Fancy Feast, not so fancy." *30 Rock* is known for shamelessly naming brands in the dialogue. In just one episode, Tina Fey mentions Starwinds Hotel several times, a not so subtle mention of Starwood Hotels. Life Alert and Geiko are also part of the dialogue, and a box of Wheat Thins crackers sits conspicuously on a desk. Leslie Moonves, CBS executive, said, "We're making more and more of those deals: the kind of cars they drive in *CSI;* the kind of orange juice they drink in *Two and a Half Men"* (Associated Press, 2005, p. TW21). The 2011 summer premiere of *Mad Men* was delayed until March 2012 because of a dispute between Matthew Weiner, the show's creator, and AMC, which wants more product placements and cuts in the episodes to allow for more commercials (Stelter, 2011, March 29).

Another form of product placement for television is the digital insertion of brands into selected versions of programs based on viewers' brand preferences. This is a legal practice, but product placement can sometimes be questionable. Christopher Turner, a clinical assistant professor of medicine at the University of Michigan, presenting a paper at the 2002 National Communication Association, pointed out that an episode of the medical drama *Chicago Hope* featured a malnourished, breast-fed baby. Dr. Turner said that the show was sponsored by baby milk products that were not advertised. He also explained that manufacturers of medical devices use television drama to interject claims for the devices. For example, he said that the A-2000 BIS monitor, which records a cardiac patient's EKG and anesthetic depth, is heavily marketed to the medical community. A story line on *Chicago Hope* had an anesthetized patient hear a female doctor make a remark about his anatomy, which he remembered when he woke up. Because of the threat of lawsuits, the offending doctor argued to install a BIS monitor as a solution to make sure that the patient is asleep. However, as Dr. Turner pointed out, the U.S. Food and Drug Administration does not allow BIS to advertise this claim (Turner, 2002).

SCHEDULING AND ADVERTISING

Despite the increase in time-shifting to watch recorded television and shows on the Internet, the use of television as an advertising vehicle is still determined by demographic characteristics or who is watching at what time. Television programming is divided into parts of the day. **Prime time** is between 8 and 11 p.m. EST on weekdays and 7 to 11 p.m. on Sundays. These are the most expensive advertising times because 75% of adults are most likely to view situation comedies, drama serials, reality television, and special reports during these hours. Daytime is between 9 a.m. and 4 p.m. EST. Daytime advertising can reach up to 65% of the adult population. Early daytime is between 7 and 9 a.m., appealing to working men and women with a wide variety of advertised products. High-profile news programs are given a separate time of day with demographics favoring the older segments of the adult population. Late-night programming appeals to younger adults, while weekends favor sports fans. Advertisers target precisely defined audiences of certain channels and programs and/or place regional or local ads within the programs.

Schedules are still designed to get viewers who tune into a popular program to stay and watch subsequent programs; thus, a new show or one with low ratings is placed after a very popular show such as *American Idol*. Network executives from NBC, CBS, ABC, and Fox who appeared on a satellite seminar from the Museum of Television and Radio explained that they create "**flow**" with their prime-time schedules. The television concept of flow has to do with viewer inertia and staying with a channel into the next program. Raymond Williams also used the term "flow," meaning a planned stream of television programs, from trailers, commercials, and public service announcements to the next program in the schedule. Williams wrote: "We can be 'into' something else before we have summoned the energy to get out of the chair, and many programmes are made with this situation in mind: the grabbing of attention in the early moments; the reiterated promise of exciting things to come, if we stay" (Williams, 1974, p. 94).

Instead of thinking about what time to air a single show, network executives build scheduling blocks from 8 to 11 p.m. (The Making of a Prime-Time Schedule, 1997). They use the **"hammock" strategy** of placing a new or less successful program before and sometimes after successful series. For example, on May 2, 2011, ABC led in the ratings with 20.9 million viewers tuned into *Dancing With the Stars*. This boosted ABC's *Castle*'s ratings, bringing it ahead of shows on the other networks (Toff, 2011, May 4). The **"tent-pole" strategy** is the opposite of the hammock technique: They schedule a successful program between two less successful programs or one less successful program and one new program. Another technique is to place series of the same or similar genre or that have similar demographic appeals back-to-back (Bellamy & Walker, 1996). The network executives also said it is important to create programs that complement other technologies such as the Internet and websites. Ratings affect when a show is scheduled, thus shows may be moved to a more or less popular night.

Most television shows open immediately on the hour or half hour with scenes from the last episode and a strong lead-in, the beginning of the **narrative** that sets the theme of the show. This is followed by a myriad of commercials—some of which are 10 to 15 seconds long—and other promotions. Unless the viewer has recorded the show to allow fast-forwarding through the commercials, that person sits through the commercials in order to be there when the next segment of the show begins. In order to follow the narrative of a show, the viewer is likely exposed to the ads. Credits at the end of the show are often accompanied in a split screen by an epilogue or previews of next week's show to keep the viewer from switching channels. To hook viewers to certain series, marathons of multiple episodes are shown in a single night for people who may be curious about a show but reluctant to commit without knowing how the series unfolded. Replays, especially of new shows, give viewers the opportunity to see something they missed.

Noncommercial Channels

Home Box Office (HBO) changed American television by eliminating commercials and repeating its programs several times throughout the week's schedule so viewers have ample opportunities to catch up with missed episodes. HBO now has seven different channels, including a Spanish-language channel. Showtime, which originally featured primarily movies, has added series like *Dexter* and *Weeds,* miniseries, and special programming uninterrupted by commercials to its schedule. HBO and Showtime do not have to attract an audience for advertisers. Although the audience for premium channels may be relatively small at any given time—compared to the mass audience that the networks must have to keep their ratings high—shows on premium channels are very popular and successful at winning awards such as the Emmy and Golden Globe. Because HBO usually produces 13 episodes per season of shows like *Boardwalk Empire,* compared with 22 on the networks, the creators have more time, artistic freedom, and bigger budgets. Shows are often shot on film with cinematic visual techniques such as moving cameras, cinematic shot-counterpoints, long takes, and sophisticated nighttime photography. They are often shot on location and have high production values. HBO also allocates huge budgets for marketing and promoting its products (Akass & McCabe, 2004). HBO is not censored in the way that broadcast networks are because it does not go over the public airways. Shows like *True Blood* have profanity, violence, and nudity but also quality acting and direction. HBO scheduled series like *True Blood* and *Game of Thrones* to have their first shows of the week on Sunday evenings with the new seasons beginning in the spring, summer, or early in the new year. In addition to feature-length films, HBO and Showtime feature original programming, and, because of the popularity of original programming, they have developed more series per season.

THE PRODUCTION OF A TELEVISION SHOW

Production Houses

Television shows are created, developed, and produced by professional production houses, most of which are located on the West Coast. The networks also have their own production houses, for example, NBC Productions and CBS Productions. The networks also produce their own news and sports programs. The networks prefer to own the shows that they air because they can eventually make huge profits by selling reruns of the shows they produced into the syndication market (Grover, 1997). Film giants such as Universal, Paramount, Disney, and Warner Brothers are production studios with big budgets where many television shows are made. The Walt Disney Company is the parent company of the ABC network. Actors and stars also may have their own production houses. For example, David Letterman has Worldwide Pants, which not only produces *The Late Show with David Letterman* but also *The Late Late Show with Craig Ferguson*. There are also a variety of independent production houses that produce only one or two shows.

Pilots and the "Pitch"

If a creator has the funds or financial backing to make a pilot, a complete pilot or a 20-minute sample of one might be made in a production house and then offered to a network or cable organization. Since it costs more than $1 million to produce a pilot for a half-hour show and more than $2 million for a one-hour show, most creators of television shows will first "pitch" an idea to the network or cable group. A **pitch** is a description of the concept of a prospective show or series; it is a brief story line presented to a network executive. Characters and settings may be described along with the kinds of viewers it might attract. Pitches are usually made by experienced writers because new writers are seldom given the opportunity.

> John Marcus, the head writer for *Taxi* and *The Cosby Show,* said in a seminar at the Museum of Television and Radio in 1996: "Executives have poker faces and skeptical attitudes. . . . Pitching doesn't invoke your skills as a writer but your skills as a salesman." David Mich, a writer for *Saturday Night Live,* who also participated in the seminar, added: "Executives do things like try on designer jeans during a pitch, or they sleep."
>
> *Source:* "From Pitch to Polish: The Collaborative Process" (1996).

The executives ask questions of the pitch, for example, what is the motivation for the story; what propels the script; what is the nature of the lead character? The executive also asks specific questions about locale and possible actors and will make suggestions as well. There are many stories about famous pitches. For example, Warner Brothers Television President Peter Roth told of the pitch for the hit show *Without a Trace,* the show about the FBI's work to find missing persons: "The pitch for *Without a Trace* was a magazine thrown on my desk with the headline WHERE IS CHANDRA LEVY? (Chandra Levy was a congressional intern in Washington, D.C., who went missing in April 2001. Her body was found 13 months later in a park in the District of Columbia.) The one-line pitch was 'Whoever finds her'" (Stein, 2003, p. 72).

Because television executives prefer to build on the successes of previous series, resemblance to other shows is often a factor in the pitch. Todd Gitlin (1983), author of *Inside*

Prime Time, coined the term **hybrid pitch,** which he described as a writer-producer trying to sell a new television series to network executives by telling them that the prospective show is brand new and there has never been one like it before and then saying that it is a blend of two familiar hit shows from the past. Gene Roddenberry, creator of *Star Trek,* pitched his show to NBC as *Wagon Train* to the stars (Meehan, 2005). *Battlestar Galactica* was pitched as an "absolutely new break-through show that would ably merge the *Star Trek* and *Bonanza* franchises" (Kubey, 2004, p. 9).

If the executives respond positively to the pitch, they will ask for an outline or a script, and—if the subsequent reaction is also positive—they will commission a pilot to be made at the network's expense. Pilots are usually made in late winter or early spring. In late spring, pilots are screened before **focus groups,** small groups of people whose comments after a screening are compiled and interpreted by a market researcher. Computer programs also enable the members of a focus group to record their likes and dislikes while they watch the pilot. Focus groups are designed to obtain perceptions of people from demographic clusters such as age, occupation, income, lifestyle, and product purchases. Because television is so competitive, data from focus groups have become increasingly important. As the season progresses, maintenance research (the retesting of regular television programs with focus groups) is conducted to measure the appeal of story lines, characters, and other factors. Many pilots never actually get on television; however, if a pilot is considered a probable winner, the network or cable company will contract with the producer for a certain number of episodes, usually 5 or 6, sometimes 10 or 11 (a half season); or sometimes 22 (a full season). The gold standard is 88 episodes or four seasons. The network's top executives announce their decisions about which new series to order and announce them to advertisers and the public in mid-May. It is in May that the broadcast networks (ABC, CBS, NBC, Fox, WB, and UPN, along with cable networks such as MTV and USA) will try to sell 75% of their commercial time for the upcoming season. In July, the pilots are screened by members of the Television Critics Association for publicity purposes. Production for the specified number of episodes also begins in July.

THE PRODUCTION TEAM

Once a series is signed on for the upcoming season, the producer of the series puts together a team of co-producers, writers, actors, directors, assistant directors, editors, and technical crew members.

The Producer

The **producer,** who is usually the senior writer, along with other writers, develops the series for the season, and oversees the creation and production of episodes, each at a different stage of development. In an article about Brian Grazer, producer of *24, Parenthood, Friday Night Lights,* and other television shows for 30 years, Mimi Avins wrote that "a producer often incubates ideas, then finds a creative team to understand and execute his vision" (Avins, 2005, p. F10). Television is a producer's medium, as Horace Newcomb and

Robert S. Alley (1983) noted in the title of their book, *The Producer's Medium,* because they found that producers were the primary figures in television. When asked, "What does a producer do?" Lee Rich, founder of Lorimar and producer of *Dallas, Falcon Crest,* and *Knot's Landing,* answered:

> A producer does exactly what it sounds like. Somebody had to put all the pieces together. Somebody else may come up with the idea and then turn it over to somebody who will do it and put it all together. A guy who is making sure it gets done, the pages are shot, and the whole thing is done on a day-to-day basis. (Kubey, 2004, p. 104)

There are many types of producers for a television series. The executive producers are the creators and senior writers who are also known as the **"showrunners"** because they oversee the television programming, tackling everything from negotiating with network executives to counseling actors to defining the creative vision of a series—and much more. For example, Shonda Rhimes *(Grey's Anatomy),* Tina Fey and Robert Carlock *(30 Rock),* David Shore and Katie Jacobs *(House),* and Matthew Weiner *(Mad Men)* are showrunners. Co-executive producers, producers, associate producers, and consulting producers also may be directors, writers, lead actors, and consultants. The **line producer** (or on-the-line producer) is the detail person who oversees the show from its concept to its production. The line producer supervises the budget, oversees the construction of the sets, and keeps the costs in line. A former line producer at CBS told me that his job was saying "no" to most requests. *CSI: Crime Scene Investigation* has four executive producers who are also writers, the lead actor, and the head director, four co-executive producers, 10 producers, three line producers, three associate producers, three consulting producers, and two supervising producers. Some of the same people hold more than one position. Information about and the names of a television program's personnel can be obtained from the program's website.

Writers

Writers are considered the most important personnel for a television program, whether it is a series, a soap opera, a news program, a movie-of-the-week, or a special. Sid Caesar, famous for the comedy shows *The Show of Shows* and *Caesar's Hour* in the 1950s, was asked about the importance of writing. His answer, an old line from vaudeville, "If it's not on the page, it ain't on the stage" is echoed by many performers of the 21st century. Caesar, whose writers for the 39 shows that he did each year included Mel Brooks, Neil Simon, Woody Allen, and Larry Gelbart, said, "Writing is the most important thing" (Kubey, 2004, p. 30).

The creator/executive producer is the senior writer in charge of the story line throughout the season, but there is a staff of 8 to 10 writers for every episode. Some senior writer/producers such as David E. Kelley *(Harry's Law)* write every script, but most senior writers develop the concept and the season story line then turn the writing for each episode over to a team of writers. Some of these writers are freelancers who write no more than two or three scripts a year, but in order to have their scripts read, they must have agents. There are also specialty writers who get called in to "punch up" a script, particularly for situation comedies.

As writers on the regular staff gain seniority, they are given the title of producer. Eventually, many create their own shows, as did Dick Wolf, creator of *Law & Order, Law & Order: SVU, Law & Order: Criminal Intent,* and *Law & Order: LA*. Wolf started out as a writer for *Hill Street Blues* in 1985, moved up to co-producer of *Miami Vice* from 1986 to 1988, and began creating his own shows, which were not outstandingly successful until he came up with *Law & Order*. Likewise, Steven Bochco wrote for *Columbo, McMillan and Wife,* and *Banacek* before he became a producer at Universal. He then joined MTM Enterprises and created *Hill Street Blues*. Many writers start out in their twenties and thirties, and tend to be very well educated with backgrounds in English literature and acting in college. The creator of a series usually becomes the executive producer and head writer.

The standard procedure for television series writers is to meet in a room to discuss the script for the upcoming episode. They talk about plot lines that may be taken from their own experiences and from news stories. Phil Rosenthal and Jeremy Stevens, writers for *Everybody Loves Raymond,* explained that they

> would come together every morning and sit around and just catch up with each other in terms of what's new or pressing. . . . We realized fairly quickly that the main source of our stories is our lives and that a lot of the humor was going to come out of the gravel of our lives. (Fernandez, 2005, May 11, p. E7)

Rosenthal's wife, actress Monica Horan, said that his exact words to her appeared in the scripts, for example, when Raymond says to his television wife Debra, "You're my girl," Horan said, "that is what Phil says to me" (Fernandez, 2005, May 11, p. E7). David Shore, creator of *House,* head writer, and showrunner, has 12 to 14 full-time writers and their assistants on his staff. The writers devise story arcs in large chunks for the season before they start writing scripts. Then they develop outlines that go to Shore for feedback; completed scripts are reworked by several writers while Shore asks a lot of questions, and a completed script has to go to Shore for final editing 8 or 9 days before filming starts.

Writers are inspired by literary figures and current events. Shore loosely based the main characters, Drs. House and Wilson, on Sherlock Holmes and Dr. Watson. House's address is 221B based on Holmes' address at 221B Baker Street. House is addicted to Vicodin; Holmes took cocaine. House has a crippled leg, but it was Dr. Watson who had a bad leg in the Sherlock Holmes stories (Jackman, 2010). Dick Wolf said that the main source for story ideas for *Law & Order* was the front page of the *New York Post* (Unger, 1997) and law reviews ("Creating Prime-Time Drama: Law & Order," 1997). Michelle and Robert King and six other writers for *The Good Wife* often ask the actors, "What do you think of doing this with your character?" Michelle King said that they consult the actors "because everything here is a team effort. The writers are very careful to service everyone" (Slate, 2011, p. 67).

Animated shows have become increasingly popular on television, none more so than the long-running show *The Simpsons*. Matt Groening, the creator, explained that all the writers get together in a rented hotel suite at the beginning of the season. There they spend a day or two throwing out ideas while a secretary records what they say and makes notes for them. In subsequent meetings, the story ideas are fleshed out, and other writers write the scripts. Groening said that the scripts get "written, rewritten, rewritten again"

(Kubey, 2004, p. 144). When Kubey asked how he learned to tell a story in 22 minutes, Groening said he learned as a staff writer for James Brooks:

> It's been the greatest learning experience in my life. I've learned more about structure, storytelling, and pacing. Everything is a writing problem to be solved, so even though these cartoons were very simple in dialogue it was a matter of learning how to tell a story and keep people interested. . . . We do storyboards about 120 pages long and our scripts vary from 40–60 pages. Once that is approved, the animation is filmed. There are 80 animators and it takes six months to do a single show. (Kubey, 2004, pp. 142 & 145)

Dramatic television programs that appear on PBS or the *Hallmark Hall of Fame* are basically movies made for television. The producers bring in the best writers they can find who tell stories, or they work with short stories or novels and find writers to adapt them for television. The philosophy of this kind of drama is to emphasize the writer and tell a story in as interesting a way as possible. They put their scripts through many drafts with suggestions from all of the production staff to "explore the world of the script and the characters and what they might do" (American Playhouse, 1992).

The Writer's Treatment

A **treatment** is an overview of the plot with details of the chronological rundown of the scenes of the prospective script with information about the setting, plot, and characters, and may include a few examples of dialogue and a few key camera shots. The Writers Guild of America suggests 10 to 15 pages of a treatment for a half-hour show; 15 to 25 pages for a 1-hour show; 25 to 40 pages for 90 minutes; and 40 to 60 pages for a 2-hour show (Hilliard, 2008, p. 401).

CSI executive producers/writers Ann Donahue, Carol Mendolsohn, and Anthony Zuiker read a lot of science and interview paramedics and crime scene analysts for their story ideas. Zuiker, the series creator, discussed the complexities of the writing process on the national, weekly public radio series, *The Infinite Mind*:

> The first thing we do is somebody will walk into the room with a kernel of an idea. It may be a piece of technology. It may be a small story line. It may be a character arc and we sort of go from there. We have six—six or seven writers in the room at one time. We'll all be in a room with a bunch of grease boards and grease pens and we'll begin to talk it out pre the research stage, and we'll talk about an opening teaser, a through-line. We'll break down several beats [scenes] of Act 1, 2, 3 and 4. We'll talk about the act outs, the spins and turns.

(Continued)

(Continued)

After we talk about all of the process of the beats we'll have for the episode, we'll go to outline stage where the appropriate writers who are assigned will jot down every beat of the episode. Then they'll go commence to writing. . . .

It's just like an outline, and once they write the first draft, it'll come in. We'll give notes. We'll get notes from the network, from our peers, from the actors, and then we'll get notes from the director and we'll accommodate some notes based on production. . . . If we need a black bottom pool vs. a white bottom pool, we'll make that adjustment. If we found a two-story house vs. a one-story house, we'll make that adjustment to reflect in the dialogue, and then every single day of shooting, we'll do small dialogue tweaks and execution tweaks until the last roll of film is run. And then we'll get to the editing room and watch the director's cut, then the producer's cut, and then the network, you know, final master, and we'll continue to do writing and ad libs and loop lines until it airs that day . . . We have to make sure that when we execute our stories that they're all forensically driven, and by using 'CSI' shots and snap-zooms, we really show the audience the intense micro. That's the one thing we keep in mind. Another thing we keep in mind is we want to make sure that it—we're always telling a great mystery with twists and turns 'cause our show really isn't so much a whodunnit but rather a howdunnit.

The challenge to writing is to be able to underwrite and to be able to write 30 percent of the dialogues so the audiences can fill in 70 percent of the subtext. We hope that we challenge people cerebrally as they watch the show, as they're able to sort of tap into the minds of our characters and what they're thinking and what are their attitudes and deal with death in a very personal level and deal with a crime that could happen on their neighborhood block.

There's no rhyme or reason. Basically we just sit back and say, "What is interesting and engaging to us? What excites us?" And we're hopeful that America will follow and they have.

Source: Television and the Mind (2002). Reprinted with permission of Lichtenstein Creative Media, Inc.

Directors

Most television series have multiple directors, sometimes a different one for each episode. Matthew Weiner, creator, showrunner, and executive director of the critically acclaimed *Mad Men,* directs the season finales. Five other men and women are the regular directors. The director sits in the room with the writers and gets the final script before the actors (unless an actor is also a producer). The director then blocks the rehearsal and the camera shots. During the taping, the director usually stays in the control room communicating with the camera operators through a microphone or via the assistant director. The assistant director often prepares the camera shots. For live television, the director sits in front of multiple monitors, selecting the best shots with great speed. Larry Auerbach, the director for *One Life to Live,* said: "Each director has a unique approach to the material, to the way he shoots it, puts it together, but you also have a producer who sits in the control room when you are doing your dress [rehearsal] and provides a third eye" (Kubey, 2004, p. 118). Directors rely on their instincts and experience to set the tone of a television show. Sometimes actors will direct an episode of the shows they star in.

Casting

The network executives may have the last word on casting, but Lynn Stalmaster, a famous casting director, said, "The director is the final voice. He must be pleased and satisfied. You're not just casting an isolated part. You have to find a blend. . . . You're orchestrating an ensemble" ("Archive of American Television: Lynn Stalmaster," n.d.). Warren Littlefield, the president of NBC entertainment in 1994, said, "Casting is everything" (Kolbert, 1994, p. C13). After the final script with well-defined characters is completed, the casting director sends a "breakdown," a description of the characters complete with production details, to agents, who send photos and résumés suggesting possible actors for the parts. Before actors audition for the network, the production studio negotiates what they will be paid if they get the part. Contracts for the actors commit them to staying for several years if the series lasts that long. Leslie Moonves, who was the president of Warner Brothers Television in 1994, said: "My concern can't solely be the best actor. I'm looking for people who are attractive. That's part of the crass commercialism the studios and the networks have to look at. I have to think, 'Am I going to have a *TV Guide* cover in six months, and what's that going to look like?'" (Kolbert, 1994, p. C18).

According to Joshua Brand, executive producer of *Northern Exposure,* the networks' first choice for an actor is always someone who has acted in a successful television show. He said that the network chief, Brandon Tartikoff, did not like Michael J. Fox for *Family Ties,* but in that case the producers prevailed ("The Future," 1993).

Many television dramas and situation comedies have ensemble acting. Barbara Miller, head of casting for Warner Brothers, described the casting problems: "Ensemble casting is particularly difficult because you really have to balance it out. It's not as if you find one person for the lead and then assign the rest of the parts" (Pourray, 1995, p. 13). Extras also have to be cast. For example, *ER*'s assistant director in charge of casting and directing the extras worked with Central Casting to find the many extras who appear as patients and their families, ambulance drivers, orderlies, and housekeeping personnel in the hospital.

Putting a Show Into Production

When production begins for a new season in July, 22 to 24 episodes have to be made. For HBO and Showtime, 12 to 13 episodes are made. There may be six or eight scripts ready to go at the beginning, but once a series is underway, there are about 8 days between conception of a script and the taping or filming of the finished product. This means very long work days that may last for 16 to 20 hours as the production staff races to complete a show for broadcast. Although procedures vary for different series, the following is the usual procedure:

After the writers have their initial meeting in the room and agree on the treatment, one of the writers makes a 10-page outline that is scrutinized by the other writers before either the single writer or some of the writers complete a draft script of about 40 to 48 pages for a half-hour episode. To allow for commercials and other messages during the broadcast, 22 minutes is the standard for a script for a 30-minute program; 44 minutes is the standard for a 60-minute program. Sometimes half the writers write the script, and the other half punch it up. Once a script is written, the actors and producers have a **table reading.** They sit around the table, and the actors read the script for the writers, producers, director, and perhaps a few network representatives. Sometimes fans will be included to listen. The actors may give some input about what works for their characters and what does not. The writers then make notes about what does not work and revise the script, often late into the same night. If they have not been present at the table reading, representatives from the network also read the script and suggest changes. After the script is revised, the actors, the director, and the camera operators have a run-through rehearsal where they block the movement and read the lines aloud with scripts in hand. All the producers watch the run-through from the front row of the studio. At the end of each scene, the actors walk up to the front row and discuss the script with the director and producers. Lines and words from the script get changed, and sometimes entire scenes are revised or dropped. As new pages get written, different colored sheets of paper are inserted into the script to mark the changes. The final production of the show for most situation comedies is in front of a live audience. Scenes are taped and retaped when there are bloopers or last-minute changes have to be made. (I am indebted to my friend Patricia Hill, camera operator, for allowing me to sit behind the producers and directors in run-throughs and filming of various episodes of *Frasier* and *Caroline in the City* at Paramount Television Studios.) The taping may take 4 to 6 hours before everyone is satisfied. The tape goes to the editors, and the show is aired about a month later.

Complicated production for a series such as *Grey's Anatomy* has a longer production schedule: 7 days of preparation, 8 days of filming, and 5 days of postproduction editing and sound mixing. *Boardwalk Empire* may take 8 days or longer to prepare, 15 to film, and several more days to edit and mix the sound. Preproduction of the next episode overlaps with the production phase of another episode, and that overlaps with the postproduction phase of the previous show.

Soap opera production is different because instead of 22 to 24 episodes, 260 must be written and produced. Agnes Nixon, long-time writer for *The Guiding Light, One Life to Live,* and *All My Children,* explained that she and the other writers determine a long-range story projection for 6 to 8 or 10 months that gets updated as needed. The projection is sent to the network for approval. Six weeks prior to taping, each episode is plotted in outline form, act-by-act, scene-by-scene, and that goes out to the network for approval. Once approved, the outlines go to the associate writers who write and edit the scripts. The directors get the scripts 3 weeks in advance, but the actors get them the night before taping. They have teleprompters, but most soap opera actors memorize their lines very quickly. They rehearse, block, and perform an episode all on the same day.

Nixon discussed network censorship when she told about wanting to do a show on uterine cancer. The sponsor, Procter & Gamble, balked, but finally told her she could do the show if she did not use the words "cancer," "uterus," and "hysterectomy." She did the show without the words and managed to get her message across. Proof of this was the many letters she received from women who said the information in the show prompted them to get medical checkups.

Nixon discussed the unwritten subtext, a very important concept in television acting:

> Subtext is a word that's in almost every scene of every outline. Subtext is what she is feeling and not saying. Sometimes, I'll start out with subtext, and it will be even more important than what she is saying, and we want to make sure that the viewer understands that though Erica is putting on a great front, she's really terrified inside. . . . This affects the camera work. Sometimes the camera will not be on the person who's speaking. What the camera shows, the audience sees. The camera says to the viewer, "Look how Erica, who is saying nothing, is reacting." (Kubey, 2004, pp. 72–77)

Sets range from a single sound stage to complicated sets and locations. Shows like *CSI, NCIS*, and *Grey's Anatomy*—supposedly set in Las Vegas, Washington, D.C., and Seattle, respectively—are filmed in West Coast studios with sets that look like the cities where they are supposed to take place. The staff, crew, and actors go to those cities every three or four months to do exterior shots for authenticity. If the writers want outdoor shots in their scripts, they often have to change the scripts and wait until the next trip to the city. (More information on sets and art design can be found in Chapter 3, "Television Style.")

After the show is "wrapped," it is sent to postproduction for editing, sound mixing, and other changes. Despite all the care that goes into producing a television show, it is normal for them to change before they air. If the network executives do not like the way the show is going, they may scratch the first few episodes, bring in new producers, and completely reshoot the show. New versions are written with new or changed characters; actors may get dropped or added; locations may be changed. *Law & Order: LA*, which began in late 2010, came back in April 2011, killed off Rex Winters, a detective played by Skeet Ulrich, and switched Alfred Molina, who played Ricardo Morales, from his part as Deputy District Attorney to that of a detective. The head of Studios USA Television, Ken Solomon, said that the networks do not wait until the November Sweeps to make changes, because "the audience very likely by then will have tuned in and tuned out" ("Auto Pilot, It's Not, as Fall Season Nears," 1998, p. D3).

SUMMARY

Television is a business that relies on audience viewership. The process of making television shows inevitably involves disappointment. Roughly eight out of ten new television shows fail. Concepts, characters, and scripts that seemed promising often do not work in production. Research audiences that form focus groups may not warm up to them. Yet sometimes there are pleasant surprises, and shows that had low expectations turn out to be quite successful in execution. Scott Siegler, a former development executive for Warner Brothers, explained why it is so hard to predict what will please audiences:

> Because it's a mass audience. . . . You can work off precedents about what's worked on television before. You can work off whatever smattering of sociological information you gleaned from whatever sources. You can let your personal judgments enter into it to some extent. . . . You can ask whether this is something that people in Georgia or Nebraska will appreciate because they'll be able to translate it into their understanding. But you never really know. And there are so many variables in programming that even when you've reached a pretty general consensus about a genre not working or a kind of attitude not working, you can never be quite sure that that rule applies." (Gitlin, 1983, pp. 22–23)

Rino Scanzoni, chief investment officer for ad buyer Mediaedge:cia, looked at it from the perspective of advertising and spin-off shows: "It's a struggle for TV networks to create 'watercooler' hits that can command ad rates of half a million bucks for 30 seconds. That's why TV viewers are seeing more spin-offs of current hits. Once viewers buy into a series, there's a real appetite for new shows" (McCarthy, 2004, p. 6B).

The love-hate relationship between the creators of television shows and the networks was comically expressed by Ellen DeGeneres, who hosted the 2001 Emmy Awards on CBS on November 4: "They can't take away our creativity, our joy. Only television executives can do that."

The television critic needs to be aware of the many economic constraints that influence television production. Television is a business and has to make a profit. However, writers, directors, actors, and even producers want their products to be of high quality, for they are creative and talented people. As a television critic, you recognize how much depends upon the mass audience and its preferences. Therefore, knowledge of the television business as well as how television style is created (the subject of Chapter 3) enhances understanding of why television is the way it is.

EXERCISES

1. Find the television ratings in *USA Today* or on the Nielsen website www.nielsen .com. (The Nielsen homepage has a link to "Television," with a link that follows to "Weekly Ratings.") Check the ratings and shares for the current week on (1) broadcast television; (2) cable; (3) syndication; (4) websites; (5) among African Americans; and (6) among Hispanics. Note how Nielsen includes DVR recording.

2. During a Sweeps Week (January, May, September, and November), examine the television schedule to determine how the programs are different at that time.

3. Find a television program that has been canceled. Go back to the ratings to see where it was ranked.

4. Watch a television commercial and describe its AQRI (arouse quick related interest).

5. Watch a half-hour or one-hour television program, paying attention to all the commercials. See if you can guess the show's demographics from the commercials.

6. Watch a half-hour or one-hour television program and note all the products that are placed within it.

7. How many products get free air time on a morning news, a game show, or a reality show?

8. Watch a show on local cable television. See how many commercials are targeted to precisely defined audiences.

9. Analyze the flow of broadcast programs from 8:00 p.m. to 11:00 p.m. and describe the building blocks. Where is a less successful program placed?

10. Select a series on HBO or Showtime: (1) Find how many times the episode is repeated during the week; and (2) find how many episodes are scheduled for a single season.

11. At the end of a television show, watch the credits and find the name of the production house that produced it.

12. Select a very successful television series, then name newer shows that resemble it.

13. Go to a television series website and look at the roles and names of the personnel (producers, directors, writers, and so on).

14. Pay close attention to the writing of a television show. How much do you, as a member of the audience, fill in what is not spoken in the dialogue?

15. Examine the unwritten subtext of a television program. How do the camera work and the acting communicate the subtext?

16. If at all possible, visit a television studio to observe the taping of a television program or a live production. Discuss what you observed and what you learned.

SUGGESTED READINGS

Gitlin, Todd. (1983). *Inside Prime Time*. New York, NY: Pantheon Books.

Jackman, Ian. (2010). *House: The Official Guide to the Hit Medical Drama*. New York, NY: HarperCollins.

Hilliard, Robert L. (2008). *Writing for Television, Radio, New Media* (9th ed.). Boston, MA: Thomson/Wadsworth.

Kubey, Robert. (2004). *Creating Television: Conversations with the People Behind 50 Years of American TV*. Mahwah, NJ: Lawrence Erlbaum.

Leverette, Marc, Ott, Brian L., & Buckley, Cara Louise (Eds.). (2008). *It's Not TV: Watching HBO in the Post-Television Era.* New York, NY: Routledge.

Marc, David, & Thompson, Robert J. (1995). *Prime Time, Prime Movers.* Syracuse, NY: Syracuse University Press.

Nielsen Company: http://www.nielsen.com

Newcomb, Horace, & Alley, Robert S. (1983). *The Producer's Medium: Conversations With Creators of American TV.* New York, NY: Oxford University Press.

Webster, James G., Phalen, Patricia F., & Lichty, Lawrence W. (2000). *Ratings Analysis: The Theory and Practice of Audience Research* (2nd ed.). Mahwah, NJ: Lawrence Erlbaum.

PART II

Formal Aspects of Television

CHAPTER 3

Television Style

The ventures of dreamland are thine for a day.

—Silas Weir Mitchell ("Dreamland")

INTRODUCTION

When we watch television, we seldom think about how it is produced, yet it is television style created by production techniques that allows us to enjoy the programs we watch. When we watch the reality show *Survivor,* we see a group of 16 men and women who appear to be stranded on an island that is miles from camp, coping with little or no convenient resources and dangerous elements. Yet, there are as many as 20 camera people, directors, producers, and others there with them. If the 16 people who play the survivor game were really alone on the island, there would be no television show about them. Because they are the invisible entities behind the show, the production professionals are not noticed by the viewers at all. As a television critic, you do not have to know the technical requirements of producing a television show, but it is useful to remember that what we see on the screen is the product of many talented people who work in the television industry. Knowing something about production techniques may help the critic talk about what is seen and heard and how it came about.

The following discussion of television style was written for this book in collaboration with Paul Monaco, film and television producer, director, editor, writer, and professor of cinema and video. He writes from an experience of professional academic and media production of 25 years.

LENGTH OF SHOT AND FRAMING

Motion picture production developed distinctive stylistic approaches during the 50 years of making movies prior to the advent of broadcast television immediately after the Second World War. Often spoken of as "film language," the stylistic choices for directors and editors may be summarized briefly. The first 30 years of filmmaking consisted of silent movies, produced without synchronous sound, so the fundamental film aesthetic developed with a strong emphasis on visual communication. As such, there are several elements of film language that were established very early in the 20th century. Visually, all shots that appear on the screen, for both movies and television, may be described as long, medium, or close. A **long shot** includes an entire human figure from the bottom of the feet to the top of the head, creating a full picture. A **medium shot** is framed on a human figure at or near the waist, so that the torso and head fill the picture, while the legs and feet are below the lower frame line and out of the picture. A **close-up shot** shows only the head. There are a variety of shots that are gradients between these long, medium, and close shots that use intermediate framing, such as the medium long shot, the medium close shot, or the extreme close-up.

What we see on television can always be thought of and described as being a long shot, a medium shot, or a close-up shot, with variants of distance from camera to subject. All types of material seen on television, and all genres of TV production, use these shots. Compared to motion picture production, strong tendencies exist in television toward medium shots. Medium shots are prominently used for news commentators, for interviewers, for talk shows, and for sports commentators when they are on air. Most live and live-on-tape production in these genres favors the medium shot. Medium shots, moreover, are favored in the production of fictional dramas and comedies produced for television. The medium shot lends itself to what is considered the most natural framing for conversation. The heart of a great deal of writing for television drama and comedy is talk. As more viewers watch television on smaller screens, it is recommended that production should shift toward closer coverage. Viewing on a computer screen or other digital devices demands more close-ups and the elimination of wider visual coverage. The newer forms of viewing are thought to be geared to a more intimate relationship of the viewer to the picture.

Photo 3.1   A medium shot on *House*.

The genres of news, talk, information programming, and commentary in particular remind us that, although television production derives in part from the traditions of motion pictures, television also derives—and some would argue more strongly—from the traditions of broadcast radio. Talk is very important on television. Television is every bit as much an audio medium as it is a visual medium. Eventually, the audio component of a production may prove more definitive of the aesthetic of the emerging media than the picture that is receding in size.

Over time, the typical style of television production developed a reliance on a medium shot that is actually framed tighter than one that is described as cutting a figure at the waist. That standard framing of a shot for television is best described as an **"elbows" shot.** TV directors and camera operators commonly use the term "elbows." Any reference to elbows frames a shot of a figure so that the lower edge of the screen is at roughly the middle point of his or her arms. A great deal of television production uses this framing. Dramas, situation comedies, and soap operas nearly always do, but the commonality of this framing to production for television spreads more widely as well.

To say that any particular shot or a frame line is standard or dominant in television production still must be understood to mean that other shots are used as well. Long shots are not as common in television production as they are in motion pictures, but they exist in all genres of television. They often serve to draw the viewer's engagement out of a comedy or a drama emotionally. Hence, they are frequently used for transitions into and out of scenes. In sports programming, by contrast, long shots are absolutely vital to portraying the action of the game, which can only be shown with a long, wide-angle shot.

MULTI-CAMERA PRODUCTION

Live and live-on-tape television is normally **multi-camera production,** meaning several cameras are in use simultaneously. Four-camera production schemes have been common in television historically for the production of both dramatic and comedy programming. Such multi-camera production schemes allow for a good deal of coverage and have been particularly useful in the confined interior settings common in much of dramatic and comedy production for television. Multi-camera production in these circumstances has been considered especially amenable to episodic programming. Traditionally, television favored such production as economical and effective; however, budgetary considerations have created a trend toward single-camera production.

REACTION SHOTS

Early in the development of motion picture production, filmmakers discovered the power of the **reaction shot,** in which a facial expression or the gesture of a person who is not talking in a scene is revealed. This capacity to fill the screen with the reaction of a figure in a scene to another character's action became more sophisticated in feature film production after the coming of synchronous sound to the movies in 1927. Production for mainstream Hollywood feature films standardized the reverse angle shot, so that an editor could choose to show a single shot on either the speaker or the listener in a conversation. This ability, to cut to a reaction shot, is definitive of one of the primary aesthetic devices available to any filmmaker. Television has made coverage of reactions even more pronounced and prominent than in the movies. Part of this is because production for television usually is more intimate than the visual coverage provided in movies made for exhibition in theaters on the big screen. Live coverage in specific television genres—such as the talk show, quiz show, public affairs programming featuring experts with differing opinions, and sports broadcasting—lends itself so well to revealing the reactions of people being interviewed, pondering a question, arguing, or responding to a play in a game.

In television comedy and drama, reaction shots have taken on increasing importance as production styles have evolved over the half century since the 1950s. Situation comedies are models of using reaction shots to emphasize the humor of a line. Because successful television is episodic, regular viewers are familiar with the characters and their relationships in a particular show. This familiarity facilitates the viewer's understanding and appreciation of these sorts of reactions. The same is true for episodic drama, and nowhere is this more evident than in the daily daytime television soap operas. Prime-time drama relies heavily on reaction shots to convey realization, discovery, and a character's coming to terms with troubling or devastating feelings or events. *Mad Men, Grey's Anatomy, House, Parenthood,* and *NCIS* are typical of exceptionally popular dramatic programs in which coverage on shots of a character's reaction to other characters and the episode's story line is vital to the style.

Multi-camera production of live talk shows, quiz shows, and sporting events, of course, lends itself to the coverage of reactions. This is true for comedy and dramatic production as well, but television production with a single camera also utilizes reaction shots. Although several directors guide the making of different episodes of *Mad Men,* for example, every episode is heavy on reaction shots, and their importance to the development of the story line and the revealing of a character's feelings is vital. This style of utilizing reaction shots so much meshes with the fact that the characters in the series—most prominently Don Draper, Peggy Olson, Roger Sterling, and Joan Harris—are strong and well-established for the viewers.

LIGHTING

"If you can't light it, you can't film or tape it." This simplistic maxim is the heart of all motion picture and television production. Once any figure or object is adequately lit so that it can be seen, a vast array of aesthetic and stylistic choices confronts the maker of film or television. The look of television production tends toward balanced lighting that avoids extremes of light and shadow and treats all figures in a scene equally. The source of light in such traditional television production has been treated as comparatively inconsequential. Lights in a television production studio hang from a grid above the action, and these lights are set to produce a common look so that generally all portions of the space are lit similarly. This mode of lighting is very different from what is used historically in single-camera film production. The use of a single camera in motion picture production requires much more time because there are far more setups. Motion picture lighting, since the early 1970s, has used lower light and permitted greater latitude in allowing light and shadow to push or pull toward greater extremes of brightness or darkness. There has even been a stylistic tendency in motion picture production toward the use of "available light," with minimal addition of lighting in certain locations. In this sense, television productions have almost always been "better" lit than movies because production for television uses more standardized and brighter lighting as a rule.

Manipulation of the lighting strongly affects the tone of a scene and the emotional mood that is conveyed by that scene to viewers. Television production, however, historically has been very modest in the use of lighting to influence tone and mood. Such a use of lighting is far more a convention of modern motion picture production. Dramatic features produced for theatrical release tend toward favoring low light, accepting what is called natural, available light for scenes, permitting the wide use of extremes of brightness and darkness and light and shadow, to create mood and emotional responses. While television production has steered away from extreme and artistic lighting schemes, the aesthetic choices about lighting are still essential to production. Cynthia Pusheck, director of photography for *Brothers and Sisters,* said the challenge of lighting eight or more actors in a scene is a challenge: "You must devise an economical way that will allow you to light it, get the coverage and maybe limit some of the angles, all while trying to create a style or mood and tell a story that the audience will grasp" (Pusheck, 2010, 49).

Because the producers wanted more intimacy between the characters for the second season of the television series *House* and to give the audience the impression that they were witnessing reality, Roy Wagner, the cinematographer, had the number of lights pulled down, and the line producer, Gerrit van der Meer, redesigned the sets. They put ceilings on all interior sets, including hallways, offices, the lobby, waiting room, and operating rooms. The ceilings enclose the spaces, and fluorescent fixtures built into the sets are the only source of light, with beams of light that can be controlled. As Wagner said, "That's important because the eye automatically goes to the brightest light in the frame. We want the audience looking at the actors" ("How Roy Wagner Reveals," 2005, p. 2). The new lighting setup gave the directors the freedom to shoot in any direction, including looking up toward ceilings. It also trimmed the budget and the time it takes to light the scenes.

PRODUCTION ON FILM VERSUS DIGITAL VIDEO

For a great many years, people in the television industry talked about entertainment shows for television being "taped," but many of the episodic dramas and comedies on TV were actually filmed. The use of celluloid film produces a "look" in which colors are more deeply saturated, detail is more precise, and the foregrounding of figures and objects is sharp. It was only in the late 1990s that any appreciable number of major episodic dramas and comedies made for network television began to be produced using digital video cameras rather than film and film cameras. The production crews did not necessarily welcome this change, and a number of long-running shows continued using film.

The industry-wide changeover to digital cameras and production had almost nothing to do with aesthetic choices or with production style. Like many producers' decisions, it was driven by economics. Film had two areas of extra cost that digital video production did not have. First, the use of film required larger camera crews, so that a four-camera production normally required a minimum of 12 camera professionals, 3 on each camera. Second, the costs of film stock and the processing of film were thought to be considerably higher than the cost of taping—even using the highest-end and most expensive digital cameras. Not surprisingly, for a while professional production personnel debated the use of the new digital technologies in the camera department. As for the preferred look in terms of color saturation, light and shadow, and detail, most professionals preferred the look of film. Many craftspeople in the industry also argued that the economic arguments for conversion to digital video production were misleading and/or mistaken. This argument advanced the notion that the hourly rental of time for digital editing was so expensive that conversion to digital production might save little or no money.

Gradually, digital cameras prevailed. The definitive influence in the final choice of digital cameras over motion picture cameras and the use of film in production for television was that digital postproduction (for editing and sound) swept away the technologies and practices of motion picture editing and double-track system sound. Motion picture and television craftspeople are famously capable of adapting to technological changes and the use of new equipment. What constituted a digital revolution in television production from the late 1990s into the early 21st century was absorbed and mastered quickly and well. Viewers did not notice when, and if, their favorite entertainment shows changed from production in film to production with digital cameras. Although the shift from traditional editing and sound technologies and practices to digital ones affected the professional workplace in television considerably, what the viewers see and hear in their homes was not necessarily changed in any perceptible way until the arrival and spread of high-definition television (**HDTV**). The picture quality of HDTV provides a delineation to the viewer's eye of a vastly improved perception of depth and a wider picture that exists in an elongated rectangular shape as opposed to the square, box-like picture of traditional television. This wider frame provides challenges to the creators of television with regard to the visual information contained in the picture and the composition within the frame that conveys that information.

STYLE, RECEPTION, AND DIGITAL VIDEO PRACTICES

Among the ironies and complexities of television style is that all the formal characteristics of picture and sound finally may depend less on what went into the television production and more on the equipment on which you view it. The goal of improving what the viewer sees and hears at home is behind the conversion from analog television to high-definition digital television in the United States that was mandated in the Telecommunications Act, passed by the U.S. Congress in 1996. Proponents of the conversion to high-definition television believe that the costs and difficulties have proven to be worth it because viewers now see a considerably sharper and clearer picture, the sound quality is vastly improved, and

Photo 3.2   HDTV is ideal for a wide long shot of a baseball game to be shown.

Source: © istockphoto.com/RBFried.

the elongation of the screen's width delivers programming in a vastly more impressive pictorial frame. It has not taken media production professionals long at all to adapt to this new, more sharply defined and wider picture of HD.

While digital production on tape has grown quickly and steadily, there are some notable holdouts in areas of production in which film is still largely preferred for image capture; put simply, the picture on film still always looks better and more nuanced visually. Once captured on celluloid with the film look, such footage must then be transferred to a digital tape format for editing. High-end commercials for many products promoted nationwide, for example, still are often shot on film. Here the preference for the film look in glossy national advertising campaigns prevails. Nonetheless, television producers have widely accepted that it is the use of camera lenses that more fully determines the "look" of any picture than whether it is recorded digitally or on celluloid.

Moreover, while the introduction of HDTV in the first several years of the 21st century has promoted the utilization of 24-p and digital video camera use for dramatic and comedy production, at the same time there is a shift away from multi-camera production to single-camera production. While the use of digital cameras saves production money at one end by replacing more expensive equipment, the choice to follow single-camera production practices increases the length of all productions and their costs. Single-camera production is a technique developed in, and associated with, the movies. The preference for it, however, may be questionable when the production in question is for television. In the late 1990s, the shift to single-camera production techniques found HBO at its vanguard. Signature HBO successes like *The Sopranos, Sex and the City,* and *Six Feet Under* were single-camera productions, and there is little doubt that these successes influenced other productions to tend toward single-camera direction and production.

To the question, "Can the average viewer recognize when he or she is seeing a single-camera production or a multi-camera production on television?" the general answer is no. Studio productions, such as talk shows and newscasts, nearly always are multi-camera productions even though they are shot entirely with digital video cameras. Multi-camera techniques lend themselves to quick cutting from shot to shot, audience coverage including an array of immediate audience reactions shots, and the ability to pull out wide on a shot in a blink of the eye. Single-camera techniques permit directors and actors more time to work through the material of a scene because there are more camera setups, and because a number of takes are required to provide adequate coverage of any scene. The single-camera technique tends to slow the dramatic action and development, and provides coverage so that a character's reactions tend to be given greater attention. Nonetheless, single-camera production had come into vogue during the first decade of the 21st century, although no specific aesthetic intention was connected to that development.

MODES OF PRESENTATION

Historically, most television production for drama and comedy has aimed at a mode of presentation like that of classic Hollywood film. Movements and focusing of the camera lens were intended to be unobtrusive. Editing generally followed patterns of continuity and the editing formulas for achieving that appearance. Disruption in the flow of the story was minimized in favor of clear and distinct break points. Television production in principle has had to follow strict points of division in order to accommodate breaks for commercials. Again, HBO, a cable network without commercial sponsorship of specific program segments, led the way toward a new form of narrative integrity and wholeness in its typical dramatic and comedy production. Here, again, however, television style is diverse and multifaceted.

Sports coverage presents an example of production decisions that are determined by the discrete nature of the game or competition itself. News coverage on television has a strong tendency toward a stylistic emphasis on immediacy, underscored by handheld camera work and a visual involvement in the developing action of any scene. With handheld camera movements, the viewer's eye follows the movements, irregularities, and pacing of the camera's lens. Handheld camera styles draw the viewer to the image, make emphatic the viewer's identification with the point of view of the camera, and thus are assumed to visually engage the viewer's emotions more. Some reality programming, such as the early reality show *Cops,* abides by this style. Such an approach to camera work emphasizes engagement, handheld techniques, and the following of action. Reaction footage is minimized in the final cutting and may not have been filmed at all because the attention of the camera work is the action as it happens in front of the police officers. *NYPD Blue,* the former weekly drama about police detectives in New York City, tended to establish a visual style based on handheld camera work and abrupt camera movements, including **swish pans** where the camera lurched in one direction or the other, but usually left to right, creating a particular "look" that became characteristic for creating transitions within a sequence. Cinematographer Roy Wagner, who employs a blend of handheld, **Steadicam** (a camera strapped to the body of the camera person), and dolly (a camera mounted on moving wheels) shots on the series *House,* said: "When the story becomes chaotic and out of control, we'll handhold the camera to create visual tension, so the audience subliminally feels a sense of urgency" ("How Roy Wagner Reveals," 2005, p. 3). From this reality style of handheld camera work, television news, live coverage, and other forms of informational programming display a strong affinity for the use of editing wipes and the blending of pictures. A moving camera, handheld footage, and swish pans (fast camera lateral movements across the screen) have become more common in television production since *NYPD Blue.*

TELEVISION SOUND AND EDITING

There is very little silence on TV. The production style for all genres and types of programming requires a sound design that is dense and unrelenting. A common term for this practice in the industry calls such sound in a production "wall-to-wall." Talk predominates on television, hearkening back to the medium's traditions which are derived from radio. Even when there is relatively less talk, music, sound effects, or what is heard as naturalistic ambient sound fills the track. Directional microphones on booms are utilized to record sound on dramatic and comedy productions. Documentaries, interviews for news coverage, and talk shows may use small, lavaliere-type microphones worn on the clothing, although wireless microphones that are carried in a pocket or attached to a belt to permit greater movement have become more common. Compared to motion picture sound, television sound is far less sweetened, manipulated, and edited. Sound effects in television production are vastly fewer and always inferior in quality to those used in motion picture production for theatrical distribution. Another factor is that the systems in the typical television sets in the early 21st century still consist of smaller and vastly inferior speakers mounted within the television set itself. To compensate, home theater setups with stereo speakers amplify television sound.

What appears most definitive and distinctive of television style is a tendency toward accelerated pacing in nearly all genres. Quick cutting is a norm, although there are exceptions to this guideline. Multi-camera production in particular favors quicker cutting, with shot lengths typically 3 to 5 seconds in duration. Longer takes are less common in television. When long takes do occur, they frequently are instances of a Steadicam, a camera equipped with a special spring-loaded rigging that combines the freedom of a handheld camera with the stability of a dollied tracking shot, moving normally with a subject. This creates the smooth, flowing appearance of the shot as the cameraman walks along.

During the 1950s and 1960s, television programming was decidedly slower-paced and more clearly based on principles of continuity than it is today. In the 1970s, cutting ratios quickened, so that shorter shots tended to be edited more quickly. As a general principle, the pace of editing has increased in all genres and types of television. However, as television programming has become as vast and as diverse as it did by the 1990s, generalizations about television style—and the prevailing aesthetic in the medium—must always be viewed cautiously. Since 2000, with digital television production in full force, the pacing and look of television programs has generally become quicker, more disjointed, edgier, and adventuresome. HBO productions such as *True Blood* and Showtimes's *Dexter* are prime examples of this, but so are series developed by the major broadcast networks such as *CSI, NCIS,* and *NCIS: Los Angeles*. Made-for-television movies followed a slower pace of development and editing than dramatic and comedic television programming. Movies are longer, complete works. Most feature films that are shown on television are an hour and a half to two and a half hours in length. Music videos and commercials tend toward fast cutting, with pacing that often may be described as frenetic. As television producers in all genres manage and manipulate time—a phenomenon that descriptively is definitive of television—it is widely observed that generational tastes appear to dictate much about editing choices and pacing. Programming that is presumed to appeal to younger viewers, especially to teenage and young adult audiences, is more fast-paced than shows, programs, and types of television aimed at a middle-aged or older demographic.

PRODUCTION STYLES

Industry professionals often say that motion pictures are a director's and cinematographer's medium, while television is a producer's and writer's medium. This generalization points to a perception that defines the differences in production styles. Traditionally, feature films made for theatrical release explore a wider range of visual looks, camera setups and movements, and engage physical space in ways that are more ambitious aesthetically. Television production is far more cautious, economical, and standardized, being dependent upon turning out material on a regular basis in a uniform way. Drama and comedy produced for TV have been intended for episodic series, and that intention drives their style. News, information, and talk programming have to be regularized to repeat daily. Sports on television is an event, although the proliferation of sports channels in the late 1990s, the lengthy seasons of many professional sports—Major League Baseball (MLB) especially, but also the National Basketball Association (NBA), the National Football League (NFL), and the National Hockey League (NHL)—and the increased coverage of major college athletics have transformed the truism of "event" programming into the programming concept of covering a different event every three hours or so.

ART DIRECTION

Television series encourage art direction, also known as production design. Studio production occurs in a defined space. Typical sets have three walls on a sound stage, usually decorated to look like familiar rooms in houses, hospitals, or offices that the characters return to over the life of a series. The fourth wall is left open for the camera equipment, lights, microphones, and a live audience if one is in the studio. Cameras are basically aimed in a forward direction like the eyes of the audience facing a stage, with side shots and close-ups as needed. The sets have open ceilings with rafters and lights. *House* is an exception to this norm with its four hard-walled, closed ceiling sets constructed to look like real hospitals. That is why viewers sometimes see the ceilings and overhead lights in the shots or follow the Steadicam, strapped to the camera operator's body, down the hallways.

Situation comedies have nearly always been taped in front of a live audience, even though the program that is shown is extensively edited after the actual taping, and normally does not air until several weeks later. The audience sits on raised bleachers on one side of the set, which normally consists of three stages built and dressed as the normal living, work, and leisure spaces of the characters. These are the places where the bulk of the show's action occurs, with another set built and added for specific scenes, in a bar or a restaurant, for example. These stages, all of which open to the camera personnel, are arranged in a line, like railroad cars, with the performance and its camera work most normally proceeding from left to right. Typically, these stages have scenery painted on backdrops to offer views out of windows from the set itself. For situation comedies, the décor and color combinations are brighter and lighter; for dramas, the look of the furnishings, the paint on the walls, and the costuming are more subdued. More reds and yellows are used in situation comedies; browns, grays, blues, and similar subdued colors are used for drama. The laboratories of *CSI: Crime Scene Investigation* are colored in blue and blue-green due to gels on the lights. Sets are detailed and dressed with props that look "natural" for the era and place, and for age and gender, as well as the economic or social status of the characters in a comedy or drama. The set created by Stephan Olson for *How I Met Your Mother* is done in shades of rust, red, and orange with the character Ted's camera collection, posters, and signs in full view. It's cluttered and conveys a masculine domain. The set for the advertising agency on *Mad Men* designed by Bob Shaw, conveys the Madison Avenue era of the 1960s. There are typewriters but no computers on the desks; the phones have dials; and there are Dictaphones. Set decorator Amy Wells found print ads for Zippo lighters and Arrow shirts for the office walls. Production designer Dan Bishop said the budget constraints caused them to shoot *Mad Men*'s restaurant scenes in existing venues like Musso & Frank in downtown Los Angeles. He said, "It would be a challenge to replicate that. They look great on film" (Roberts, 2007, p. 63).

Prop masters are in charge of selecting appropriate properties on the sets, and makeup artists and costume designers decorate the actors for their parts. The actors in *Mad Men* are authentically dressed in 1960s style with the women in crinolines, sheath dresses, angora sweaters, and pearls, while the men have hair slicked with Brylcreem and wear skinny ties, white shirts, and cuff links. Much attention is paid to details, whether it is a foamy cocktail or a plastic typewriter cover, and everyone smokes. On *Glee,* set in contemporary times, Jane Lynch, who plays Sue Sylvester, averages nine track suits, that are purchased in mall stores, per episode.

The production designer or art director works hard at balancing any number of considerations. The driving aesthetic for such choices is naturalism, with a strong emphasis on creating spaces that the viewer will take as appropriate to, and believable for, the particular characters and episodes. Successful comedies and dramas run for years and then go into syndication, when they may be telecast daily. The distinct spaces where these dramas and comedies occur are very detailed parts of their overall aesthetic value.

To save on production costs and to avoid problems that arise from shooting outdoors, many television shows use **green screens,** that is, actors are placed in front of a blank green screen and realistic backgrounds are superimposed in postproduction. Studios create virtual, three-dimensional exteriors using high-definition footage shot in distant locations. Green-screen digital special effects recreate historical scenes such as castles and fantasy locales.

Nonetheless, when thinking about the styles in television production, and, at some point, commenting on a few of the differences between the production look of movies as compared to television, a very basic and historic fact stands in the way of reaching any simple conclusion about television style. Because of their fundamental photographic nature, motion pictures and television aesthetically are considered to be strongly "naturalistic." From the inception of each of these media until the mid-1960s, however, production and presentation in them was in black and white. Little seems less natural than a visual world perceived and seen only in black and white, but many of the most highly regarded movies in motion picture history and all the classic television productions of the 1950s and early 1960s were in black and white. Moreover, reruns of *I Love Lucy* and *Gunsmoke,* for example, still entertain television audiences into the early 21st century. The telecasting of black-and-white classic feature films and significant historical documentaries on television has only grown with the proliferation of cable and satellite television and their many new channels.

The norms of spatial production design in drama and comedy produced for television tend to be stage-like, commonly with the action opened up toward the imaginary fourth wall of a set where the action occurs. The cast essentially plays to the cameras, much the way stage actors play to their audiences. Lighting for depth perspective and the use of filming techniques such as selective focus or deep focus have traditionally been minimized in production for television. Again, by the late 1990s and into the early years of the 21st century, HBO productions, notably series like *The Sopranos* and *Boardwalk Empire,* as well as special productions like HBO's *John Adams* and *The Pacific,* pushed production for television toward motion picture artistry and its visual and performance aesthetic.

So much of what is on television is news, information, interview, and talk programming, and in these genres the stylistic conventions are standard. The set itself is generally functional, relatively unembellished, and the commentators, hosts, and guests are foregrounded. This means that their figures are prominently lit and that the backgrounds do not detract or draw attention away from their prominence in the frame. Such programming typically finds a satisfactory look and stays with it. There are differences, of course. The *Late Show With David Letterman* is produced in an older theater owned by CBS and, not coincidentally, located on Broadway in New York City. *The Tonight Show* on NBC with Jay Leno is produced in a large studio in Burbank, California, and the production style is distinguished by beginning each show with shots revealing the entire studio, sometimes showing camera operations, and always zooming in to the host with a sweeping crane shot as he emerges on stage. More serious talk formats, such as *The Charlie Rose Show* on PBS, utilize more minimal spatial and set design. Rose's interviews take place against a minimalist black background. Serious interview shows and political and informational talk on television do not use an audience. Daytime talk shows and various similar genres, where talk is primarily with celebrities and entertainers, nearly always feature the audience in some way, typically taking the show's host into the audience at some point to interact with selected audience members in a great many of the shows.

THE SPLIT SCREEN

By the late 1990s, television news and informational programming on television in the United States discovered the split screen. Sometimes this is used purposefully, for example, to have a reporter at a location in one box discussing an event with the anchor in the studio, who is in the rest of the pictures. Other uses of the split screen appear more arbitrary or capricious. Splitting the screen is easy with the technology and frequently seems done for no other reason than that it can be done. A simple informational scroll of information in a line across the bottom of the screen—typically with stock prices, or the local weather—is a modest gesture that does not really split the screen.

Split screen use appears most effective on informational shows in which adversaries are discussing a public issue in debate style, and the screen is split between them for the conduct of what constitutes their debate. Perhaps even more so because they are separated physically and joined from different locations only as a visual convention on the TV screen, this visual format lends itself to the style of cross-talking and escalating exchanges that often seem to turn angry.

Any consideration of the style and aesthetics of television must keep in mind that the antecedents of television come as much, or more, from broadcast radio as they do from motion picture production. Sound is continuous in all types and genres of television. Silence is dead air, and even "natural" pauses in speech or response, whether in interviews, commentary, or delivering fictional lines, are to be minimized. Part of the aesthetic of television is the constancy of sound, which in some instances, such as news coverage or reality shows like *Cops,* demands a prominent track of ambient location sound.

DIRECTORS

In motion picture production, successful directors gain recognition and fame. Their names appear prominently in the credits of a movie and on the marquees of the movie theaters. Such attention is not granted to television directors. If their productions are multi-camera, their work may be even more intense and demanding than directing for the single camera. Directors of sports television must be utterly engaged in what is going on in the game, quick-witted, and make instantaneous decisions. Their work is facilitated by the ensemble of veteran professionals around them. This is a slick business, whose positions are reserved for the best and the most reliable. Simultaneously, the director in live sports gives camera operators directions—"pan to the right," "get tight on the manager in the dugout," "hold a shot on the backfield," and so forth—while following the game and calling for the technical director, who works at a control board called a switcher, to take the correct shot and transmit it out to the audience. All this happens in a relative flash. The director also needs to be able to spot good reactions from fans in the stands, or at least amusing ones, for example someone who has fallen asleep in the late innings at a boring Major League Baseball game.

Studio multi-camera direction for talk shows or game shows is similar, but far less stressful. The action is predictable. Audience members at a show's taping most likely have been selected and seated by a production assistant well before the taping begins. Directing a newscast is even more predictable, unless breaking news interrupts the planned broadcast and the director must make an immediate decision about when to interrupt the newscast, how long to stay with the incident occurring in real time, and how to instruct the editor to use whatever camera coverage of it is available.

When there is multi-camera dramatic and comedy production for television, the director must watch a large television screen with the pictures from each of the four cameras on that screen at once (called a quad-split), while simultaneously being engaged with what is going on with the characters. Directing is about camera setups, movements, and angles, but it more deeply must be about what is going on with the characters and where each character's arc is in the story. Thus, directing most clearly for television drama and comedy comes down to being about capturing people and what is going on with them to fit the purposes and goals of the particular show. Television **situation comedy** directors must develop an uncanny feeling for a joke and also have a sensitive feel for catching a reaction shot from one of the other characters. For drama, something similar is the challenge, but the director watches for expressions of feeling and tension and is sure to cover those while also having made certain that appropriate reaction shots are covered for another character.

ACTORS

Television actors often have theater acting backgrounds, but acting for television is altogether different from acting in the theater. There are fewer rehearsals, with many last-minute changes and often little time to memorize lines. In the first few rehearsals before the camera crews arrive, actors may be relatively free to move about on the sound stage in accordance with where they feel they need to be. If the camera cannot make an adjustment, the actors change their movements to help out the camera operators. Often the floors of the sets are marked with quarter-inch paper tape that shows an actor where to stand and which way to angle his or her body, but the tape is removed before the cameras shoot. The directors block the actors to the furniture in situation comedies so that they do not look down when performing. Also, the blocking is for the director of photography so he or she lights where the actors will be. The actors (and the production staff and crew) for dramas put in extremely long hours, as many as 16 in one day, with many starts and stops while keeping consistency of character. They have to return to the set, bringing themselves back into character with the same voice, movement, and gestures.

SUMMARY

The stylistic commonalities in television are many. The genres of production for television, however, are vastly diverse. Whatever is made for television and shown on television always is seen in a circumstance that varies greatly depending on the quality of the particular set on which the viewer is watching. Has the horizontally expanded screen of HDTV and the brighter, more numerous pixels and more crisp resolution of the picture promised by digital television vastly changed the viewing experience? At a simple, surface level, the answer is yes. But at a more complex depth of analysis, the question remains open.

Television is about story and character. Any director of television understands that his or her job is less setting the cameras, framing the shots, and composing them than it is in understanding and conveying to viewers the sense of the story and what is going on with the characters in it. This is true for all television drama and comedy, but also for the news, informational reporting, celebrity coverage, talk shows, and whatever reality television may claim to be recording and portraying.

EXERCISES

1. Select examples from several types of programming—a situation comedy, a drama, a national or local news broadcast, a talk show, a game show, and/or a sports event—and turn off the picture and listen to a show for 10 minutes. How much have you lost in your experience without the picture?

2. Record some situation comedies and dramas or watch them online, then view them a couple of times to carefully determine and write down the use of close, medium, and long shots in the productions. What differences do you perceive between comedy and drama with regard to the use of close, medium, and long shots?

3. Analyze the same shows that you used for exercise No. 2 and time the individual shots in the show. What do you perceive as the differences between comedy and drama in terms of the length of shots and the pacing with which the show is put together?

4. Again, using the same situation comedies and dramas, look carefully through them for the reaction shots. How frequently are reaction shots used? What patterns do you perceive in situation comedies and dramas? How are they different?

5. Watch a talk show to see how many reaction shots there are: of the host, of the guests, of the audience. Watch a public affairs show on which guests or a panel representing different points of view are featured. See how many shots are reactions of someone when another person is talking. Watch a sports event throughout, such as a complete baseball or football game, and see how much coverage there is on players, coaches or managers, and fans in the stands.

6. Select an episode of a situation comedy with which you are familiar and watch it, concentrating on the number of reaction shots used on a character who is not talking. Do the same for an episodic drama.

7. What is the look of a particular show on television? Is the lighting bright or dark? Can you clearly see the characters at all times, or do the characters move into shadows where their features are obscured?

8. How would you describe the production design of any particular show on television? What do the sets, locations, or costumes suggest to you? What information is conveyed to you by the design elements? If it is a comedy or a drama, do the sets mesh with the mood or the theme of the program? If it is a nonfiction show, do the sets convey a sense of seriousness, authority, and/or objectivity?

9. When you are aware of a camera movement, either in toward a subject or out and away from it, or movement that follows a character from left to right or from right to left, can you explain what appears to be the motivation and intention of the camera being put into motion? Does this movement serve to reveal something in the scene to the viewer, or does the camera movement appear to be about mood and feeling?

10. Select a show with which you are familiar and have watched many times. Select one actor from the show and comment on the consistency of character (appearance, voice, movement, gestures, and attitude) over time.

SUGGESTED READINGS

Caldwell, John T. (2008). *Production Culture: Industrial Reflexivity and Critical Practice in Film and Television*. Durham, NC: Duke University Press.

Kingdon, Tom. (2004). *Total Directing: Integrating Camera and Performance in Film and Television*. Los Angeles, CA: Silman-James Press.

Musberger, Robert B. (2010). *Single-Camera Video Production*. Boston, MA: Focal Press.

Shelton, S. Martin. (2004). *Communicating Ideas With Film, Video, and Multimedia: A Practical Guide to Information Motion-Media*. Carbondale, IL: Southern Illinois Press.

Ward, Peter. (2003). *Picture Composition for Film and Television* (2nd ed.). Boston, MA: Focal.

Zettl, Herbert. (2011). *Television Production Handbook* (11th ed.). Belmont, CA: Wadsworth.

CHAPTER 4

Television, the Nation's Storyteller

Sing to me of the man, Muse, the man of twists and turns

driven time and again off course, once he had plundered

the hallowed heights of Troy. . . .

Launch out on his story, Muse, daughter of Zeus

start from where you will—sing for our time too.

—Homer *(The Odyssey)*

INTRODUCTION

As you have seen in previous chapters, television is a producer's medium, and most producers are the creators and writers of the stories that are told on television. Both fiction and nonfiction television tell stories, thus this chapter relates the important characteristic of television as a story-making medium. All television tells stories whether they are through drama, comedy, news, reality, game, or cooking shows. As a television critic, you will analyze the characteristics of narrative and the ways in which stories are crafted to fit the television medium. If you are a student of television production, this chapter will help you develop the stories you want to tell.

Paul Bloom, a professor of psychology at Yale University, said that imaginative events have power because we do not have to make choices since they are made for us: "We can get the best of both worlds, by taking an event that people know is real and using the techniques of the imagination to transform it into an experience that is more interesting

(Continued)

67

Structure and systematic organization are extremely important in television narrative. Because of frequent interruptions during the programs and week-long gaps between episodes, familiar structure enables viewers to stay with the stories. Time constraints for broadcast television require most stories to fit into 30- and 60-minute time slots, with the stories themselves taking up no more than 22 or 44 minutes, respectively. Half-hour shows are broken into two acts, while hour-long shows are broken into four acts. This allows for the commercial breaks and other interruptions. Programs on premium subscription television such as HBO are also broken into acts, although there is more flexibility because an episode is not interrupted by commercials. Formats are repeated week after week because television programming, for the most part, is episodic. Series and serial television have groups of recurring characters whose essential qualities and basic situations remain the same from episode to episode. In series television, novel events do occur, but the characters and their strategies and actions tend to remain similar. There is usually a resolution to a dilemma or problem in a single episode, but conflicts in interpersonal relationships may not get resolved. In serials, especially in soap operas, the situations continue from episode to episode. Each program in a series and serials is composed of segments with a format holding the segments together, providing them with continuity and narrative progression. Like dramatic series, news programs are structured with breaking news stories early in the program followed by weather, sports, and human interest stories. News programs can be seen as a unified body exhibiting themes and patterns with heroes and villains. Narrative devices emphasizing community and rituals are used in news writing. News is put into frameworks that are easily understood and anticipated. Documentaries are structured as narratives, while sporting events are structured as rituals with stories about heroic players interspersed with the games.

Television's narratives and characters are familiar and reassuring to the audience. Paul Monaco explained, "Stories are best for television when they are highly accessible, easily understood, fall within a range of plausibility, and strike viewers as familiar enough to fit easily into patterns of repetition. . . . They are best liked and most admired precisely in those instances in which a familiar formula is taken and modified slightly" (Monaco, 1998, p. 6). Bloom said, "Stories are similar because people have similar interests. The popularity of themes having to do with sex and family and betrayal, for instance, is not due to some special feature of the imagination, but rather because people are obsessed, in the real world, with sex and family and betrayal" (2010, p. 165).

STORYTELLING AND THE HUMAN CONDITION

Storytelling is an ancient tradition. From the oral storytelling tradition of Homer to the stories told around the fireplace in the past to the electronic hearth of television today, people have enjoyed and participated in a narrative tradition. Narratives probably originated with human signifying practices, that is, the human ability to describe with language events and people in their absence. James Watson and Anne Hill (2003) define story as a social ritual that has the power to bring about a sense of shared experience and of social values. They quote Michel de Certeau's *The Practice of Everyday Life* (1984): "Narratives 'articulate our existences'; indeed, we as social, communal animals, are 'defined by stories'" (Watson & Hill, 2003, p. 187). Narratives take many forms, for they may be stories told orally or written, or they may be visual stories told in stained glass windows, tapestries, or carved doors of churches and cathedrals. Many cultural and religious rituals are based on sacred narratives. For example, the story of American independence from Great Britain is celebrated on July 4; the Christian story of the birth of Jesus is marked each Christmas Day on December 25; the story of the rededication of the holy temple in Jerusalem after the Jews' victory over the Syrians in 165 BCE is celebrated during Hanukkah (or Chanukah) for eight days in November and December. Older stories are regenerated into newer versions. Shakespeare's *Romeo and Juliet* has provided the theme for many stories about star-crossed lovers; the legend of King Arthur and the Knights of the Round Table has been the basis for stories about chivalry, a quest, magic, and heroism; Homer's story of the Trojan Horse is a model for fooling an enemy. Themes from ancient stories, such as the prodigal son, the fall from innocence to experience, resurrection and redemption, weaker persons defeating stronger forces, selling one's soul to the devil, succumbing to a temptress, and so on, proliferate in contemporary stories. As Roderick Hart pointed out in his discussion of narrative, "Sometimes these stories are complex, springing from deep cultural roots; often, stories told today are but updated versions of centuries old tales . . . they awaken within listeners dormant experiences and feelings" (Hart, 1989, p. 133).

The Good Wife's ongoing plot about Alicia's indecisiveness about staying with her husband or having an intimate relationship with her boss, Will, is reminiscent of Shakespeare. *TV Guide* writer Ileane Rudolph wrote,

It's exhibiting many of his [Shakespeare's] hallmarks, complete with star-crossed lovers and a purloined letter. (Or make that voice mail.) "It's Romeo and Juliet!" says a delighted Josh Charles, whose Will Gardner has spent the early part of Season 2 reeling from having his declaration of devotion to Alica Florrick . . . married object of his desire rebuffed . . . or so he thinks. "Like with Romeo and Juliet, our audience knows there was miscommunication between Alicia and Will after a third party stepped in," says Margulies [who plays Alicia] . . . "But our characters don't." (2010, p. 23)

Photo 4.1 Alicia and her unfaithful husband, Peter, in *The Good Wife*.

Like most scholars, Walter Fisher, a rhetorician, made the assumption that humans are essentially storytellers and proposed in his book, *Human Communication as Narration: Toward a Philosophy of Reason, Value, and Action,* that "all forms of human communication are most usefully interpreted and assessed from a narrative perspective" (Fisher, 1989, p. ix). He wrote:

> The world as we know it is a set of stories that must be chosen among in order for us to live life in a process of continual re-creation. [The] narrative paradigm sees people as storytellers, as authors and co-authors who creatively read and evaluate the texts of life and literature. A narrative perspective focuses on existing institutions as providing 'plots' that are always in the process of re-creation rather than existing as settled scripts. Viewing human communication narratively stresses that people are full participants in the making of messages, whether they are agents (authors) or audience members (co-authors). (Fisher, 1989, p. 18)

People tune in to television to be told stories, but they have a familiarity with the narrative forms in which the stories are told; they relate to these stories against a backdrop of the stories they know and become the coauthors, so to speak, in the story development. In order for a story to be successful, it has to engage the audience's own sense of narrative. This includes the ability to defer one's gratification, to supply connectives among the parts of the story, and to perceive events as significantly related to the point of a sequence or the entire story.

When my sons were young, I read bedtime stories to them every night. They enjoyed hearing the same stories over and over, often speaking the lines from the books before they were able to read them. My older son and daughter-in-law read to their daughter Elizabeth every night, often the same stories that I read to my sons. Elizabeth also loved the stories on television—*Clifford the Big Red Dog, Arthur (the Aardvark)*—and, when she was only 3 years old, she could expertly pronounce "aurora borealis" after seeing the Disney movie *Balto* (the story of a sled wolf-dog in Alaska). Like other children, she learned to produce and process stories at an early age. She enjoys repeated reading and viewing of stories and often tells me the stories that she has heard and watched. Now, at the age of 10, she enjoys television stories about dogs and cats on Animal Planet and shows on Nickelodeon such as *iCarly, Victorious,* and *Bigtime Rush* that have activities on their websites. I am an avid reader of both fiction and nonfiction, yet I also regularly tune in to television stories. My favorites are *The Good Wife; NCIS: Los Angeles; Parenthood; CSI: Crime Scene Investigation; Army Wives; Project Runway;* and *Masterpiece Classics, Mystery,* and *Contemporary*.

The *Masterpiece* dramas, which are usually based on novels, and the made-for-television movies are self-contained and have closure, unless the movie is a pilot for a series. The difference between a self-contained novel or television movie that has closure at the end and a television series is that while a series episode may have closure of a given problem, there is seldom closure for the personal stories of the characters. As I watch series television over time, I learn about the characters, their relationships, and their ways of solving problems. They may solve a crime, figure out how the crime was committed, find a missing person, save someone's life or take it, separate and reunite, marry, have babies, divorce, and so on, but the series continues each week with the same main characters and their ways of living and working together. Even when a series comes to an end, there is seldom closure.

The exception was *M*A*S*H*, which in 1983 after 11 years on the air, had a 2½-hour finale celebrating the end of the Korean War with Hawkeye, B. J., Major Houlihan, Colonel Potter, and the rest of the 4077th Mobile Army Surgical Hospital returning home. (It was the highest-rated single program of all time, with 106 million viewers.) The last episode of *The Sopranos* was in 2007, but people still discuss the ambiguous ending on various websites. At the end of the last show, Tony Soprano goes into a diner and sits at a booth. Each time the door opens, there is a bell. After other customers enter, Tony's wife, Carmela, comes in; then A. J., their son, arrives. A man comes in and sits at the counter, glancing over at Tony. Then we see the daughter, Meadow, having trouble parking. The man at the counter walks past Tony on his way to the bathroom. The bell rings again, Tony looks up at the door, and the screen goes black. That is the end. What does it mean? Did the screen go black because the man shot Tony? Does it mean that Tony will always have to be on the look-out for an assassin? Or does it simply mean "that's all, the series is over"?

THE NATURE OF NARRATIVE

Narrative recounts one or more events, thus a story is a series of events arranged in an order. Narrative can be about one event, as in "the hamster died" or "Marian left Simon." If an event is not recounted, then the expression of it is not a narrative. "Marian is the daughter of S. P. Haddock" is not a narrative because there are no events expressed in this sentence. It is assumed that a narrative will be expressed by someone to someone; a storyteller relates a story to an audience. Thus, a story can be viewed as being expressed in such a way that an audience can interpret its meaning. Whether the story is told as comedy or drama, news or sports, cooking instructions or infomercials, there has to be a pattern that viewers can anticipate. When an audience has expectations about what might happen, the narrative plays on those expectations. Narrative can be either fiction or nonfiction as long as events are ordered and recounted. A dramatic series on television is based on narrative, but the news, reality shows, and sporting events also have narrative structure. A narrative has two parts: (1) the structure that comprises the recounting of one or more events; and (2) the communicative act that involves the production and reception of the story.

A story almost always has temporal elements. Some of the events in the story may occur simultaneously; some may be successive; some may go back and forth in time. "Marian left Simon as he boarded an airplane to New York" has a simultaneous temporal element. "After Simon left for the airport, Marian began to pack to leave him" is an example of successive events. "As Marian packed her suitcase to leave Simon, she reflected on the times in the past when they had been happy" is an example of going back and forth in time. In each case, the stories consist of at least one transformation from one state of affairs to another. Sometimes the events in a story may be linked by cause and effect. "Marian left Simon because he never helped with the dishes" is an example of causation.

The sequence of a narrative has to be structured in a systematic way in an order that makes sense to its audience. This allows the events, characters, and themes to develop and move forward in a coherent fashion. The television narrative should draw the viewers in, engage them, and keep them watching the program. Stories are structured so the scenes build on one another as the viewers gradually learn more about a character and/or the plot. Each stage of the narrative has a logical place and meaning in the sequence, and each stage influences the next one. The television critic can ask why the events are arranged in a certain order and why they started at a certain point and ended at another.

NARRATIVE THEORIES

Aristotle's Narrative Theory

Narrative theory can be traced back to ancient Greece. Aristotle's *Poetics,* written in 330 BCE, is a treatise on the making of a dramatic work of art. Aristotle explained that drama is defined by its shape, composition, manner of construction, and purpose. While character, thought, dialogue, song, and spectacle were considered important, Aristotle said that plot is the most important part of the narrative. He said that plot is the unified arrangement of the incidents, which must have a beginning, middle, and end. Television programming appears to most strongly follow Aristotle's advice, with tightly structured scripts that usually have to be 22 or 44 minutes long. Aristotle also said that unnecessary people and incidents should be omitted from a story's plot. Aristotle's guidelines are familiar to viewers of television in the 21st century. Television scripts must present the conflict in the first few minutes of the first act along with the hero, antagonist, and other essential characters who are related to the problem. The successive act(s) present complications and other incidents, and the final act usually presents a solution to the problem. We expect the familiar structure of the beginning, middle, and end; we expect unity of plot; we anticipate seeing only the essential characters with whom we are familiar; and we enjoy stories not only for the pleasure they give, but also for the order they offer. When the resolution is carried over to the next episode, the viewer is motivated to tune in next week to satisfy a desire to know what happens.

Propp's Narrative Theory

Vladimir Propp (1968), an early 20th-century literary theorist, influenced narrative theory with his 1928 book *Morphology of the Folktale,* although it was not translated into English until 1966. Morphology is the study of structure and forms which Propp developed into 31 functions of characters from the perspective of their fundamental meanings in a story. Propp argued that stories always contain the function of the **lack** and/or *villainy.* The story then proceeds to other functions, such as the hero and the villain joining in direct combat resulting in the defeat of the villain. When the hero's task is resolved, the lack is fulfilled, and Propp's last function has the hero marrying the princess and receiving an honor, such as ascending the throne. In other words, an initial equilibrium or harmonious state of a place or character is disrupted, most often by a lack of something or a villain. The narrative charts the course of the disequilibrium and ends with a resolution that restores equilibrium. A lack may be a missing person who is the subject of a search by FBI agents. If found, the missing person is restored to the family, and equilibrium is achieved. A lack may be overcome when police detectives find a criminal—the villain—and bring that person to justice. A person may lack love and a satisfactory relationship that can be achieved by meeting a desirable person. A teenager may lack the use of the family car until proven responsible enough to use it. Lack is also related to desire or wish fulfillment. If what is desired or wished for is not present, then there is a lack. Villainy does not have to be a person but could be an animal or an earthquake or some natural or unnatural event that disturbs equilibrium. The movement to restore equilibrium drives the narrative forward, linking events together, providing insights and meaning, and fulfilling the desire to overcome the lack or the villain.

Barthes's Narrative Theory

The literary critic Roland Barthes (1974) described narrative as having a hermeneutic code. Hermeneutics is the science of interpretation. The stages of the **hermeneutic code** enable an audience to interpret and follow a story as follows:

First, there is an *enigma* that causes us to ask a question about the narrative's development: Who committed the crime? Who will win? How might a character react to a piece of news? How might a relationship develop? The enigma engages our interest and causes us to want to see how it is resolved. The enigma is like a riddle that teases us to guess the next piece of information to be revealed. Second, there is a delay that stalls or postpones the solution to the enigma. The delay sequence may keep the enigma open, causing us to dwell on it as suspense builds. Third, a resolution to the enigma is found, thus satisfying our curiosity and giving us pleasure.

Most narratives have an intricate series of enigmas, delays, and resolutions, with one resolution creating another enigma. For example, the criminal's identity is now known, but will he or she get caught? This drives the narrative forward and sustains our interest. Not only do situation comedies and dramas follow these patterns, but quiz shows, the news, reality shows, and sporting events are also structured in these ways. A quiz show has an enigma of who will win the prize. A reality show engages us in an enigma, delay, and resolution as people, events, and actions cause the candidates for the prized position to be eliminated. For example, the enigma on *The Bachelor* is which woman will he select? Will his parents like the woman he has brought to meet them? (This presents another enigma.) They say that they like her because she is an old-fashioned girl, but then he brings a second woman home to meet them. This produces a delay and another enigma—will they like her? They do not like the second woman that much, but he spends an evening in the hot tub with her (delay), and picks her over the woman of his parents' choice, thus resolving the main enigma: Who will get selected to be his bride? A sporting event has the "who will win?" enigma. When there is more than one event leading to a bigger prize, the enigma builds suspense over time. Mine That Bird, a remarkable but underdog racehorse, won the Kentucky Derby in 2009. The enigma was "Will Mine That Bird win the Preakness Stakes, the second race for the Triple Crown?" The media provided many delays with stories about how the horse's owner pulled him in a horse trailer behind a pickup truck 1,700 miles from New Mexico to Kentucky, whereas the other horses were flown in or brought in expensive horse vans. Suspense built up until the day of the race, but Mine That Bird came in second on a muddy track at the Preakness.

Barthes also described an **action code** that makes complex ideas and feelings immediately recognizable to the audience while, at the same time, their significance becomes apparent in the narrative. This requires the audience to understand the action code within the context of the narrative, thus becoming the coauthor of the story. In other words, the audience senses what will happen next. When Silvio in *The Sopranos* drives Adriana—who has been an informant for the FBI—into the woods, the viewers sense that he is going to kill her. How do they know this? She thought he was taking her to the hospital to see her fiancé, Christopher. Because he did not drive to the hospital, because the woods are isolated, and because she has been an informant, the viewer interprets the situation and recognizes, along with the character Adriana, what the course of action will be. Of course, the viewer has learned, by watching the series, that the characters in *The Sopranos* execute their enemies as a way of obtaining revenge. Silvio is Tony Soprano's right-hand man and would logically be sent to do the dirty deed. The enigma of what will happen to Adriana now that she has told Christopher that she has been giving information to the FBI is delayed as she imagines that she is driving away with her suitcase in the car to enter a witness protection program. Carina Chocano, television critic for the *Los Angeles Times,* wrote: "The moment remains open to interpretation. But it at least hints at the idea that Adriana went to her death like a soldier" (Chocano, 2004, p. E25). When Silvio pulls into the woods, the viewer understands that she will be shot in an act of cold-blooded murder. Chocano wrote that Adriana "suffered like Antigone," thus comparing her story to Sophocles' play *Antigone,* written in 442 BCE. In the play, Antigone, the daughter of Oedipus, was executed (sealed alive in a tomb) by her uncle, the King of Thebes, because she buried her brother Polynices, who died fighting Creon's army. Creon considered him a traitor for whom state law forbade burial. It is a classic story of conflict of loyalty to family versus loyalty to the state.

NARRATIVE STRUCTURE

Narratives rely on conflict and oppositions in their structures. Certainly the masculine/feminine opposition is used most frequently in both situation comedies and dramas. Other oppositions that are widely used are work/home, legal/illegal, life/death, good/evil, healthy/sick, competent/incompetent, tolerance/intolerance, trust/distrust, and so on. The oppositions that create conflicts on *True Blood* are human/vampire, life/death, love/hate, and day/night as the main characters—human and vampire—fall in love with one another, kill others, love or hate one another, and live during night and day or only at night.

Narrative structure provides a tendency for stories to fall into predictable patterns or formulas. Some formulas are unique to certain television genres and particular shows. The crime show will have a crime solved at the end; harmony will be restored in the family situation comedy; a life will be saved in the hospital, a case will be decided in court, and so on. Formulas that were successful in previous shows are repeated in new shows. Conventions are used that viewers recognize and come to expect. A **convention** is any kind of social or cultural practice used in a narrative that has a meaning that is shared by members of a culture. A musical signature at the start of a television program or a news reader looking directly into the camera are common conventions. Lyrics to songs played during the narrative provide a subtext to the story. As Watson and Hill (2003) point out, "Knowledge of conventions on the part of the audience and recognition when convention is flouted suggests an active union between encoder and decoder" (p. 188).

In order to keep an audience coming back each week to a series, multiple story lines, often without resolution, are developed and interwoven into the narrative structure of an episode. *Hill Street Blues,* on the air from 1981 to 1987, established this pattern with its ensemble cast, stories set within an institution (a police station), several intersecting story lines per episode, story arcs covering several episodes, and literate, witty writing (Stempel, 1996). *Hill Street Blues* had as many as seven story lines going on in one episode. When it did not get good ratings for its first season on the air, NBC renewed the show with the caveat that it had to complete at least one story line per show. You can see this pattern on many shows today. Crimes get solved and court cases are settled, but workplace relationships carry over for many episodes.

To aid viewer memory or to assist viewers who have missed an episode, script writers put in information that repeats previous episodes. Situation comedies recap the narrative situation after a commercial break to reorient viewers. The familiar "previously on . . ." is standard practice for the beginning of a drama series. As a series continues, some story lines are brought to closure and new ones are introduced. Because writers have an entire season to tell a story, some story lines continue throughout the season, and, in some cases, to the next season.

Another form of structural repetition is the inclusion in the narrative of a number of redundant signs that reinforce a point, a character's personality, a theme, and suspense. These may be in the setting, costumes, details in the dialogue, and action. This kind of redundancy provides texture and tone for the audience and deepens the consistency and believability of the narrative. These are known as social codes and are discussed in more detail in Chapter 6, "Rhetoric and Culture," as cultural signs that are used conventionally for viewer recognition and meaning.

Narrative structure is also adapted to short sequences of action and rapid editing. This is done to try to prevent viewer zapping or channel-hopping. It is hoped that the viewer will not want to lose involvement in the ongoing narrative. *NCIS* has very rapid images in black and white at the start of each act that reflect characters in events in the previous act. The effect is almost subliminal because the visuals are so rapid.

It is impossible to separate art from the business of television. The objective of narrative is to attract viewers to the programs and hold them there during the show and keep them returning each week.

INTERTEXTUALITY

Viewers are more likely to engage with a television program when they experience pleasure. One source of pleasure is recognition of references to other television programs or characters or events. Reference to or connection with other "texts" outside of the present one is known as **intertextuality.** If viewers recognize and understand an allusion, they can become party to it as an inside joke. Intertextuality is often used as a device for parody and has been around in television for many years. Carol Burnett was known for her parodies of movies, television shows, and commercials on her comedy show. Her most famous intertextual parody was a skit called "Went With the Wind," in which Burnett imitated Scarlett O'Hara. In the movie, *Gone With the Wind,* Scarlett makes a dress out of green velvet drapes because she no longer has beautiful dresses. In her television show, Carol Burnett came down the stairs in green velvet drapes with the curtain rod still attached and sitting on her shoulders. When Harvey Korman, playing Rhett Butler, told her, "That gown is gorgeous," she replied, "I saw it in the window and I just couldn't resist it." (You can still see this skit on the Internet.) There are instances of intertextuality in many scripts, not necessarily for parody. On an episode of *Army Wives,* when Pamela and Chase decide to remarry, Pamela has no wedding dress, so her friends alter a dress for her to wear. When she gushes over it, her friend says, "It won't win a prize on *Project Runway"* (a reality competition show also on Lifetime).

Intertextuality describes both the interpretive practice exercised by viewers and a strategy consciously used by television producers. Ott and Walter (2000) describe intertextuality as a stylistic device that writers and producers deliberately employ to invite a particular response. One reason for the popularity of the animated show *The Simpsons* is the parody created by many references to other texts. *The Simpsons* deliberately invites viewers to tap into their knowledge of news stories, politics, current events, celebrities, literature, old movies, and other television programs, especially programs about families. In each half-hour episode, *The Simpsons* incorporates 15 to 20 allusions to outside events ranging from

The Odyssey, Antiques Roadshow, Hitchcock movies, and *Mad Men* to physicist Stephen Hawking talking about black holes. Intertextuality credits viewers with the experience necessary to make sense of these allusions, offering them the pleasure of recognition.

Collins attributes intertextuality as a hallmark of postmodern cultural production. He quotes Umberto Eco's description of the "already said"—that is, intertextuality—as the most distinguishing feature of postmodern communication. Revivalism in architecture, vintage clothing, antique furnishings, and so on are forms of recirculation and appropriation of older forms functioning in the present day. Collins writes, "There is no other medium in which the force of the 'already said' is quite so visible as in television, primarily because the already said is the 'still being said'" (Collins, 1992, pp. 333–334).

CHARACTERS

Although Aristotle believed that plot was the most important part of a story, characters and their interrelationships dominate television stories. Characters, like the structure of the plots, however, also fall into formulaic types. Viewers recognize characters on television when they are acknowledged **social types,** defined by Reed, a sociologist, as "collections of real people who resemble one another in ways that could be quantified and measured if we wanted to do it" (Reed, 1986, p. 14). Characters may be popular ideal types and folk generalizations, representing the kinds of people one is likely to encounter superficially. Social types have certain noticeable behaviors and attributes that observers can easily identify and remember. Examples of well-known social types are rednecks, bullies, hillbillies, yuppies, hippies, Southern belles, groupies, snobs, gangsters, cowboys, bosses, maids, butlers, and so on. Because they are no more complicated than they have to be and have limited and predictable functions, they are likely to be minor characters on television. They are represented visually as well as through spoken accents, stock dialogue, and language.

Characters have to be introduced, their personalities defined, and their relationships to one another, to place, and to time have to be established. Characters are appealing because of their traits. The main characters have several traits, while minor characters may have only one or two traits. Character traits may be appearance, attitudes, skills, preferences, psychological drives, and any other specific quality created for a character. The three main characters on *Men of a Certain Age* have distinctive personalities, but each one develops strengths as the series progresses. Joe (Ray Romano) is a divorced father who owns a party store. Gradually he overcomes his insecurities about dating and qualifying for the senior golf tour. Terry (Scott Bakula) is a charming bachelor who dates younger women and has not had steady employment since he was a minor actor. Gradually he adjusts to full-time employment as a car salesman and recognizes the worth of a relationship with a woman closer to his age. Owen (Andre Braugher) is a sweet but stressed husband and father who works for his father whom he still calls "Daddy." Gradually he takes over the business and learns to be authoritative. The three friends meet each morning for breakfast, confide in one another, and share teasing and advice. Viewers learn who these characters are in the same way that people make friends with each other. A friendship evolves out of understanding who the other person is over a period of time. So viewers gradually understand who Joe, Terry, and Owen are—slowly and with admiration for their abilities to grow. Their personalities are consistent, but they evolve. As with long-term friendships in which friends reveal more of their personalities, television characters also become better known to us as the series progress.

Consistency of character traits causes audiences to know the character and to look forward to seeing him or her each week. Viewers know that the main characters of a television show will be back again next week to experience similar conflicts and repeat similar acts. Actors portraying television characters often become celebrities, and sometimes their fans confuse the actors with their characters. When a show goes off the air, viewers miss the characters because they have become part of their lives. They regard many television characters as their friends.

Television scriptwriter Madeline DiMaggio also teaches scriptwriting. She advises creating back stories for characters, giving them a biography of significant events that happened in their lives before the television story unfolds. Although the back stories may not be part of the script, they are important in understanding the development of a character and may even help the writers determine locales and other characters. Many television program websites have back stories for the show's characters.

Because scripts for television programs are so tightly controlled, there is little time to show a character's personality except through action. Robert Hilliard explained, "Not only do the qualities of the characters determine the action, but also character is revealed through the action" (2008, p. 396). The choices a character makes, especially at moments of crisis or conflict, bring out the qualities of the character. Character relationships, which are so important in television drama, reveal a character's personality and compelling characteristics. Also,

Photo 4.2 Three friends, Joe, Owen, and Terry, meet every morning for breakfast and conversation in *Men of a Certain Age*.

because of the intimacy provided by television close-ups, the characters' inner feelings can be seen but not necessarily spoken about. We saw in Chapter 2 that this is known as a **sub-text**. Marg Helgenberger, who plays crime scene investigator Catherine Willows on *CSI,* said, "It's a different style of acting because you look at the evidence without speaking and the audience knows what you are feeling" (The William S. Paley Television Festival, 2001).

Viewers know that the lead characters in a series will be back again the next week to experience similar conflicts and repeat similar acts. Most viewers tend to be more connected with the characters than with the plots, and they tune in week after week to see what adventures they will encounter and how they will resolve the enigmas that occur. By watching series and serials on a regular basis, viewers form a relationship with the characters and often identify with them. They see them go in and out of relationships, get married, have children, go to work, fight crime, settle disputes, enjoy leisure activities, and, of course, they see them encounter some form of disequilibrium and try to bring balance back into their lives. Each semester when I teach television criticism, I ask my students why they watch the shows they watch. Every semester different students offer the same answer as their predecessors: "Because the characters on television have such interesting lives, and we can vicariously live their lives." In other words, the television characters bring pleasure through identification and entertainment through vicarious experiences.

Characters in plays and made-for-television movies must have their character traits established early in the script because there is not an entire season to develop them. Usually there is just one protagonist whose desire or lack catalyzes the story in these programs. Although there are delays in the narrative, there will be a resolution at the end of the program because there is no continuation unless it gets followed up later by a sequel. There may be more characters in a mini-series. For example, HBO's mini-series *John Adams,* based on David McCullough's biography, had a large cast of historical characters including Thomas Jefferson and Benjamin Franklin, but the prominent character was John Adams. From modest beginnings as a farmer to high status as president of the United States, Adams was an independent man with reverence for the law and a commitment to liberty. He was a lawyer whose first appearance in the series occurs after the so-called Boston Massacre. He agreed to defend the British soldiers in court but refused a lucrative post under the British rule and subsequently joined the newly created Continental Congress. His character, as portrayed by Paul Giamatti, was marked by contradictions. At once humble and frugal, he was also ambitious and had a desire to be recognized. Married to Abigail (Laura Linney), his confidant and advisor, for 54 years, he was often separated from her as he fulfilled his duties. This outstanding production received the Emmy award for best mini-series in 2008, including best actress for Linney and best actor for Giamatti. There were also archetypical and mythical themes such as initiation, the journey, separation, loss, and ascension.

ARCHETYPES

Television characters are often modeled after classical **archetypes** such as heroes and villains, father and mother figures, leaders and sidekicks, wise elders and foolish youths, loyal friends and deceiving associates, and so on. Plots may be based on archetypal themes such as a journey, heroic action, the antihero, the fall, and redemption. Images such as circles, gates, and bridges can be archetypal. Archetypes are recurrent patterns of actions, character types, or identifiable images whose expression is an unconscious product of the collective experience of the entire human species, an unconscious mental record of such experiences, the collective unconscious.

> The Swiss psychiatrist Carl G. Jung developed a theory of myth based upon his theory of the collective unconscious which he defined as, "a part of the psyche which can be negatively distinguished from a personal unconscious by the fact that it does not, like the latter, owe its existence to personal experience and consequently is not a personal acquisition. . . . The contents [of the collective unconscious] have never been in consciousness, and therefore have never been individually acquired, but owe their existence to heredity. . . . The content of the collective unconscious is made up essentially of archetypes." (Jung, 1971, pp. 59–60)

Through analysis of thousands of patients' dreams, Jung discovered a striking similarity among ancient myths, dreams, and symbols of widely separated civilizations and cultural groups. He found that the images and structures of the collective unconscious manifest themselves in regularly repeating forms that he named *archetypes*. He believed that these mythical images were present in all people, becoming activated in visual form in dreams and myths. He believed that they express desires, urges, and fears common to people of every age. People react to archetypes because they stimulate images that are already in their collective unconscious. Archetypes depict some eternal quality, some enduring feature of the human race. When people find them in a story, they experience immediate recognition.

Jung wrote that archetypes "indicate the existence of definite forms in the psyche which seem to be present always and everywhere. Mythological research calls them 'motifs' . . . literally a pre-existent form" (Jung, 1971, p. 60). An archetype is a narrative pattern, a model, or a prototype reflecting cultural patterns that reveal and shape a person's psychic and social life. Some archetypes have human form, such as the hero, a monster, Earth mother, temptress, the innocent, unfaithful spouse, a magician, a martyr, or a warrior; some are experiences, such as a journey, a quest, a task, initiation, descent, ascent, the fall, or redemption; some are things, such as a bridge, fire, a door, or water; and some are metaphors, such as a mandala or magic circle, light and darkness, or heaven and hell. There are too many archetypes to discuss fully here, but they can be found in the many writings of Jung and his followers. On television, heroes are obvious, as are villains, innocents, and temptresses. One archetype that deserves more consideration—because it appears so often on television programs—is the trickster, known for sly jokes, malicious pranks, preference for physical satisfaction above intellectual pursuits, the power to change shape, and sometimes a dual nature (half animal, half human). The trickster, although usually a negative type of hero, may transform what is meaningless into something meaningful (Samuels, Shorter, & Plaut, 1986). Jung identified the trickster in fairy tales such as *Tom Thumb* and *Stupid Hans,* but he also discussed the trickster in Native American mythology, often as a shaman or in the form of a coyote (Jung, 1969). The characters Tracy on *30 Rock* and Wilfred on FX's *Wilfred* are comic tricksters, whereas in a drama, the trickster may be a clever criminal or a jealous rival.

Robert R. Smith found many archetypes in nonfiction television, such as tests of bravery in sporting events; wisdom in statements by government and world leaders; redemption in reports of medical breakthroughs and scientific advancement; Armageddon in news about floods, hurricanes, pollution, and starvation; paradise in holiday celebrations or vacation stories; and Dionysus (god of wine and revelry) in stories about rock concerts, parties, and other celebrations. Television is a natural medium for archetypes because of its visual appeal to a mass audience (Smith, 1976).

Rituals are also archetypal. Recreational, national, and celebratory events on television, such as the World Series, the Super Bowl, the Olympics, presidential inaugurations, royal weddings, state funerals, Macy's Thanksgiving Day parade, and tragic disasters, unify the audience as a collective body who observe and participate in these rituals from afar through a communal focus. These are narrative occasions as announcers and anchors tell the stories as the events unfold. Football players take on heroic dimensions in massive stadiums; inaugural rituals with visual and musical symbols of patriotism remind viewers of the stability and continuity of government and nation; state funerals, such as the 1963 funeral of President Kennedy, the 2004 funeral of President Reagan, and the 2007 funeral of President Ford; and televised accounts of tragedies such as the *Challenger* disaster, the Oklahoma City bombing, and especially the fall of the World Trade Center Twin Towers on September 11, 2001, enable the television audience not only to collectively mourn their loss but also to reinforce a strong sense of national unity. Meyrowitz (1985) explained that we respond to television images as if we were seeing them firsthand, thus physical presence is no longer required for the firsthand experience. Television is truly a "window on the world." The obsessively repeated images of tragedies on television burn them into our minds so that they seem to happen again and become part of our collective memories.

MYTH

Myth and archetype tend to overlap, although myths are more closely related to individual cultures. Myths are important for television criticism because they have formed the foundation for narratives throughout the ages. Mythical themes occur and recur in narratives because they represent life experiences, beliefs, values, and behaviors that organize social interaction. Myths are generally known as fictitious tales, often with primitive or ancient origins, involving supernatural characters embodying timeless virtues and values. These virtues and values tend to be ideas to which people already subscribe. Myths offer examples of right and wrong, explain baffling or frightening phenomena, and provide models of good and evil. They are, according to R. Slotkin, "stories drawn from a society's history that have acquired through persistent usage the power of symbolizing that society's ideology and of dramatizing its moral consciousness—with all the complexities and contradictions that consciousness may contain" (Jasinski, 2001, p. 383). Rollo May explained that "a myth is a way of making sense in a senseless world. Myths are narrative patterns that give significance to our existence. . . . Myths are like the beams in a house: not exposed to outside view, they are the structure which holds the house together so people can live in it" (May, 1991, p. 15). Myths are also based upon the norms of a culture and acceptable ways of resolving conflict. René Wellek and Austin Warren's definition of myth includes the notion of human origins and destinies: "Myth comes to mean any anonymously composed storytelling of origins and destinies: the explanations a society offers its young of why the world is and why we do as we do, its pedagogic images of the nature and destiny of man" (Jasinski, 2001, p. 383). Each society has its own myths that are related to its history, values, and beliefs. According to Roderick Hart, there are four characteristic types of myths based on their functions. *Cosmological* myths explain "why we are here, where we came from, what our ancestors were like" (Hart, 1990, p. 315). These myths come from family members, school books, church, films, and television. *Societal* myths "teach one the proper way to live" (Hart, 1990, p. 315). These may be stories of famous people, such as George Washington's refusal to lie and Abraham Lincoln's love of school and his long walks through the snow to get there. Although the facts of the myths may be erroneous, the "truth" of their messages is not. *Identity* myths preserve a culture's distinctiveness and provide a sense of collective identity. Stories of immigrants coming to America and succeeding in the fulfillment of their dreams and stories of the dedication of the United States to freedom and opportunity distinguish the nation from closed and authoritarian societies. *Eschatological* myths "tell people where they are going, what lies in store for them in the short run . . . and in the long run" (Hart, 1990, p. 318). These myths may promise success through hard work, discovery of a cure for disease, a heavenly reward, or an eternal punishment.

Bronislaw Malinowski, a cultural anthropologist, defined myth as "a body of narratives woven into a culture which dictates belief, defines ritual, and acts as a chart of the social orders" (Malinowski, 1961, p. 249). Joseph Campbell, the author of 13 books on myth, believed that there were two orders of myth: "the mythology that relates you to your nature and to the natural world of which you're a part. And there is the mythology that is strictly sociological, linking you to a particular society" (Campbell, 1988, p. 28). The former is a motivating power or a value system that is universal because it is of one's own body and of nature. The latter has to do with specific societies. In other words, a person is both a natural woman or man and a member of a particular group. Robert Scholes and Robert Kellogg (1966) in their book, *The Nature of Narrative,* use the terms "myth" and "traditional narrative" synonymously because this was the meaning of the Greek word "mythos." They further refined the definition of myth by elucidating three types: (1) the imaginative folktale designed to amuse an audience; (2) a legend, a quasi-historical tale of ordinary or fantastic events; and (3) the sacred myth, an expression of and justification for theology, manners, and morals (p. 217). The latter is the most tradition-bound of all forms of narrative in any culture and, as an embodiment of religious truth, is not to be tampered with or changed. Scholes and Kellogg pointed out that "traditional and rigidly preserved stories lend themselves to alteration or adaptation; they become rationalized and humanized or fancifully exaggerated. . . . myth, in yielding up its special characteristics, dies only to be reborn. Because mythic narrative is the expression in story form of deep-seated human concerns, fears, and aspirations, the plots of mythic tales are a storehouse of narrative correlatives—keys to the human psyche in story form—guaranteed to reach an audience and move them deeply" (Scholes & Kellogg, 1966, p. 220).

Earlier in this chapter, contemporary television narratives were described as forged from "older stories" and "themes from ancient stories." Today, myths can be found in our rituals, the visual arts, architecture, books, music, and on television programs. Television stories often have mythic themes already shared by large segments of the population. Television narratives often have characters, situations, and plots taken directly from known myths or mythic motifs. The enormously popular series *The X-Files* was analyzed by Leslie Jones as entirely mythical. Jones found that all the stories in the series were based on three myths in multiple versions and variants: "There's something in the woods," "There's something in the house," and "There's something in the government," depending upon the location of that week's story (Jones, 1996, p. 81). Jones described the equal weight given to each of the three categories in the episodes of *The X-Files* as "a kind of narrative osmosis, as characteristics of one category seep into another and all narrative traits become interchangeable. We find monsters of myth, space, and conspiracy equally out in the wilderness, at home in the sewers, and bagged, tagged, and filed for reference in the warehouses of the Pentagon" (Jones, 1996, p. 83).

Desperate Housewives has a weekly theme narrated by Mary Alice, a character who is dead. On December 4, 2005, the theme was "return of the prodigal son." At the conclusion of the episode, Mary Alice said in voiceover:

> The stories are as old as time itself. The prodigal son who returns home, the father who forgives him, the jealous wife who tricks the husband who trusts her, the desperate mother who risks everything for the child who needs her, and the faithless husband who hurts the wife who loves him so deeply. Why do we listen again and again? Because these are the stories of family, and once we look past the fighting, pain, and resentment, we occasionally like to remind ourselves that there is absolutely nothing more important.

The popular series *Lost* was based on thematic myths with archetypes such as fate versus free will, good versus evil, and faith versus reason, but as the showrunner, Damon Lindelof, said, "If there's one word that we keep coming back to, it's redemption. It is that idea of everybody has something to be redeemed for, . . . But in order to redeem yourself, you can only do it through a community. . . . In many ways 'Lost' is a mash-up/remix of our favorite stories, whether that's bible stories from Sunday school or 'Narnia' or 'Star Wars' or the writings of John Steinbeck" (Manly, 2010, pp. 2–3). One of the characters, Desmond, came to the island on *Lost* when his boat was blown off course. Desmond spent years trying to get back to the woman he loved—Penny, short for Penelope. Penelope was the wife of Odysseus in *The Odyssey*.

Leading characters in television programs are often heroes with supernatural powers or superior abilities. Television series like *Fringe, Supernatural,* and *Medium* feature characters who use their supernatural powers for the good of humankind. On the other hand, Kensi Blye, one of the lead characters on *NCIS: Los Angeles,* is a slender, feminine, and, of course, beautiful woman who can subdue a criminal much stronger and heavier than she is. Kensi is an NCIS special agent, not a goddess or an Amazon, but she has superior abilities that enable her to bring down criminals fearlessly. Athletes in sports may be seen to have superior abilities, consequently becoming heroes or fallen heroes. Barbaro was a racehorse who became a hero to thousands of admirers. Undefeated in previous races, he won the Kentucky Derby in 2006 by a thrilling 6½-length triumph. He was the favorite to win the Preakness Stakes on May 20, 2006, but suffered a life-threatening injury, shattering his right hind leg at the start of the race. Because of his heroic status, people sent cards, flowers, carrots, and apples to him following his surgery. The University of Pennsylvania School of Veterinary Medicine, the site of his surgery, convalescence, and eventual death, set up a website with reports of Barbaro's progress, photographs of him, and a link for people to send messages to the stricken horse, their fallen hero (http://www .vet.upenn.edu).

Campbell wrote that there are two kinds of deeds that mythical heroes perform: the physical deed, in which the hero performs a courageous act in a battle or saves a life, and the spiritual deed, in which the hero experiences the supernormal range of human spiritual life and returns with a message. He described the "usual hero adventure" as beginning with a lack—something has been taken from someone or something is lacking in normal circumstances. The hero takes off on a series of adventures beyond the ordinary to recover what has been lost or to find a remedy. It is a cycle of going and returning. The basic motif of the hero's journey is to leave one condition and discover that which will enable a movement to a richer or more mature condition (Campbell, 1988).

The antihero is also a familiar character in television programs, from Archie Bunker to Gregory House, even Bart Simpson. These are deeply flawed characters with some quality that redeems them. Some have dark pasts, like Don Draper on *Mad Men;* some are self-destructive like Grace Hanadarko on *Saving Grace.* As Jeanne McDowell said,

> What redeems these characters for audiences is that all have aspects of their personalities that viewers identify with in some way. . . . Audience acceptance of Dexter Morgan surprised even his executive producer and executives at Showtime, who weren't sure how the series was going to be received. . . . "At the heart of his appeal may be that his victims seem to deserve the justice he doles out, and each murder is self-revelatory for him in his journey for humanization," [said Sara Colleton, executive producer of *Dexter*]. (2008, p. 49)

Reality shows are often mythical in nature. *The Amazing Race* is a journey in which the contestants vie with one another to reach a destination with a prize at the end. *The Bachelor* and *The Bachelorette* are variations on the prince or princess selecting the best person to wed. *The Biggest Loser* is about defeating the monster—obesity. *Project Runway* is a Cinderella story in which the designers transform their models into beautifully dressed, coifed, and made-up beauties.

Television and myth are intimately related in many ways. Traditional tales of gods and heroes, folklore and fairy tales, and villains and supernatural forces are sources for television narrative. The patterns of characters in myth inform the destiny of the characters modeled on these myths. As you can see, there are many ways to analyze the mythical roots of characters in television stories.

Photo 4.3 Don Draper and his ambitious protégé in *Mad Men*.

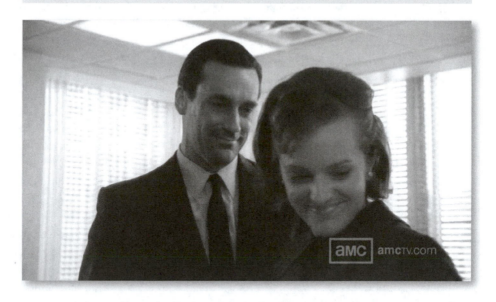

Photo 4.4 A fairy tale moment on *The Bachelorette*.

Modern descriptions of narrative patterns were cited by Craig Tomashoff, who interviewed creators of television series. Mike Royce, co-creator of *Men of a Certain Age,* described "The Trap" as trapping a group of people in an elevator or as hostages in a bank or a hospital. He said the device works because (1) it is shot in one location to save money and (2) it forces the characters to deal with one another. Bill Lawrence, co-creator of *Cougar Town,* cited "The Lie" when he said, "There's always the episode with the lie that snowballs. . . . Whether it's 'I told my parents I run my own restaurant but I'm really a busboy, and now they're coming to visit,' or 'I wanted that woman to like me, so I told her I know a celebrity and now she wants to meet him,' this is a sitcom staple." Howard Gordan, executive producer of *24,* described the lie as "The People Who Are Not As They Appear to Be" otherwise known as "moles." Stephanie Savage, executive producer of *Gossip Girls,* explained "The Vacation" as a special episode to send the cast out of town: "We get so used to seeing characters—it's fun and fresh and shocking to see them in another place." Carter Bays, co-creator of *How I Met Your Mother* calls it "The Date or The Unexpected Crazy Night Out" plot." After the date, comes "The Wedding," then "Having a Baby" or vice versa. Tomashoff also identifies the familiar "Gimmick" as spinning familiar stories in unfamiliar ways. "Writers may develop a dream sequence in which outrageous things seem to happen" or have the characters play parallel characters to themselves, and, of course, use flashbacks or flashforwards (2011, p. 10).

CLOSE ANALYSIS OF NARRATIVE STRUCTURE

Another way you can examine how a story is told is by examining a program scene by scene. Michael Porter defined a scene as a part in which all of the units are held together by continuity of time or place or parallel action in separate locations or a sequence of shots unified by a theme. He asked four questions of a scene in a television serial, either situation comedy or drama: (1) What does a scene tell about the story? (2) What does the scene tell us about the character? (3) What does the scene tell us about the setting? and (4) What would happen if this scene was not here? Could I still understand the story? He examined scenes according to event, character, and details of the setting. These can be any kind of physical or mental action for events, any person or personalized entity for character, and any evocation of place for the third question. These are described in terms of functions, with 15 functions for plot and 7 for character. Sometimes the setting may have a function as well. Porter also found that narrative analysis "focuses on how a culture presents the myths of a society to the members of that society" (Porter, 1998, p. 140).

SUMMARY

The stories told on television challenge, tease, guide, and please the audience. There are stories that offer archetypal models, myths and folktales, and morals and models for living. Roger Silverstone wrote, "Our stories are social texts: drafts, sketches, fragments, frameworks;

visible and audible evidence of our essentially reflexive culture, turning the events and ideas of both experience and imagination into daily tales. . . . Narratives tell us how it is and it is how they tell us" (Silverstone, 1999, pp. 41 & 46). The television critic William Henry once wrote, "I run to television for solace. In times of personal turmoil it provides familiarity, emotional connections, and the promise of resolution" (Kubey & Csikszentmihalyi, 1990, p. 184). Television is the nation's storyteller. Understanding of narrative gives you, as a television critic, insight into how these stories are told and how they relate to social and cultural life.

EXERCISES

1. Describe the narrative according to its beginning, middle, and end on a news program.

2. Describe the "lack," according to Propp, in a situation comedy and tell how equilibrium is restored.

3. Watch a drama, a reality show, or a soap opera and identify the enigma, the delay, and the resolution.

4. Find an example of an action code (such as the one described in *The Sopranos* example) and describe how you sensed what was going to happen.

5. Watch a drama and describe its narrative structure.

6. Watch *The Simpsons* with a friend and list all the instances of intertextuality in one episode. See if you both find the same or different ones.

7. Look up a television program's website and read the back stories of the characters.

8. Who is your favorite character on television? Explain why you like this character.

9. Give some examples of social types on situation comedies.

10. Discuss a particular character in a drama or situation comedy, and describe how the character's relationship with another character or characters reveals his or her personality.

11. Cite an instance of an archetypal trickster in a situation comedy and in a drama.

12. Describe archetypes in nonfiction television, such as sporting events, news, and reality shows.

13. Give an example of an archetypal ritual found on television.

14. Find a myth in a television drama and relate it to some deep-seated human condition.

15. Find examples of The Trap, The Lie, The Vacation, The Gimmick, and The Date. Ask of each one, Is it credible, familiar, too obvious, and/or enjoyable?

16. Try to analyze the structure of a 30-minute television program of your choice on a scene-by-scene basis, answering the four questions posed by Michael Porter.

SUGGESTED READINGS

Aristotle. (330/1995). *Poetics*. Cambridge, MA: Harvard University Press.

Barthes, Roland. (1974). *S/Z* (trans. Richard Miller.). New York, NY: Hill and Wang.

Campbell, Joseph. (1988). *The Power of Myth*. New York, NY: Anchor Books.

Jung, Carl G. (1969). *Four Archetypes: Mother/Rebirth/Spirit/Trickster*. Princeton, NJ: Princeton University Press.

Jung, Carl G. (1971). *The Portable Jung* (R. F. C. Hull, Trans.). New York, NY: Viking Press.

Propp, Vladimir. (1968). *Morphology of the Folktale* (2nd ed.) (L. Scott, Trans.). Austin: University of Texas Press.

CHAPTER 5

Television Genres

"And the Emmy goes to Modern Family for the Outstanding Comedy Series!"

"The Emmy for Outstanding Lead Actress in a Drama Series goes to Julianna Margulies in The Good Wife!"

"The Emmy for the Outstanding Reality/Competition Show goes to The Amazing Race!"

INTRODUCTION

The Emmy awards, perhaps the most important popular awards given to television programs, actors, writers, directors, and creators, are given in categories representing **genres**—comedy; drama; mini-series; reality/competition; made-for-TV movie; variety, music, or comedy; children's programs; animated programs; game shows; talk shows; commercials; and nonfiction programming. When a creator of a television program pitches a new show, it is identified as a situation comedy, a drama, a reality–adventure show, and so on. For television professionals, genre has been central to the organization and structure of the production industry. Although television shows are often blends or hybrids of these categories, for example, the docudrama, the "dramedy," and the "mockumentary," television programming continues to be based on the concept of genre. Television is known for its inventiveness in developing new genres, for example, the reality show. Another important aspect is the formulaic nature of television programming, which enables large numbers of people to recognize familiar types. Producers and viewers alike assume that genre categories exist and that they know what they are. The genres that prevail on television are those that yield a regular profit for their producers. As a television critic, you will recognize the genre, its conventions, and its departures from conventions when you conduct your analysis and evaluation.

Genre is a French word that translates into English as genus, family, or kind. It is a form of classification. In literature, the major genres are comedy, tragedy, novel, poetry, drama, prose, and nonfiction. In film, some major genres are romantic comedy, science fiction, horror, disaster, and film noir. In television, we recognize broad genres, such as situation comedy, drama, reality shows, talk shows, news programs, and commercials, as well as subgenres, such as daytime soap operas, detective or police **procedurals,** family melodramas, magazine–news shows, reality and reality–competitions, and docudramas, as kinds or types of programming. These tend to be tried and true formulae that have certain predictability and familiarity.

The opening sequence usually follows a familiar pattern. For example, in the police or detective drama, a crime takes place followed by detectives arriving on the scene and canvassing witnesses. A situation comedy usually opens in the same locale, for example, a family's kitchen or living room or an office or a coffee shop with a dilemma expressed by one or more of the characters. Because they are series, viewers recognize the locales as well as the personalities of the characters. Although each television program has its unique qualities, each one may be classified according to some genre or combination of genres.

The formula for a genre is based on certain familiar narrative conventions or common features that make it relatively easy for audiences to follow. Genre conventions prompt viewers to enjoy a program in a certain way. Conventions include program formats, sub-genres, general characteristics, character types, and types of plots. The television audience not only recognizes conventions but also comes to expect them in particular genres. The audience also recognizes when conventions are flouted. This reveals the active union of viewers and television shows. As television programming continues to develop different approaches, traditional conventions are altered and blended with other genres to evolve into new genres and conventions. What is important is acceptance of certain basic assumptions and how much sense a new genre makes.

TELEVISION GENRE, PRODUCTION, AND SCHEDULING

Genre is also used to organize the actual production process in the television industry. Comedies tend to be produced inside studios, with the final production presented in sequence before a live audience, followed by postproduction editing. Dramas tend to be produced more like films in that they are shot out of sequence, often filmed with a single camera, in studios and on locations, followed by postproduction editing. Comedies are produced to fill 30-minute segments, while dramas are usually in 60-minute time slots. Furthermore, genres are used to determine placement on television schedules. Soap operas and children's television are aired in the morning or early afternoon; some talk shows are in the morning or afternoon; while situation comedies are broadcast in early prime time for "family" viewing. Crime shows or adult dramas come later in the evening after the "family hour," presumably after the children are in bed. Morning news magazine programming takes place early in the morning before the workday begins, and local and world news programs come around 6 or 6:30 p.m. when the workday ends, and at 10 or 11 p.m. before bedtime or late-night talk shows.

THE RULES FOR CLASSIFYING GENRES

There are certain "rules" for classifying genres that relate to both cultural norms and production constraints. Such "rules" allow the mass audience to easily understand and follow familiar conventions. Viewers orient their reactions to what they see according to their expectations that have been generated by their knowledge of and experience with the genre. They expect to be amused by a situation comedy like *30 Rock* or *The Office* but not necessarily by a detective show like *CSI: Crime Scene Investigation*. They do not presume that a western such as *Justified* will have singing and dancing as they might in a musical. It is, however, difficult to isolate the characteristics that distinguish one genre from another because they change from season to season and from program to program.

Genres and their conventions change as cultural norms develop. Cultural themes reflect societal norms in a given time. Former situation comedies such as *I Love Lucy* or *The Dick Van Dyke Show* featured married couples who slept in twin beds. The men had careers and the women were homemakers who got themselves into funny predicaments. Today, women on television have careers, may be single parents, and have sexual relations. Couples may be gay as well as straight. Regardless of changing norms, a situation comedy has always been expected to be funny and often has laughter on the soundtrack. In the past, recorded laugh tracks were used, but today most laughter comes from a live audience in the studio watching the final performance. Indeed, the actors may even pause in their dialogue to allow for audience laughter. The audience is expected to laugh along with the studio audience, recognizing the humor in the dialogue or physical actions. Some situation comedies are not filmed in studios and may not have laugh tracks at all. Furthermore, what constitutes a comedy is not always clear, even to the professionals.

> The popular *Desperate Housewives,* a show that is 60 minutes long, won the 2006 Golden Globe Award for Best Television Comedy although it is seldom funny, and it is not filmed before a live audience. Perhaps this is why the 2006 People's Choice Awards nominated it for Best Drama. Which genre is it? This show deals with divorce, illness, death, murder, juggling career and parenting, and outrageous behaviors on the part of some of the characters in the manner of a television drama series, but it is also about friendship, love, domestic problems, comeuppance, and learning from situations in the manner of a situation comedy. The better classification would be "dramedy" because it fuses elements of both comedy and drama; therefore, it is a **hybrid genre.** Marc Cherry, the creator of the show, calls it a "comedy-drama." Sometimes situations on *Desperate Housewives* provoke laughter, but more often we react to it with surprise, curiosity, and shock.

Joanne Ostrow, television critic for *The Denver Post,* wrote that hybrid shows were examples of "**genre bending.**" She wrote, "Producers desperately seek ways to stand out in the increasingly competitive entertainment world, [and] the result is the number of hybrid experiments" (Ostrow, 2001, p. 1E). This brings home the point that the competitiveness for ratings is usually the driving force behind the push for novelty. A spin-off of *JAG, NCIS,* a crime procedural about a Navy Criminal Investigation Service, has been a top-rated action drama for several years. It blends solving murders of Naval and Marine personnel with humor generated by a quirky team of special agents. Steve Sternberg, vice president for audience analysis at the media-buying agency, Magna Global, said, "I think 'NCIS' is one of those rare shows that effectively combines drama and humor and it hasn't lost a step creatively" (B. Carter, 2008, November 17, p. 1).

GENRE AND TELEVISION CRITICISM

As television critic, you need to know about genres and conventions to be able to discuss expected audience responses, the conventions of formats, and characteristics of subgenres, characters, and plots. You will be able to recognize genre hybrids. You will ask how a genre helps us to understand the narrative and how to identify and analyze the features of a program or a series. Knowledge of genres and conventions also explains an audience's ability to tune in to a new program midway through it and recognize the character types and progression of the plot. Genres, as discussed in *Key Concepts in Communication and Culture,*

> limit the meaning-potential of a given text, and they limit the commercial risk of the producer corporations. But they are constantly transformed by the addition of new examples, so that in the end you have to conclude that there's no such thing as a "typical" Western, even though you can recognize one when you see it. (O'Sullivan, Hartley, Saunders, Montgomery, & Fiske, 1994, p. 128)

The characteristics of the subgenres especially tend to be reflective of cultural norms, concerns, and fears that change as times change. Topics such as sexual relationships, fertility, addiction, and homosexuality, which could never have been the subjects of situation comedies or daytime talk shows in the past, now are commonplace on television. Since the destruction of the Twin Towers of the World Trade Center in New York City by Al Qaeda operatives on September 11, 2001, and other terrorist acts around the world, the war on terror has been incorporated into many television dramas.

The history, features, and changes in genres are subjects worthy of an entire book, and there are several good ones (Creeber, 2008; Edgerton & Rose, 2008; Geraghty & Jancovich, 2008; Kaminsky & Mahan, 1985; Mittell, 2004; Rose, 1985). There are also books devoted to single genres, especially comedy, drama, talk shows, children's programming, science fiction, and reality shows. To present the aspects of genres in an efficient manner, Table 5.1 was developed to describe the genres, the subgenres, and common features or conventions in recognized genres. It is difficult to arrive at a finite list of all the genres and even more difficult to specify their individual characteristics. Yet, because television industry practice and viewer anticipation follow genre designations, it is important to include this information here. However, this table must include the disclaimer that these "rules" are frequently broken. The table is extensive but not all-inclusive because there are so many subgenres with differing characteristics. Some of the genres are self-evident and even have their own channels, for example, Food Network, Country Music Television, Cartoon Network, Home Shopping Network, and SOAPnet. A discussion of the characteristics of each of the genres follows.

COMEDY

Situation Comedy

Situation comedies have been the staple of television programming for a long time. Although many pilots are made, few make it onto the air. Because reality shows are cheaper to produce, they often get picked over situation comedies. Yet situation comedies are less expensive to make than dramatic series. A situation comedy is usually located in a domestic or workplace setting. Therefore, the same set can be used over and over, and a limited number of actors are employed, although the casts of very successful shows demand and receive extremely high salaries. The family and workplace settings are convenient places to bring people together. In the workplace, people have a common goal to get a job done, thus they have to interact with one another. The workplace provides an opportunity to develop characters of different backgrounds, ethnicity, gender, and race.

Situation comedies are generally known as escapist fare and provoke laughter through jokes, humorous dialogue and situations, and slapstick. As series, they are broadcast at the same time each week for 30 minutes during the television season and tend to be complete in each episode. The characters are the same each week, although there may be a guest actor playing the role of an outsider who sets the plot in motion. There may be a lead actor, such as Steve Carell in *The Office,* although usually there is an ensemble of actors playing the family or the staff in the workplace. The plot customarily involves some minor enigma, lack, or a test, known as "the problem of the week," for example, getting a date, having a disastrous date, avoiding a visit by an in-law, losing something valuable, forgetting an anniversary, wrecking the family car, buttering up the boss, coping with jealous coworkers, or convincing a coworker to cover up a mistake. The enigma or lack gets resolved after a delay by the end of the episode, and usually there is some sentimental reconciliation, a lesson learned, or moral growth. Equilibrium is achieved in 30 minutes, so there is a happy ending that the audience has come to expect. The basic nature of the characters and their situation is reaffirmed.

The main characters are likeable, and audiences identify with them because the foibles of the characters are recognized as similar to their own shortcomings. Carl Reiner, who wrote, directed, and produced many outstanding situation comedies, such as *The Dick Van Dyke Show,* said it was important for the characters to have "warmth." "You laugh easier when funny things are happening to nice people" (Rose, 1985, p. 117). James Burrows, winner of 10 Emmys and director of *Cheers, Will & Grace, Frasier,* and many other situation comedies, echoed Reiner when he said, "The successful key to a situation comedy is to create warmth which transfers to the audience. Good shows are stories told from the heart" (O'Donnell, 1996). In his book *Comic Visions,* David Marc wrote, "sitcoms depend on familiarity, identification, and redemption of popular beliefs" (Marc, 1989, p. 24). While the situation comedy endorses cultural norms, it may also advance certain new ideas.

The late Sheldon Leonard, producer of many successful situation comedies such as *The Andy Griffith Show,* said, "We can, within a framework of good showmanship, advance valid social comments, valid ethical concepts, valid generalizations about the human condition which have meaning for the audience" (Rose, 1985, p. 119). In the situation comedy

Table 5.1   Genres, Subgenres, and Their Conventions

Genre	Subgenre	Conventions	
		Format	Characteristics
Comedy	Situation comedy	30 minutes, usually filmed before a live audience and edited later	Provokes laughter through jokes, humor in dialogue, or slapstick. Domestic or workplace setting.
	Animated comedy	30 minutes, animation with voices, often celebrity voices	Provokes laughter through parody, sight gags. Multiple story lines, intertextual references.
	Variety comedy	60 minutes, live before an audience	Provokes laughter, enjoyment. Comic skits, musical numbers.
Talk show	Nighttime talk shows	60 minutes, recorded before a live audience. Broadcast late at night 5 nights/week	Provokes laughter, entertainment. Opening monologue, improvisational and scripted dialogue, skits, music. Desk for host, sofa for guests, performance space in studio.
	Daytime talk shows	60 minutes, recorded before a live audience 5 days/week	Informative, sometimes shocking, guests reveal sensitive and personal experiences. Host and guests sit on chairs on the stage. Studio audience reacts boisterously.
	Informational talk shows	Usually 60 minutes	Informative discussion of current topics, conversational, face-to-face, and interviews
News	National and world news	Usually 30 minutes, live with recorded segments	Informational, anchor announces news with prerecorded reports, brief news clips.
	Local news	Usually 30 minutes, 60 minutes in some large markets	Similar pattern regardless of place of origin, brief recorded clips and field reports
	News-talk	Usually 60 minutes	Informational, 3–4 in-depth stories, news staff stays with story and asks questions

	Conventions	
Characters	Plot	Examples
Ensemble actors, one or more leads, often stereotypical, guest stars	A dilemma or test is solved by the end of show. Learning or moral growth.	• The Big Bang Theory • The Office • Glee • 30 Rock • Modern Family
Cartoon characters, regulars and guests	Domestic dilemma, event, or parody of real life.	• The Simpsons • South Park • American Dad
Ensemble cast, guest host	Satire and parody	Saturday Night Live
Single host, band leader, and sometimes a sidekick. Celebrity guests, exotic animals.	Topical humor and variety	• The Tonight Show • Late Show With David Letterman • The Late, Late Show • The Daily Show
Host and guests who are often ordinary people, sometimes high-profile celebrities	Explores cultural oddities, usually domestic	• Dr. Phil • The Ellen DeGeneres Show • The View • The Talk
Single host with experts, sometimes celebrities	Topics: current issues, books, films	• Charlie Rose • Meet the Press
Anchor sits behind desk, network field correspondents report live or recorded	Global, national current events, business, human interest, health advances	• ABC News • CBS News • NBC News • Fox News
Two or 3 anchors and sportscaster, mixed gender and race, they also chat "happy talk."	Local news, "breaking news," about crime, accidents, disasters, lifestyle, sports, weather. Larger markets may include some global news.	Local television stations
Host with other staff reporters	Global, national current events, business, and health news	NewsHour With Jim Lehrer

(Continued)

Table 5.1 (Continued)

Genre	Subgenre	Conventions	
		Format	*Characteristics*
	24-hour news	24 hours of news, both live and prerecorded	Informational news repeated throughout the day, other news on captions, special reports
Magazine show	News-talk-entertainment	1–3 hours with prerecorded segments	Informational and entertaining news, interviews with authors, celebrities, politicians, health professionals. Segments about food, music, fashion, new products.
	Investigative or public affairs	60 minutes, prerecorded	Informational, entertaining, shocking stories with reenactments and interviews
	Celebrity news	Information about film and TV stars' private and professional lives, 30–60 minutes	Male and female hosts announce stories with prerecorded, edited segments.
Drama	Crime shows, detective/police/FBI, forensic science	60 minutes recorded outside and on indoor sets, episodic	Audience follows case step by step, anticipates the outcome. Case is solved within the hour, interpersonal conflicts may carry over to subsequent shows. Character and dialogue are central to show. Usually set in urban area. May use flashbacks. Emphasis on law, order, and justice.
	Workplace drama	60 minutes recorded outside and on indoor sets, episodic	Audience follows several events, anticipates the outcome. Workplace crisis or conflict is usually settled within the hour. Set in hospital, law office, courtroom. Interpersonal attraction between and among people at workplace. May have flashbacks.
	Family drama	60 minutes recorded outside and on indoor sets, episodic	Audience identification with characters, familiar conflicts, set inside home and surroundings in the present time.
	Hybrid dramas	60 minutes recorded outside and on indoor sets, episodic	Family drama fused with mystery or science fiction. Audience anticipates outcome, may identify with characters.

	Conventions	
Characters	Plot	Examples
everal different anchors in shifts, orrespondents are prominent	Global, national current events, business, health, and human interest news	• CNN • Headline News • Fox News • MSNBC
wo anchors, one male, one female who iterview guests plus other talent reading ews, weather, human interest stories. nchors chat, tell personal stories.	Multiple segments similar in layout to a print magazine	• *Today* • *Good Morning America* • *The Early Show*
nchor with field correspondents	Usually one primary story about an event, scandal, illegal or immoral acts.	• *60 Minutes* • *48 Hours* • *Nightline* • *20/20*
osts are youthful and attractive.	Stories about the stars to reveal them as people who date, marry, divorce, have children.	• *E! News* • *Insider* • *Access Hollywood*
nsemble cast with character development ver time. Major and minor characters, ixed gender and race.	Crime is committed or person goes missing; law enforcers arrive at scene, interrogate witnesses, examine evidence at crime scene or in laboratory, make arrest, solve crime, find missing person.	• *Cold Case* • *NCIS* • *Criminal Minds* • *Prime Suspect* • *Law & Order: SVU* • *The Closer* • *The Mentalist* • *CSI* • *Bones*
nsemble cast, young attractive women nd men with few older adults, mixed cially. Interpersonal relationships evelop over time.	Crisis or conflict, teamwork to arrive at a solution within the hour, interpersonal affairs carry over.	• *House* • *Grey's Anatomy* • *Mad Men* • *Damages* • *The Good Wife*
nsemble cast with young adults, ildren, some senior citizens	Multiple interpersonal conflicts carry over from week to week.	• *Brothers and Sisters* • *Friday Night Lights* • *Parenthood* • *Smallville*
ead actor(s) with ensemble cast	Dilemma may or may not be solved within the hour, may be crime, espionage, or interpersonal conflict	• *Fringe* • *True Blood*

(Continued)

Table 5.1 (Continued)

Genre	Subgenre	Conventions	
		Format	*Characteristics*
	Telefilms	Audience may have familiarity with story. Mini-series over 3 or 4 nights or 90- to 120-minute movie, possible pilot for a proposed series.	Audience identification with characters. Adapted from a well-known book or original screenplay. Full-length drama, may be romantic, adventure, or melodrama.
	Docudramas	Audience may know something about the biographical person but expects to learn more. Audience is expected to know it is watching impersonations, not file footage. Blend of fact and fiction. Miniseries over 3 or 4 nights or 90- to 120-minute movie.	Based on a true story, biography or crime in dramatic form, includes imaginary dialogue. Often melodramatic.
Soap opera	Daytime drama, some nighttime drama	30–60 minutes, daily, continuous serials. May run for years. Audience has to stay tuned to follow narrative.	Interpersonal relationships, domestic crises, overlapping storylines, cliffhangers
Science fiction		• Feeds audience imagination • 30–60 minutes, episodic • Some are on Syfy channel	Usually takes place in the future and in space, features fantastic technology. Stories reflect contemporary problems of the present such as nuclear threat, racism, multiculturalism, ecology.
Reality shows	Competition, talent, real lives	Encourage audience voyeurism. Usually 60 minutes, usually episodic, almost never appear as reruns.	Ordinary people compete for expensive prizes. Competitive, winners chosen by group vote or judges. Real-life police responses to crime, sting operations.
Sports	Football, basketball, baseball, hockey, tennis, golf, soccer, water sports, volleyball, Olympics	Audience sees live broadcast of full-length games.	Sports announcers describe and comment on the game.

	Conventions	
haracters	Plot	Examples
ctors may or may not be famous. Heroes nd villains.	Characters established and followed through story to the end.	• Band of Brothers • The Pacific • Mildred Pierce • Little Dorritt • Upstairs/Downstairs • Downton Abbey
ome resemblance to actual people, actors ay not be well known.	Tends to rely on family melodrama, a specific time in the life of a famous person, often features mature and personal topics such as spouse abuse or eating disorders.	• Justice for Natalee Holloway • William and Kate • Cinema Verité • John Adams • Temple Grandin • You Don't Know Jack
egular cast of familiar characters, ttractive young adults, a few older dults. Familiar setting in homes or work laces.	State of equilibrium is disturbed, rarely a solution or a climax that ties loose ends. Resolution is endlessly deferred.	• The Young and the Restless • As the World Turns • General Hospital • The Bold and the Beautiful
nsemble spaceship crew, aliens	Heroes save humanity from aliens and Armageddon.	• Battlestar Galactica • Supernatural • Dr. Who • Falling Skies • Terra Nova
on-actors audition for places and pportunity to compete.	Contestants are given tasks to complete in blocks of time; contestants are eliminated by group members, judges, or authority. One team or one winner emerges. Police arrest offenders.	• The Biggest Loser • American Idol • Dancing With the Stars • Survivor • Cops • The Bachelor • Project Runway • The Amazing Race
ive competition	Stays on the air until a winner emerges.	Network and sports channels' coverage of various sports such as Super Bowl and college bowl games, NBA, World Series.

(Continued)

Table 5.1 (Continued)

| Genre | Subgenre | Conventions | |
		Format	Characteristics
Children's television	Live and animated programming	30 minutes, 5 days/week, daytime; appeals to children of various ages	Ranges from educational entertainment to cartoon violence.
Game shows		Television audience can match answers or guesses with contestants, 30–60 minutes. Recorded in front of live audience, weekly or daily.	Contestants compete for prizes within the program or over several weeks.

Note: Other genres are mostly self-evident: religious broadcasting, shopping networks, food networks, award shows, music performances,

Conventions		
Characters	*Plot*	*Examples*
Often has familiar characters such as Big Bird	Educational programs have combination ensembles of puppets and live actors. Cartoons have heroes and villains.	• *Sesame Street* • *Scooby Doo* • *SpongeBob SquarePants* • *Arthur* • *Electric Company*
Host and attractive woman to work the game board. Contestants.	Categories of quiz questions. Correct answers increase value of prizes, suspense is built as contestants struggle to give correct answers.	• *Jeopardy!* • *The Price Is Right* • *Wheel of Fortune* • *Minute to Win It*

movie channels, History Channel, Discovery Channel, Nova, Nature, Animal Planet.

about a television news staff, *Murphy Brown,* not only did the lead character (played by Candice Bergen) have a child out of wedlock, but in a later episode, Murphy had breast cancer and subsequent surgery for which she chose a lumpectomy rather than a mastectomy. Breast cancer was also a theme in some of the last episodes of *Sex and the City* as Samantha (Kim Cattrall) lost her hair due to chemotherapy. These problems were not treated as comedy but rather as real-life situations. Thus, the situation comedy, though generally funny, also enables the audience to identify with real-life situations and embrace the characters as more human.

Animated Situation Comedy

Animated situation comedy has once again become popular on prime-time television, especially since *The Simpsons* became a regular series in 1990. Animated situation comedy tends to have everything a human comedy has—a family, an ensemble of regular characters who do things to provoke laughter, multiple story lines, a "problem of the week," and restoration of equilibrium at the end of 30 minutes. Spin-offs of *The Simpsons* include *South Park, Family Guy, Futurama,* and *American Dad. The Simpsons,* which began as 30-second inserts in *The Tracey Ullman Show* in 1987, has been running as a regular 30-minute series since 1990, winning 24 prime-time Emmys, holding the record for the longest-running situation comedy, and surpassing the longest-running prime-time animation series, *The Flintstones.*

Photo 5.1   Bart and Lisa Simpson

Animated situation comedy is characterized by parody and satire. The brochure for the Museum of Television and Radio's seminar on *The Simpsons* describes it as "a gonzo attack on mainstream television, melding sharp, clever writing with animation to reinvigorate the conventional sitcom format as a cartoon satire on contemporary America" (Creating Prime-time Comedy, 2003, p. 9). The references to television, film, literature, social topics, organized religion, political figures, and advertising give the show its special edge. To appreciate this aspect of *The Simpsons,* a viewer has to be familiar with classic films like *Citizen Kane* as well as television's *Mad Men.* The Simpson family watches a lot of television, thus there are many references to actual series. On one episode, the little sister Lisa is trying to make new friends while on vacation at the seashore by telling them about hermit crabs. One child asks Lisa, "Did you learn that from a teacher?" "No," said Lisa, "I learned it on *Baywatch.*" These intertextual references are enhanced by the audience's knowing complicity and recognition of famous guest voices such as Halle Berry, Kristen Wig, Joe Mantegna, Kareem Abdul-Jabbar, the architect Frank Gehry, and former Prime Minister Tony Blair. To understand the intertextual humor, the audience has to be familiar with the events, names, voices, films, and television programs that the show parodies. In one episode, Lisa gets in trouble because a career test indicates that her future work should be that of a homemaker. The school principal asks her, "What are you rebelling against?" Her response refers to Marlon Brando in *The Wild One* when she says, "Whattaya got?" It is possible to enjoy *The Simpsons* without intertextual recognition, but when the allusions are caught, the enjoyment is enhanced. Thus, children and adults alike enjoy the show. Because it is an animated cartoon, it gets away with antics that might not be acceptable in human situation comedy.

Variety Comedy

The **variety comedy** shows of the past, such as *Your Show of Shows* with Sid Caesar and Imogene Coca or *The Carol Burnett Show,* had a regular host, an ensemble cast, music, and humorous skits. While many variety comedy shows have come and gone, *Saturday Night Live* has been on NBC since 1975 with weekly guest hosts, including Sting, Queen Latifah, and Jane Lynch, an ensemble cast of improvisational comics who do impersonations and put on funny and satirical skits, and breakout musical acts. This show has launched the film and television careers of comic performers like Steve Martin, Eddie Murphy, Dan Aykroyd, Bill Murray, Adam Sandler, Tina Fey, and Amy Poehler. It is telecast live before an audience in New York City at 11:30 p.m. and has followed the same formula since its inception. The skits, performed by the ensemble cast as well as the guest host, satirize current events, politicians, newscasters, or relationships.

TALK SHOWS

Nighttime Talk Shows

Steve Allen launched the nighttime talk show genre in 1954 with comedy, music, and guests on *The Tonight Show.* When Johnny Carson became the show's star in 1962 and remained there for 30 years, it became a late-night institution. The format Carson used has hardly changed. There is a single host sitting behind a desk who talks to guests who are sitting on a sofa. The host has a sidekick or a band leader with whom to banter, and there is a performance space for musical numbers. The guests may be celebrities, politicians, or zoo keepers who introduce exotic animals to the host.

Writers meet with the host to develop a "script" that is placed on the host's desk, but much of the dialogue is improvisational. As Rob Burnett, head writer on the *Late Show With David Letterman,* said, "Everything is planned and nothing is planned" (Writers Guild of the East, n.d.). The late-night talk shows are taped before a live audience earlier in the evening and broadcast late at night, after the news, five nights a week. Each show opens with a monologue, usually a parody of that day's newspaper headlines, followed by talks with guests who may be promoting films or books or themselves (Arnold Schwarzenegger announced his candidacy for governor of California on *The Tonight Show* with Jay Leno), musical events, and comic skits. Letterman does remote acts outside the studio, but they are filmed and edited in advance. These late-night talk shows are 60 minutes long.

Bernard Timberg called this "television talk" rather than "television talk shows" because it is a special kind of talk. "It is often directed to an individual in the studio (guest or side-kick) but also, simultaneously, to a national television viewing audience of millions" (Timberg, 2000, p. 359). He also indicated that television talk

> begins and ends with the host. Talk shows are, to use the words of one producer, "he" or "she" shows. The producers and talent coordinators line up guests and topics for "him" or "her"; the writers write lines that will work for "him" or "her," to be spoken as he or she would speak them. The tone and pacing of everything that happens with the show is set by the host. (Timberg, 2000, p. 361)

Daytime Talk Shows

Daytime talk shows are taped before a live audience for 60-minute time slots, five days a week. The host and guests tend to explore cultural oddities. Sometimes the guests are famous, and sometimes they are people who reveal sensitive problems, usually domestic or criminal, and disclose their most private experiences to the host or hostess. Jerry Springer and Maury Povich, whose talk shows bear their names, emphasize the vulgar and crude, often with fistfights between guests, nasty repartee, and outbursts from the audience. Often these people are from marginalized or stigmatized groups. They may be incest or rape victims, unwed mothers, transsexuals, prostitutes, or people with incurable diseases. In some cases, the guests and the studio audience have been rehearsed. Media psychologist Dr. Phil, on the show of the same name, teaches through interpersonal discussion and psychological analysis of his guests. The audience can observe how others with problems and personal conflicts in relationships work through them. Daytime talk shows may highlight moral conflict and confrontation between and among the guests and sometimes the audience members. The approach is to "tell all" no matter how distressing.

The Ellen DeGeneres Show, winner of 31 daytime Emmys, where Ellen DeGeneres discusses topical issues with guests ranging from A-list celebrities to First Lady Michelle Obama, invokes laughter with her stories and videos, often about animals, and gains support for humanitarian causes. *The View* and *The Talk* are morning talk shows featuring women who discuss events of the day and interview guests. All three of these shows give away prizes to the audience. *The View* has been satirized on *The Simpsons* and *Saturday Night Live*. A Walmart 20-minute infomercial that looked a lot like an episode of *The View* had four women chatting about its big box stores.

Information Talk Shows

Information-oriented talk shows include discussion of current issues, books, films, and other serious topics. They are conversational and guest oriented. Charlie Rose, on *The Charlie Rose Show,* leads serious discussions with one or more guests who sit at a table with him. The viewing audience gains information from experts. *Meet the Press* has been on the air for 60 years. It features political news and interviews on Sunday mornings.

Photo 5.2 Ellen DeGeneres and Taylor Swift on the talk show *Ellen*.

NEWS

News includes the elements of "timeliness, consequence, prominence, rarity, proximity, conflict, change, action, concreteness, and personality" (Metzler, 1979, pp. 23–24). News reporting is interpretative and creative, therefore it is a symbolic strategy that contains an attitude toward the events that are recounted (Wilkins & Patterson, 1987). Communication satellites, relay stations in space, carry press agency news feeds and global television, bringing news from remote regions around the world and up-to-the-minute reporting from conflict zones. Interviews, correspondent reports, and actual footage are structured to fit the news format and time.

National and World News

The national half-hour news report at the end of the workday follows a standard format of news stories sprinkled with advertisements for remedies for indigestion and headaches. An anchor sitting at a desk reads the news reports with taped or live visual images to convey the stories. Satellite transmission of images allows the viewers to feel a sense of immediacy and involvement. Network correspondents report from Washington, DC, the White House, Capitol Hill, the Pentagon, and from around the globe. Cuts in budgets have reduced the number of correspondents in the field, resulting in "parachute journalism." Correspondents based in a foreign city have to fly at a moment's notice to a location where the news is breaking (Foote, 1998). National news anchors have become stars. Former anchors from the three networks—ABC, CBS, and NBC—Peter Jennings, Dan Rather, and Tom Brokaw, respectively, became institutions in our living rooms. Katie Couric, a star from NBC's *Today,* became the anchor on *CBS Evening News* until 2011. Diane Sawyer is the anchor of *ABC World News,* and Brian Williams is the anchor on *NBC Nightly News.*

When CNN, the 24-hour news channel, appeared in 1980, the three networks redefined their approach to news to compete.

> Assuming that viewers watched the big stories before the evening news was broadcast, networks opted for more reflection, stylized reporting, longer trend stories, and a hint of "infotainment." What they lacked in immediacy and news-gathering ability around the world, they tried to make up for with a well-regarded anchor name and segments. (Foote, 1998, p. 12)

In addition to national and international current events, the nightly news also includes segments of business news, advances in medicine, and human interest stories, all of which are very brief.

Local News

The local news is usually on for 30 minutes before network national and international news and late at night before the nighttime talk shows. Local news broadcasts tend to have a similar format regardless of their origins, thus the local news in New York City resembles

Photo 5.3   *NBC Nightly News* anchor Brian Williams.

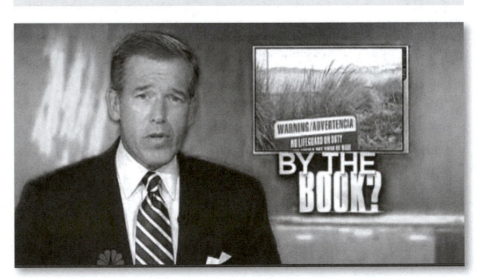

the local news in Los Angeles. Typically, there are two or three anchors behind a desk, a man and a woman plus a sportscaster. Often one or more of the anchors is African American, Hispanic American, or Asian American. In addition to reporting the news, the anchors chat with one another. The weather person is not behind the desk, but rather he or she appears to be standing in front of a map for the weather spot on the program. Promotions and lead-ins are used to grab viewer attention ("Arson suspected in home fire. News at 6 o'clock."). Local news often emphasizes "breaking news," with live images of car chases, people being carried by stretcher to a waiting ambulance, burning buildings, and so on. In addition to crime and disaster news, local stations usually have some soft news ("Fireman rescues kitten from sewer pipe"). In addition, there is health news, local and national sports, and celebrity items. Local news from large urban areas has some national and international reporting.

News-Talk

PBS's *The NewsHour With Jim Lehrer* is on five nights a week for 60 minutes. It has in-depth news stories, usually only three, with reporters staying on the story for greater under-standing. Lehrer stops and asks questions during each report. The stories are about national and international news, business news, and education, and there are interviews with heads of state, writers, and politicians. When the stock market report comes up, the reporter tells the audience what it means. A seminar at the Museum of Television and Radio in 1989 included Lehrer and his former co-anchor Robert MacNeil, who said, "We intended our show to be different. . . . to expand time devoted to a story to fit its importance. [You] stay with the topic or interview until you find its importance." They do not consider their audi-ence elite, but very broad in scope. Lehrer said, "We do not assume a certain body of knowl-edge in the audience. We are very basic, we use maps and other information helpful to understanding the issue. We ask, 'would so-and-so understand this and would he care?'" (*MacNeil/Lehrer NewsHour,* 1989).

Other news talk shows are more specific in their focus. Network and cable channels feature shows with pundits—self-appointed experts, who express their own opinions and argue with one another about issues of the day.

24-Hour News

The Cable News Network (CNN) began to broadcast news 24 hours a day, seven days a week in 1980. Although it had anchors, emphasis was placed on the news, not on person-alities, and the correspondents' reports were given importance. News bureaus were set up across the United States and around the world. In 1982, Ted Turner initiated a second CNN service, *Headline News,* with updated newscasts every half hour. When President Ronald Reagan met Mikhail S. Gorbachev at the summit that would signal the end of the Cold War, CNN had 17 correspondents onsite. By 1989, CNN was available in 65 countries. In 1991, CNN was the only television network operating live from Operation Desert Storm in Iraq and Kuwait.

Other 24-hour news channels emerged—MSNBC and Fox News—to challenge CNN. Although CNN had fallen behind Fox News and MSNBC in the ratings, it recovered to lead in the ratings with its coverage of the earthquake and tsunami in Japan and the fighting and NATO airstrikes in Libya in the spring of 2011. MSNBC's president, Phil Griffin, said, "This is where CNN excels. This is in their bull's eye, and they've done a great job. Even Fox News, which dominates them, gets beat by CNN at times like this" (B. Carter, 2011, March 23, p. 1).

MAGAZINE SHOWS

News-Talk-Entertainment

News-talk-entertainment shows are generally on in the early morning. To attract the working audience, 22 minutes of commercial-free hard news is reported at 7 a.m. The next hour, from 7:30 to 8:30 a.m., has hard and soft features aimed at a female audience, and the next half hour is aimed at senior citizens, with health-oriented pieces. The content includes interviews with celebrities, authors, politicians, and doctors. Consumer advice, health news, cooking tips, film reviews, and fashion are presented by the anchor-hosts and guests. Much of the fare is light-hearted, and the anchor-hosts, usually one woman and one man, chat with one another. More serious news is handled by a regular news reader, and another regular on the show talks about weather. These multiple segments are similar to a print magazine, for they are short, informative, and basically entertaining. *Today* has been on NBC since 1952. Ann Curry, Matt Lauer, and Al Roker are the stars who go outside to chat with the crowd that gathers as early as 5 a.m. in Rockefeller Center. In the summer, they have live music on Fridays. *Today* added a fourth hour hosted by Kathy Lee Gifford and Hoda Kotb, who talk about fashion, dating, and diets. *Good Morning America,* the CBS *Early Show,* and *Fox and Friends* follow a similar pattern. Needless to say, these news-talk-entertainment shows are very competitive.

Investigative or Public Affairs

Investigative or public affairs television shows were developed "to offer an alternative to the television presentation of news" (Stark, 1997, p. 188). Each of these shows has one or more anchors and investigative field reporters. They may focus on single or multiple stories of a scandalous or disturbing nature, such as kidnapping, organized crime, unsafe food in restaurants, scams, and frauds, although sometimes they do positive profiles on people who have done good deeds, recovered from adversity, or are effective leaders. They may use taped footage, but some are inclined to use reenactments with actors. *60 Minutes* has been on the air since 1968, and reporters such as Morley Safer and Steve Kroft have been with the show for many years. Diane Sawyer joined the show as its first woman in 1984. When she left in 1989, Lesley Stahl replaced her. When host Harry Reasoner introduced the first broadcast of *60 Minutes,* he said, "It's kind of a magazine for television, which means it has the flexibility and diversity of a magazine adapted to broadcast journalism" (Stark, 1997,

p. 189). The first show had a story mix of political campaigns, conflicts between police and citizens, an animated film, and a humorous essay. In later years, *60 Minutes* altered its focus with fewer lighter features and more investigative pieces. In keeping with popular tastes, it also featured profiles of film stars and athletes. Steven Stark wrote, "*60 Minutes* changed the face of programming and journalism. . . . [it] made journalists into national icons" (Stark, 1997, p. 189). *60 Minutes* spawned a trend in news magazine shows. *48 Hours* covers one story with multiple angles; whereas *Dateline* is known for its surprise visits and hidden cameras. *20/20* features sensational stories, often using reenactments.

Celebrity News

The 21st century has seen an increased obsession with the lives of celebrities, and many television shows concentrate solely on the private and personal lives of film and television stars and their fashions. *Entertainment Tonight,* or *ET,* began in 1981 with Mary Hart and John Tesh in an upbeat, gossipy, and glitzy show about the stars, award shows, new films and television shows, and musicians. Soon other shows followed—*Insider, Access Hollywood,* and an entire cable channel, E! Entertainment Television—devoted to entertainment news, reality shows, and re-runs of *Sex and the City*. Described as "hysterical cheer" and "tabloid TV," the fast-paced style of celebrity news shows with attractive and young female and male hosts revealing the intimate details of the lives of the stars has influenced the style of local news programs and reality shows.

DRAMA

Drama on television may be serial, a mini-series, or a single play that may last for one hour or several hours spread over a fixed number of nights or weeks. Drama is the most varied, complex, expensive, and popular television genre. Series drama tends to be formulaic, whereas mini-series and single plays are formatted to fit the allotted time in the schedule. Series consist of 22 to 23 episodes per season on the networks and 12 to 13 episodes on cable channels. Because a single episode of a drama series costs millions to produce, the plots may be self-contained with a resolution at the end of the hour. This is convenient and cost-effective for reruns because viewers do not have to know what happened in the previous episode. Not all series are self-contained, however, for unresolved issues keep the viewers tuning in to find out what happens next.

Most dramatic series have ensemble casts of actors who play the same roles from week to week. Audiences prefer familiar characters and story lines. In a study conducted by the Corporation for Public Broadcasting to find out why American audiences were not watching imported British dramas more frequently, participants in focus groups said that because they did not know the characters, it required too much effort to watch a new program with so many new actors. Their preferences were for familiar characters, sets, and story lines (Kubey, 2004). Familiarity with the characters and narrative structure also enables the audience to pick up a story line when the holiday seasons interrupt series for several weeks.

Crime Shows (Detective, Police, FBI, and Forensic Science)

The crime series are 60 minutes long, starting at point A with an enigma (a murder, a missing person, a theft, a rape, a kidnapping, or an arson in an urban or suburban area) that is resolved (by detectives, the police, military special agents, FBI agents, or forensic scientists) at the end of the hour at point B. Although they are part of a series, individual episodes can stand alone because of the resolution at the end of each show. Since September 11, 2001, terrorism has become a common theme on crime shows, especially those that feature the FBI.

Crime shows have ensemble casts playing crime fighters who have skills and weapons and know how to use them. These characters also have interpersonal relations with one another. While a crime gets solved, the suspense and conflict in these relationships are not necessarily resolved at the end of an episode, carrying over to the next week. The casts are usually mixed in gender, race, and age, with characters who develop some depth over time. However, these shows are not so much about crimes but rather about those who try to solve them, thus they depend upon characters and their dialogue. Although each individual crime series has its own uniqueness, they tend to follow a similar structure: (1) a crime is committed; (2) the detectives-police-special agents-FBI-crime scene experts arrive at the scene to view the body or fire or other criminal act; (3) they interrogate witnesses and family members and follow the leads; (4) they search for and ultimately detain or arrest the suspects; and (5) they solve the crime.

Sometimes there will be internal conflict when the police or detectives disagree or go beyond the boundaries of their duty. The Internal Affairs Bureau (IAB) officials, although on the side of the law, are often depicted as villains who get in the way of the detectives who are trying to solve a crime. Some of the crime shows have original takes on procedurals. *Cold Case,* set in Philadelphia, is about investigating unsolved murders from the past, and *Bones* is about a forensic anthropologist who has an uncanny ability to read clues in victims' bones. Both of these series feature female leads, Emily Deschanel on *Bones* and Kathryn Morris on *Cold Case. Criminal Minds* features FBI profilers who track criminals to try to prevent them from attacking again. *The Mentalist* is about a former psychic who is a consultant to the California Bureau of Investigation (CBI) and with his sharp skills of observation helps solve crimes.

The crime scene investigator characters of *CSI: Crime Scene Investigation* collect evidence that they examine in the laboratory and almost always examine bloody, bruised, and mutilated corpses with medical examiners explaining the cause of death. A trademark of these shows is expensive equipment donated by publicity-seeking manufacturers (a $50,000 forensic microscope and a $500,000 ballistic identifier on *CSI*) and special visual effects known as "snap-zoom" that snap into a body or zoom into a piece of evidence (Gliatto, 2002, pp. 113–115; Stein, 2003, p. 72). The viewer looks at the evidence along with the characters in the show. Correct scientific vocabulary, often in Latin, is used for realism.

Over the years, the characters on shows like *NCIS, CSI: Crime Scene Investigation,* and *Law & Order: SVU* have developed through both their work and personal lives. Each character has a personal story that affects how he or she acts in investigations. Essentially, crime series emphasize law, order, and justice as well as the determination and ability of law enforcement officials.

Workplace Drama

Workplace dramas are about groups of professional people in a hospital, law firm, advertising firm, government office, or the military. An ensemble cast of young and attractive men and women with a few older adults is likely to be racially mixed. The characters they play undergo personal growth over time in both their work and their personal relationships. The settings provide the work-related action as well as the characters' personal affairs. In most workplace dramas, several events occur simultaneously, with work-related crises or conflicts usually settled within a 60-minute episode, while the personal affairs continue over several episodes.

The hospital has been a popular setting for television workplace dramas with various illnesses, accidents, last-minute surgical saves, compassionate doctors, and a multitude of patients who provide opportunities for guest actors. *Grey's Anatomy* follows a group of young, attractive doctors through their surgical residency at a Seattle hospital and the older doctors who guide and harass them. *House* has a lead actor, Hugh Laurie, who plays Dr. Gregory House, a brilliant diagnostician with a dysfunctional personality, who delivers surly, acerbic lines with a wry sense of humor. He supervises a group of young doctors and argues with the hospital administrator about a single case on each episode.

Mad Men has a long, unfolding narrative about advertising professionals in the 1960s. At the center is Don Draper, a secretive, brooding womanizer who is the successful creative director in the firm. The show is known for its authenticity of sets, costumes, products, and outmoded standards. There were no sexual harassment laws in the 1960s, thus Draper's imperfect colleagues get away with gawking and making remarks about the women who work, mostly as secretaries, in the office.

Workplace dramas also take place in law firms, two with strong women in charge. *Damages* has the ruthless Patty Hewes, while *The Good Wife* has Diane Lockhart, the firm's managing partner. *The Good Wife*'s star, however, is Julianna Margulies, who plays Alicia Florrick, an associate attorney and the wife of a politician whose affair with a prostitute ruins their marriage. Alicia's teenage children engage in a lot of social media on their computer at home that reflects current norms in society.

Family Drama

Family dramas are melodramas, for they depict ordinary suffering as special and meaningful (Deming, 1990). Personal life as revealed through close relationships is at the core of melodramatic narrative that also is replete with extraordinary conflicts and catastrophes (Ang, 1990). Chris Barker describes melodrama as having "a heightened sense of the dramatic, with a focus on emotions and 'life's torments.' . . . viewers are propelled along a roller-coaster ride of emotional ups and downs" (2008, p. 323). *Friday Night Lights,* which has won numerous prestigious awards, was about a Texas high school football team, the coach and his family, and the small town of Dillon. The football coach faced many challenges as did the various high school students. It was about family, relationships, and community. *Parenthood* is a drama about a big family of three generations whose lives are closely intertwined. Each character experiences crises, but the family supports one another in admirable ways. One of the children has Asperger's syndrome, and the young actor's realistic portrayal of it is impressive. Although the individual members of this family have flaws and difficulties, the unity of the family is at the center of the series. The families in these two series are educated, live in nice homes, and are White, middle-class, although African American characters are integral to their lives and are portrayed as friends and partners. Viewers who write about them on various websites identify with them and indicate that they are important in their lives.

Hybrid Drama

Hybrid dramas on contemporary television are police or family dramas blended with elements of other genres, often science fiction or the supernatural. *Medium* was a self-contained, hour-long drama that was part family drama and part crime procedural and featured a mother of three young daughters who is married to an understanding and helpful husband. She works for the district attorney because her dreams reveal the identities of killers, and she has visions of their crimes when she confronts suspects and crime scenes.

HBO's summer series, *True Blood,* is a Gothic Southern satire that incorporates a multitude of genres—family and workplace drama, crime procedural, comedy, science fiction, and fantasy. It also has plenty of sex, mayhem, and blood. The human family consists of Sookie and her brother Jason, Sookie's best friend Tara, and Tara's cousin Lafayette. The vampire "family" has many members, for it is a dynasty headed by a queen. The workplaces are two bars—a human bar owned by Sam, who is also a shape-shifter, and a vampire bar run by Eric and Pam, who are vampires. The crimes, mostly murders by vampires, are investigated by an imperfect sheriff and Jason, who gets involved with a woman who turns into a panther. The comedy is satiric, as the vampires represent the disenfranchised of every type of person, and there is a fanatic anti-vampire cult. The supernatural elements center on the romance between Sookie, a human with telepathic abilities who is related to fairies, and Bill, the 173-year-old vampire, but there was also a minor romance between Hoyt, a human, and Jessica, a vampire. There are also love triangles, between Sookie and two vampires, Bill and Eric, and between Sookie, Bill, and his former vampire lover. The show embraces mythology, especially with an ancient goddess who builds a temple and conducts orgies. This series is one of HBO's most-watched shows. Producers of shows with a supernatural twist apparently believe that the American public is concerned with death and interested in mystical stories.

Teleplays and Telefilms

Teleplays or telefilms cover a wide variety of stories, for they may be based on well-known books, historical characters or events, or original adventure, romantic, or melodramatic scripts. They may be in the format of mini-series spread over three or four nights, or a 90- to 120-minute movie that could also be a pilot for a proposed series.

Imported teleplays from England are shown on PBS's *Masterpiece Classics, Contemporary,* and *Mystery!* There is no *Masterpiece* on British television; rather, the shows that appear on PBS are dramas from England's BBC, Channel 4, and other television stations. *Masterpiece Theatre,* which started in 1971, had dramatizations of classic literature, history, and contemporary stories, such as *David Copperfield, Great Expectations, Pride and Prejudice, Little Dorritt,* and *House of Cards.* Hosted by the venerable Alistair Cooke for 20 years, these programs often stretched over 2 to 8 weeks and featured well-known British actors such as Derek Jacoby and Miranda Richardson. Now there are three variations of *Masterpiece—Classic, Contemporary, and Mystery! Classic* continues the tradition of the former *Masterpiece Theatre,* with *Downton Abbey* and *South Riding. Mystery!* features short series, such as *Prime Suspect, Foyle's War, Sherlock, Miss Marple,* and *Inspector Lewis,* which run from 2 to 6 weeks. *Mystery!* also features famous actors, such as Helen Mirren. *Contemporary,* as the name suggests, has stories set in the 20th and 21st centuries, such as *Endgame* and *Framed.* These programs come from PBS affiliate WGBH in Boston, which originally promised to present a fair number of American works or productions but rarely did so. A producer said, "It's cheaper to import productions which the BBC or other British companies have already done" (Stark, 1997, p. 174).

Hallmark Hall of Fame has high-quality dramatic productions on network television with reruns on the Hallmark Channel. HBO has adaptations of books and films that run for 2 or more weeks, such as *The Pacific, John Adams, Mildred Pierce,* and *Too Big to Fail* as well as original dramas.

Docudrama

Once a staple of network broadcasting, the made-for-television movie is now more likely to be a docudrama on a cable channel about a biographical person or event. These films are based on a true story, biography, or crime such as *William and Kate,* about the romance of Prince William of England and Kate Middleton, shown a week before their royal wedding, or *Justice for Natalee Holloway,* the second Lifetime docudrama about the disappearance of a young woman in Aruba in 2009. Viewers are expected to know they are watching impersonations, not file footage, and that these films are a blend of fact and fiction. They tend to rely on family melodrama and mature topics such as spouse abuse, eating disorders, and other private topics and personal stories.

SOAP OPERA

The soap opera could be considered a subgenre of the drama, the melodrama, but it has become so prevalent and popular that it is considered a genre unto itself. As a genre, soap operas are best known for daytime dramas such as *The Young and the Restless;* however, nighttime serials such as *Parenthood* have soap opera qualities. Daytime soap operas are daily, 30- to 60-minute, continuous serials without end, running year-round for many years. Because they are performed daily, the actors have little rehearsal time. They are performed in broadcasting studios, taped, edited, and aired 2 weeks later. The settings are urban or suburban, but nearly all the action takes place indoors. Open narratives with unresolved stories keep the viewers coming back. Agnes Nixon, creator of *All My Children,* said her philosophy for viewers was "Make them laugh, make them cry, make them wait" (Stark, 1997, p. 204). Many fans record the soaps when they cannot watch them at scheduled times, but they also have the SOAPnet channel that repeats those in syndication.

"Soap operas," Robert C. Allen explains, "implicitly assume they will never end, and they very seldom produce narrative closure within a given episode. Every plot line continues across a number of episodes. . . . Soap operas disperse their narrative energy among a constantly changing set of interrelated plots, which may merge, overlap, diverge, fragment, close off, and open up again over a viewing period of several years. Individual episodes advance the plot incrementally, but no one watches a soap opera with the expectation that one day all of the conflicts and narrative entanglements will be resolved so that the entire population of the soap opera universe can fade into happily-ever-after oblivion." (Allen, 1992, pp. 107–108)

Soap opera casts are very large and may include as many as 40 regular cast members who have an array of melodramatic problems. The young adults have ideal bodies and faces and wear the latest fashions. Steven Stark summarized some conventions of the soaps:

Women who want to get pregnant never can, but those who don't want to usually end up with a child, even after a presumedly safe one-night dalliance. Amnesia is almost as frequent as the common cold. No one accused of murder is ever the guilty party. The parents of characters often are not the 'real' parents. . . . People get killed in accidents, only to have long-lost twins somehow mysteriously show up months later, when an actor or actress playing the character returns to the soap from another engagement. . . . Characters seldom talk on the telephone, preferring instead to drop in on people, even if they have to drive a long distance. (Stark, 1997, pp. 205–205)

The soaps are known for taking on major social and personal issues, for example, mental illness, spouse abuse, interracial romance, date rape, homosexuality, and infertility. In an attempt to attract younger viewers, according to Seiter and Wilson (2005), soap opera narratives also have supernatural story lines such as demonic possession and witches and angels wreaking havoc on townspeople. Soap operas are popular among high school and college students as well as older adults. How popular they are was made clear when I supervised a graduate project on soap operas and asked undergraduate students in my large film and television class to be subjects in three categories: nonwatchers, moderate watchers, and heavy watchers. In a class of 100, only 1 student was a nonwatcher of soap operas.

A soap opera in Venezuela is facing censorship from the government. *Chepe Fortuna* features an unscrupulous secretary named "Venezuela" who has a dog called "Little Hugo," an apparent reference to Venezuelan President Hugo Chavez. The character Venezuela is associated with illegal activities and vulgarity. The Venezuelan telecommunications regulatory agency Conatel accused the soap opera of promoting political intolerance and said it should be taken off the air.

Source: Government demand soap opera end (2011).

SCIENCE FICTION

Science fiction as a genre is easily recognizable because the action usually takes place in the future and often in space, although this is not always the case. When science fiction is set in the future, the societies tend to be utopian, that is, progressive and positive, or dystopian, that is, apocalyptic and pessimistic. Plots tend to be about saving humanity from aliens, although sometimes the aliens are peaceful. Both aliens and humans utilize fantastic technology. The best-known science fiction television program was *Star Trek,* in which an ensemble of mixed ethnic and racial characters explored outer space but also dealt with contemporary problems of the present day, for example, racism, nuclear warfare, overpopulation, multiculturalism, and ecology. *Star Trek* spawned four prime-time series.

REALITY SHOWS

The proliferation of reality shows in recent years may cause people to think that they are a new phenomenon; however, the reality show can be traced back to 1973. (A case could be made for *Candid Camera,* which began in 1948, as the first television reality show. The show's surprise contrivances were set up without the contestants' knowledge until the end when they were told, "Smile, you're on *Candid Camera.*") The first modern reality show was the PBS series *An American Family,* a documentation of the daily life of the Loud family that included the parents' divorce and the son's coming out as a gay man. Seven months of filming resulted in 12 weekly 1-hour installments. *An American Family,* however, did not immediately bring about other reality shows. (A 2011 HBO show, *Cinema Verité,* was about the Loud family and the making of *An American Family*.) *Cops,* a half hour of edited footage taken by camera and sound professionals who ride along in a squad car as the police answer calls, began in 1989 and is still running on Saturday nights on Fox. Each week the veteran reality show gives its audience "a dose of unscripted chaos" from various cities and towns around the nation with "cops breaking up domestic squabbles, cops hassling drunks, cops busting down doors, cops bagging bad guys" (Farhi, 1998, p. 21). Nothing is rehearsed, for the people in the police squad car do not know where they are going until they get the call from police headquarters. *Cops,* like many reality shows that followed it, is cheap to produce because there are no actors or sets.

There is a vast array of reality-based entertainment on television with many subgenres—dating, make-overs, and various competitions for jobs, talent, designers, and winning races. There is a preoccupation with testing, judging, coaching, transformation, and rewarding. Real people appear in both scripted and unscripted narratives in which they are often rejected while viewers watch their humble grace in defeat and their emotional trauma. Talent competition encourages viewer interaction because viewers get to text votes for their favorites. Television executives like reality shows because they are much cheaper to produce than comic or dramatic series, and prizes are often donated in exchange for naming the products on the air.

The trend in hour-long reality shows began in 2000 with *Survivor,* a blend of soap opera elements, quiz show, and adventure program, which spawned many imitators. *Survivor* has a very large production crew—more than 20 camera people and 13 editors. Three hundred

Photo 5.4 The three finalists, Kirstie Alley; the winner, Pittsburgh Steelers football player Hines Ward; and Chelsea Kane, with their *Dancing With the Stars* partners.

hours may be taped to be edited for a single 42-minute episode (Simon, 2005). Romance and rejection are featured on *The Bachelor* and *The Bachelorette,* while the world of business is the theme of *The Apprentice.* Makeovers are popular themes in *The Biggest Loser* (obese people try to lose weight), *Extreme Makeover* (contestants undergo plastic surgery), and *Extreme Makeover: Home Edition* (homes are refurbished). The top-rated *American Idol* has inspired many copycat shows that stress talent competition and both nice and harsh comments from the judges. A recent trend has been addiction reality shows such as *Celebrity Rehab, Intervention, Relapse,* and *Hoarders,* that may feed into viewers' desire to see people fail. A variation on hoarding is TLC's *Extreme Couponing,* a show that features people who use coupons to buy and stockpile excessive amounts of grocery items. The ratings-phenomenon, *Jersey Shore,* a favorite of viewers between the ages of 12 and 34, features "loud, vulgar, salon-tanned, and gym-bulked numbskulls who drink, brawl, belch, and use foul language" (Stanley, 2010). Snooki, Mike ("The Situation,"), Jennifer ("JWOWW"), Deena ("The Blast"), Vinny, Pauly D., and Ronnie spar, party, and hook up. *Jersey Shore* has given new life to MTV, which had lost viewers after it stopped showing music videos. Bill Carroll, executive at Katz Media Group, said, "MTV requires not just strong ratings or profits to succeed—it must also be a timely cultural force." MTV is "a go-to destination for advertisers and marketers" (Flaherty, 2011). MTV has developed new programming in a variety of genres—reality, animation, series, and movies—designed to keep it relevant to its demographic.

In most cases, the production process manipulates and contrives the action on these shows. Contestants on some shows vote to eliminate fellow players, and they can be quite cruel to one another. Reality shows encourage audience voyeurism as viewers watch people undergoing difficult tasks, competing with one another, and being humiliated, rejected, or victorious. Audiences like to watch reality shows because, as Ron Simon explained, they refer "back to the commonplace world we experience and live in every day and especially how real people interact in undirected situations" (Simon, 2005, p. 180). Viewers also are likely to feel superior to the contestants and judge them as uncouth and disgusting. The popularity of reality shows may reflect the urge for a sense of contact with what is real rather than what is fiction.

SPORTS

Television is a very popular medium for watching sports. One can watch practically any sport on one of the cable sports channels or subscribe to specialized events such as baseball games and boxing matches. Networks preempt regular programs to broadcast basketball tournaments, college and professional football, horse racing, and specialized sports like the Olympics. While one game is being broadcast, regional "splits" show another game that is being played simultaneously, or inserts keep viewers informed of the progress of other games. Viewers can watch live games, interrupted by commercials, through to the finish while listening to sportscasters describe the plays and comment on the players. Television has changed sports because instant replays cause time-outs. In professional baseball, pitchers' mounds were lowered in 1969 to make it harder for pitchers to strike out batters, thus making the sport more visually appealing (Bellamy & Walker, 1996). Sportscasters such as Bob Costas and Billy Packer have become celebrities who bring life to the games.

CHILDREN'S TELEVISION

Children's television uses age as its defining characteristic. It may be aimed at toddlers, young children, preteens, or teenagers. It incorporates other genres—comedy, drama, game shows, talk shows, cartoons, and news. PBS's *Teletubbies* is for very young children, while *Sesame Street* with its well-known characters like Big Bird, Kermit, and other Muppets (meant to be the emotional voices of children) is for preschool and kindergarten children. PBS has a large variety of daily animated programs, for example, *Arthur* and *Clifford the Big Red Dog,* with stories about sharing, acceptance of others, and friendship. Disney, the Cartoon Network, and Nickelodeon channels are aimed at young children and teens. *SpongeBob SquarePants* appeals to both teens and adults. Discovery's *Kids* features science for young people. Norma Pecora pointed out that commercial stations have catered to 6- to 11-year-olds because they could pressure their parents to buy things, whereas preschoolers had no consumer value (Pecora, 2005). With the introduction of cable channels, teens became more important to the market, thus tween shows such as *iCarly* and *Victorious* provided outlets not only for stories but also related websites with games. The 2006 merger of WB and UPN into a new channel, CW, was done to attract young viewers and advertisers.

The Children's Television Act of 1990 requires all television broadcast stations to program for the educational and entertainment needs of the young audience. The Three-Hour Rule was added in 1995, requiring broadcasters to program an average of 3 hours of age-specific educational programming each week (Pecora, 2005).

GAME SHOWS

Game shows either ask competing contestants questions or get them to do something to win very large amounts of money (*Jeopardy!, Wheel of Fortune*) or prizes such as cars, furniture, and vacations (*The Price Is Right*). They feature a host, usually male, an attractive woman assistant, and preselected contestants on a studio stage filled with a spectacle of flashing lights, bright colors, and carnival-like sound effects. These shows are taped live in front of an audience and are on the air daily or weekly. Some of the game shows have been on the air for many years—*Jeopardy!* since 1964 and *The Price Is Right* since 1973. Prior to 1967, all game shows were on prime time, but they were moved to daytime and prime-time access, the alleyway to prime time at 7:30 p.m. (NBC's *A Minute to Win It* is on prime-time). The viewing audience can match wits with the contestants with its own answers. The answers must be given within seconds, so there is no time for reflection. Competition, winning, and materialism are the values featured in these shows. Like so many other genres, game shows have their own network, GSN, The Game Show Network.

Photo 5.5   Contestants in *The Newlywed Game*.

OTHER GENRES

There are many other genres, but their characteristics are self-evident, for they focus on a single theme: movie channels, History Channel, Discovery, Animal Planet, award shows for film and television, religious broadcasting, shopping networks, food networks, country music, and so on. The Weather Channel drew record numbers of viewers in 2005 as devastating hurricanes hit the southern part of the United States and in 2011 during the severe flooding in Vermont. There is a cafeteria of genres on today's television, something for everyone, that supports the importance of television in our lives.

As a television critic, you will examine the characteristics of the genres in light of society and culture. The television medium stresses immediacy, thus context and culture are extremely important. Jason Mittell pointed out, "Genres operate in an ongoing historical process of category formation—genres are constantly in flux, and thus their analysis must by historically situated" (Mittell, 2004, p. xiv). Mittell emphasized that genres do not come from the television texts but rather from the television industry, its audience, and historical context. He asks us to look at a genre's operative coherence. "Does a given category circulate within the cultural spheres of audiences, press accounts, and industrial discourses? Is there a general consensus over what the category refers to in a given moment? Do so-called 'subgenres' play a useful and widespread role in classifying, interpreting or evaluating programs?" (p. 11). Mittell suggests that we examine circulating generic practices and the ways they are culturally operative. In other words, what do they mean to a specific audience and why do people enjoy and regularly watch genres? How do they derive pleasure from genres? Horace Newcomb, in a similar approach, asks, "What is the relation of television's stories and storytelling strategies to American society and culture?" (Newcomb, 2005, p. 25). This question, according to Newcomb, together with asking "How does television tell its stories?," is central to the study of television. He supports the idea of examining industrial practices and ideological formation contained within genres. Social issues are treated in genres, but you, as a television critic, need to be aware of how the same social issue is shaped differently in different genres.

SUMMARY

Genre is an acknowledged form of television industry categorization that is recognized by viewers who develop certain expectations about what they watch and enjoy. Successful genres on television are those that bring in profits for their producers. Genres and subgenres, of which there are many, have formulaic conventions that render them identifiable. As society changes, so do the genres and their conventions. Television blends and bends genres, but the viewing audience continues to recognize the various characteristics within them. The television industry organizes production of shows according to genre and schedules them accordingly. Knowledge of genres enables a television critic to understand how a television story is told, organized, and resolved. Such knowledge also enhances the television critic's awareness of the relationship of television storytelling to society and culture.

EXERCISES

1. What are the conventions of genre? Select a favorite television show, identify its genre, and describe the conventions.

2. How are genres used in the television scheduling process?

3. Select any genre and list your expectations of it before you watch it.

4. Why is it important for the television critic to know about genre?

5. Why is a situation comedy generally cheaper to make than some other types of programs?

6. What are the genre characteristics of plot in a situation comedy?

7. How do intertextual references on *The Simpsons* enhance viewer enjoyment?

8. Why are talk shows called "he" or "she" shows?

9. Watch the national and international evening news to see how much of it is news and how much is infotainment. List the news stories and list the infotainment stories. Now watch PBS's *The NewsHour With Jim Lehrer* for one of the stories you watched on the national and international news. Compare and contrast the coverage.

10. Select a crime procedural series (police, detective, forensic science, FBI) and record your thinking as you watch it. Do you participate in examining the evidence and selecting a suspect? What led you to your selection? Did you pick the same one that the characters on the show did?

11. Select a workplace drama (hospital, law firm, advertising agency). Describe how the story is more about character and dialogue than workplace.

12. What is a hybrid drama? Give an example and identify the genres in it.

13. Watch a daytime soap opera and count the number of characters and plot lines in a single episode.

14. Select a reality show. What elements of the commonplace world do you observe? How does it reflect our cultural norms? If there are judges, evaluate their criticisms. Why do you think it is popular with viewers?

15. Watch a sporting event on television with and without a sportscaster's comments. Describe the differences in your experience of watching the game.

16. Select a children's television program and estimate the age of the children at whom it is aimed.

17. Select a science fiction show and describe its characteristics. Does the story take place in the future? In space? Is it utopian or apocalyptic?

18. Watch a game show and try to give answers to the questions. How do you compare with the contestants? Why do you think the contestants know so much about what seems to be trivial information?

SUGGESTED READINGS

Creeber, Glen (Ed.). (2008). *The Television Genre Book*. London, England: British Film Institute.

Edgerton, Gary R., & Rose, Brian G. (2008). *Thinking Outside the Box: A Contemporary Genre Reader*. Lexington: University Press of Kentucky.

Geraghty, Lincoln, & Jancovich, Mark. (2008). *The Shifting Definitions of Genre*. Jefferson, NC: McFarland.

Itzkoff, Dave. (2009). Ground Breakers. *Emmy*, *31*(6), 29–37. (A good article about *The Simpsons)*

Kaminsky, Stuart M., & Mahan, Jeffrey. (1985). *American Television Genres*. Chicago, IL: Nelson-Hall.

Mittell, Jason. (2004). *Genre and Television: From Cop Shows to Cartoons in American Culture*. New York, NY: Routledge.

Rose, Brian G. (Ed.). (1985). *TV Genres: A Handbook and Reference Guide*. Westport, CT: Greenwood Press.

PART III

Theoretical Approaches to Television Criticism

CHAPTER 6

Rhetoric and Culture

We make our meaning together with a text, we wrestle with what we see and talk back to it, and we become more fully ourselves in the process.

—Edward Hirsch (1999, p. 260)

INTRODUCTION

Rhetorical criticism and cultural criticism are different intellectual practices with very different pasts. **Rhetoric** had its beginnings in classical Greece 2,500 years ago, whereas cultural studies had its current roots in Great Britain in the 1970s. Rhetoric locates and analyzes what are the available means of persuasion and information and how they work; cultural analysis examines the strands of meanings that can be made from discourse and how they relate to social practices. Rhetoric examines the intention of symbolization; cultural criticism examines the struggle and conflict over meaning. Neither rhetoric nor cultural studies is monolithic, however. Both practices have a repertoire of methodologies, some more explicit than others. Each practice can be useful to you as a television critic, or combinations of the methodologies may yield answers to questions one asks about television.

There are areas of overlap, as exemplified in Thomas Rosteck's book *At the Intersection: Cultural Studies and Rhetorical Studies.* Both rhetoric and cultural studies "address specific and parallel questions about culture, critical practice, and interpretation" (Rosteck, 1999, p. viii). Rosteck cited Cary Nelson and Dilip Gaonkar, whose review of some early cultural studies concluded that "cultural studies has been deeply, if broadly, textual and rhetorical in its methodology" (Rosteck, 1999, p. 9). Both perspectives recognize that meanings are related to particular contexts. Rosteck wrote:

> Rhetorical studies offers a mode of analysis for thinking about how texts are produced (intent), what they are (textuality), and what they do (consumption/ effects.) A more properly "rhetorical cultural studies" recognizes that the perspectives of rhetoric define an approach that holds in suspension text and producer, text and reader, text and society. . . . Cultural studies . . . delivers to rhetorical studies a richer and more fully realized model of how discourse is

always a product of wider social formations and reflects necessarily the materialization of the ideology that gave birth to it. It offers a more sophisticated sense of the text-history-audience-critic relationship and also the crucial relationship between texts and critical methodologies, namely how history and ideology shape readings and critical work. . . . The ideal relationship between rhetorical studies and cultural studies is one of mutual critique and transformation. (Rosteck, 1999, p. 22)

This chapter describes salient aspects of rhetorical criticism and cultural criticism. As a critic of television, you can pick and choose various aspects from one or the other or from a blend of both. What is most important is what you ask about a television program or series. The tools to find the answers to those questions may then be sought out.

RHETORIC

Rhetoric is a twofold field of study: rhetorical criticism and rhetorical theory. Since this is a book about criticism, rhetorical criticism will be the main focus, although it is apparent that rhetorical criticism is grounded in theories.

Rhetoric is the study of symbols and how they are used to influence. Rhetorical criticism focuses on the conception, composition, presentation, and reception of messages that tend to be persuasive in nature, although they may also be informative. It is also a humane field of study of the choices made by persuaders, informers, and audiences as they work to co-create meaning and sustain human sociality. It is, thus, a cooperative art that brings senders and receivers of messages together in an attempt to bring about voluntary change or enlightenment. Classically conceived, rhetoric is concerned with systematic principles of idea development and reasoning, known as invention, organization, style, presentation, and ways to recall information, known as memory, all of which are phenomena that a critic can uncover and observe. It is believed that the success and significance of the messages are related to the methods used to develop and present them. A rhetorical critic identifies and explains how the methods of message development work to persuade or inform an audience.

The Good Wife is a television series about the lives of the characters in a law firm and the cases they take on, ranging from class action suits to defending alleged murderers. When one of the attorneys makes a persuasive speech to a jury, it is natural and appropriate to rhetorically analyze and criticize the arguments, evidence, and emotional pleas contained within the speech. When *Parenthood*'s Zeek Braverman (Craig T. Nelson) teaches a moral lesson to one of his grandchildren, the persuasion in his words and deeds is readily apparent to most viewers. These persuasive messages of television programs can be rhetorically analyzed, for they are, in essence, discourse, that is, spoken or reported talk that sets forth ideas about a subject.

What, then, of television programs such as *CSI* or *The Office* that have entertainment as the major focus for both their creators and their audience? Is it possible to use the concepts of rhetoric to analyze and criticize television programs when persuasion may not be so apparent? What about the background sounds (sound effects and music) and the images of television? Can they be analyzed according to principles of rhetoric as well? This chapter attempts to answer these questions, define television rhetoric, and introduce some aspects of rhetoric that can be used to analyze television.

First, it is necessary to understand what rhetoric is and how the rhetorical critic applies principles of rhetoric to a message. Rhetorical studies have been an important part of education since ancient Greece. Contemporary theories of rhetoric have been derived and adapted from the major treatises of classical writers such as Aristotle and Cicero. Throughout history, rhetorical theorists developed principles of rhetoric to try to understand the discourse of their own times—in assemblies, war councils, royal courts, elections, legal courts and councils, in the church, and in the marketplace. Mostly, they dealt with words because the messages were verbally conveyed, but many also dealt with the character of the speaker or treatise and presentational elements as well. Today, we communicate with images, sounds, and, of course, words, and we have adapted principles of rhetoric to understand the visual, aural, and verbal elements of messages.

Classical Rhetoric

Aristotle's definition of rhetoric has been an enduring one and, because of its extensive scope, has been used to justify rhetorical analysis of media. He defined rhetoric as "the faculty of discovering in the particular case what are the available means of persuasion" (Aristotle, 333 BCE/1932, p. 7). Because the political and judicial systems placed prominence on oral persuasion in Aristotle's Greece, his theory of rhetoric was based upon observing persuasion in politics, in the courts, and in ceremonies. In *Rhetoric* (333 BCE), he laid out certain principles and classifications of persuasion in the context of occasions—courtroom proceedings, public ceremonies, and legislative and political activities. Aristotle viewed persuasion as an instrument of social adaptation, for it enabled people to live in society using strategically selected and stylized speech to influence one another. Rhetoric was very important in Greece, for people used it to debate internal problems as well as to decide which values were important in society. Through persuasive discourse, people attempted to reason together, to discuss ideas, and to make decisions regarding their lives. People such as Alexander the Great, who chose a career in public life, studied with teachers of rhetoric, including Aristotle, to learn how to choose message content (invention), how to arrange the content (arrangement), how to stylize the content into clear and impressive language (style), how to recall the content (memory), and how to present (delivery). These five categories were classified by Roman rhetoricians and are known as the canons of rhetoric: invention, arrangement, style, memory, and delivery.

Such a rhetorical system seems pragmatic and formulaic, but Aristotle's major contribution was invention, the development of ideas and the selection of content, namely proof. If one were to persuade, it was assumed that one had to prove an argument. Aristotle classified proof into two categories: *inartistic,* that which a persuader could refer to but not have to control—such as documents, wills, contracts, torture, situations, and even physical qualities—and *artistic,* that which a persuader could create or manipulate. Artistic proofs were of three major types: **ethos,** the speaker's character, integrity, and goodwill—known in contemporary terms as "source credibility"; *pathos,* the persuader's appeals to the emotions of the audience and the situation; and *logos,* the persuader's appeals to the rational side of the audience as well as their ability to process information.

Logos means "word" in Greek and probably comes closest to the contemporary meaning of communication as an interactive process during which the speaker and audience create and share intellectual meaning. Aristotle's two forms of *logos* were proof through examples and proof through **enthymemes.** Examples enabled the persuader to generalize and prove through citation of evidence that was meaningful to the audience, while enthymemes enabled the persuader and audience to co-create reasoning by interactively coming to a conclusion. The audience was an essential component of Aristotle's rhetoric, for the persuader not only appealed to an audience, but the audience completed the reasoning process by supplying missing elements.

Television advertising uses both forms of logos, especially enthymemes. A commercial for yogurt uses the song "Itsy-bitsy, teeny-weeny, yellow polka dot bikini" with an image of a yellow polka dot bikini hanging on the wall. A woman walks past the bikini while eating yogurt several times, wearing different outfits to suggest the passing of time. The commercial ends when she takes the bikini off the wall and gets into a convertible with a friend. The audience is expected to fill in the rest of the proof, namely that eating yogurt has enabled her to lose enough weight to fit into the bikini.

Aristotle's approach to rhetoric was pragmatic, but it also carried with it the cultural ideal of Greek society, that humanity should strive for excellence and to live life in a morally responsible way. The Greek work *telos,* meaning end or completion, stood for an optimal moral end. In ancient Greece, a person tried to achieve his or her telos by the end of life because by such an achievement, that person would experience moral excellence and contemplative happiness, and others would bestow virtue upon him or her. The Greeks considered rhetoric as the means that moved people toward a telos of moral excellence, for the end of rhetoric was the formation of public character in those with the potential for moral action.

Rhetoric Through the Ages

Many of Aristotle's principles and classifications were carried over and elaborated upon throughout history by a succession of rhetoricians such as St. Augustine (426), who developed the study of preaching for the clergy; Francis Bacon (1623), who incorporated scientific theory-building into the study of rhetoric; François Fenelon (1717), who stressed the social character of rhetoric and the use of communication to instruct and inform; and George Campbell (1776), a Scottish theologian who drew upon the works of early psychology to analyze audiences and developed four ends of speaking "to enlighten the understanding, to please the imagination, to move the passions, or to influence the will" (Golden & Corbett, 1968, p. 145).

These early forerunners of contemporary rhetoric offered rich and important ideas that may be adapted to the analysis and criticism of television. Although Aristotle limited his rhetoric to the discovery of the means of persuasion, later rhetoricians recognized information as a form of rhetoric. One way of describing the function of rhetoric without wedding it to persuasion or information was expressed by Donald C. Bryant, who wrote that the function of rhetoric is "adjusting ideas to people and people to ideas" (Bryant, 1953, p. 420).

Intentionality

Whether the desired purpose of a message is persuasion or information, intentionality is often seen as the key focus of rhetoric, although not all rhetorical theorists agree. Aristotle laid the groundwork for the concept of intentionality with his teleological view of nature. Intentionality as activity is explicit in the work of contemporary philosopher John R. Searle (1979, 1984), who wrote that intentionality is "the feature by which our mental states are directed at, about, or refer to, or are of objects and states of affairs in the world other than themselves" (Searle, 1984, p. 16). Searle put it another way when he wrote quite simply, "If I have an intention, it must be an intention to do something" (Searle, 1984, p. 1). Rhetoricians note that **intention** carries with it the notion of consciousness because a person plans "for the purpose of obtaining some specifiable outcome" (Arnold & Bowers, 1984, pp. 875–876). In other words, intention is the purpose and end desired from an audience; however, it is not always possible to know the exact intention of a communicator. Thus, Arnold and Bowers modify the notion of intention to mean an *attributed* intention.

We assume that a scriptwriter for a situation comedy has the attributed intent to provoke laughter from an audience, or that a writer for a soap opera has the attributed intent to involve the viewer in a situation so he or she will tune in next time to find out what happens. In more obvious cases, we assume that a television commercial has the attributed intent to have the viewer remember the brand name, to have a positive attitude toward it, and to buy the product. There may be other more subtle attributed intentions in television fiction and nonfiction such as influencing attitudes and beliefs or reinforcing values and cultural norms. There may even be subconscious intentions that could be derived from a critic's interpretation. Remember the statement from Sheldon Leonard in Chapter 5, where situation comedies were discussed as a genre. Leonard, the producer of sit-coms said that good television can advance valid social comments, valid ethical concepts, and generalizations about the human condition.

The Symbolic Nature of Rhetoric

Rhetoric by its nature examines the symbolic, that is, symbols or words and images that stand for something else. As humans we generate symbols and expect others to know the meaning of the symbols. Symbols rely upon connections that are not necessarily causal. The word "cow" symbolizes a four-legged bovine mammal, but it is an arbitrary symbol that we have learned to mean a four-legged bovine mammal. The same animal is symbolized as *vache* in French and *Kuh* in German, neither of which resembles the English symbol "cow." The English language might have assigned a different symbol, for example, "ballerina," and that would have been the name that people learned to identify a four-legged bovine mammal.

Symbols stand for ideas and acts, that is, they stand in the place of ideas and acts, and, most significantly, symbols are created to signify something. The symbol © was created to signify "copyright," but one has to learn this meaning or it means nothing. Visual symbols such as a couple embracing or a father playing ball with his son may stand for a value such as love. It has been said that meanings lie in people, not in words, thus if a word or an image stimulates a recognition of something familiar in the audience's experience, then communication takes place. What symbols are attended to by an audience and how they are received is dependent upon a variety of factors—the perceptions, experiences, needs, and uses that an audience makes of television.

Television rhetoric works to shape audience expectations by conspicuously promoting programs and attempting to direct viewer perceptions through images and words. Although viewers choose what to treat as messages, television rhetoric actively attempts to shape those choices. It is, indeed, a circular situation, for television creators tap into cultural norms to attract an audience, and the audience in turn responds to them because they are agreeable, that is, some of the time. As we will see in the section on cultural studies, an audience can also choose to resist or negotiate meanings.

The Rhetoric of Kenneth Burke

A rhetorician who greatly influenced 20th-century rhetoric was Kenneth Burke. He defined rhetoric as "the use of words by human agents to form attitudes or induce actions in other human agents" (Burke, 1950/1969, p. 41). He said that whatever form rhetoric takes, it is "the use of language as a symbolic means of inducing cooperation in beings that by nature respond to symbols" (Burke, 1950/1969, p. 43). He contributed the idea of *identification* to rhetoric, that is, when people share a common substance or properties—citizenship, physical objects or attributes, occupations, friends, common enemies, activities, beliefs, and values—they unite by sharing a common substance, or in Burke's term, they become consubstantial, which means of the same substance. Burke added, however, that people share substance only momentarily because each person is unique. He wrote that identification was the key to persuasion: "You persuade a man only insofar as you can talk his language by speech, gesture, tonality, order, image, attitude, idea, *identifying* your ways with his" (Burke, 1950/1969, p. 21). Identification can be on a conscious level. For example, Jennifer Aniston's hairstyle on *Friends* influenced a great many women to get their hair cut in the same style. On the other hand, Burke believed that identification can be subconscious or unconscious. For example, a person who buys a fancy bicycle may be subconsciously identifying with Lance Armstrong, seven-time winner of the Tour de France bicycle race, even though the bicycle was purchased to go back and forth to school.

Burke developed his concept of identification because he believed that people are basically divided or estranged from one another, therefore, they communicate in order to eliminate that division. Through identification with a common substance, people may transcend their differences and unite in a common attitude or behavior. As Robert Heath explained,

By sharing common symbols—particularly those which relate to personal identity and role—individuals can be brought together. The key to using this strategy is to discover abstract terms high in the hierarchy of our vocabulary. The formula went this way: the higher, and therefore more abstract, the term [or symbol], the greater its appeal because it could encompass the identities of more people. (Heath, 1986, p. 17)

The Cosby Show, with its all–African American cast, was not only enormously popular in the United States but also in South Africa during *apartheid.* Perhaps the reason for its popularity in a country divided by racism was that the higher symbol that the show emphasized was family and not race. Dennis Ciesielski pointed out that Burke anticipated "the postmodern concept of the transcendent signifier in his observation that all action is symbolic of other action, all signs hold further implications" (Ciesielski, 1999, p. 244).

Although Burke stressed language, he included in rhetoric many other forms of discourse, including nonverbal activity, literature, and art. Art, he said, instructs people about their moral and social responsibilities. In a seminar that Burke taught when I was in graduate school, he told us that his definition of rhetoric included television. Identification between a viewer and a television program is usually a matter of preference for a certain character or the recognition of a situation in the program as being similar to the viewer's, but identification has the capability to influence the viewer to become involved to the point where he or she may adopt certain ways of speaking, clothing styles, mannerisms, or even attitudes and behaviors.

Burke described communication as a form of courtship whereby its form is an arousing and fulfillment of desires. He wrote, "A work has form insofar as one part of it leads a reader [viewer] to anticipate another part, to be gratified by the sequence" (Burke, 1931/1957, p. 124). This is exactly what television does, as stated in the desire/satisfaction formula in Chapter 1: Television executives and producers try to know what it is that the audience desires and then satisfy that desire in order to maintain an audience following. Burke's rhetoric is too complex to include its details in a single chapter. He offers a myriad of ways to examine rhetoric, many of which are suitable and useful for television criticism. There are several good books on Burke's theories of rhetoric and studies that use his various approaches to criticism such as the Dramatistic Pentad, cluster analysis, terministic screens, the representative anecdote, and the demonic trinity. The titles of these and other books on rhetorical criticism can be found at the end of this chapter.

There are other methods of rhetorical criticism that may be adapted to television. Contemporary rhetorical criticism has expanded in light of new contexts and cultural development. Rhetorical critiques may focus on types of argumentation, rhetoric as prophesy (Darsey, 1997), celebrity rhetoric (Redmond & Holmes, 2007), apologetic rhetoric (Towner, 2010), or discourse analysis (Lorenzo-Dus, 2009). We have already examined two other forms of analysis that are bases for rhetorical critiques—narrative and genre. Thematic rhetoric (Bormann, 1990; O'Donnell, 1988) comes from a theory called "fantasy theme analysis." This could be useful in analyzing television narrative, which tends to be thematic. The critic finds specific themes and puts them together to find a general and accepted type or myth that suggests an abstract rhetorical vision for the community, such as "the American Dream," "Freedom," or "Salvation." Visual rhetoric examines symbolic actions enacted primarily through visual means. Visual rhetoric addresses "culturally derived ways of looking and seeing and endeavoring to influence diverse publics. . . . Visual rhetoric seeks and produces communities of viewers, spectators, witnesses, and participants through actions visualized in various forms" (Olson, Finnegan, & Hope, 2008, p. 3). As you can see, there is overlap in the various kinds of rhetorical criticism, thus often such criticism becomes eclectic. Both rhetorical and cultural criticism can be used to examine belief systems that form interpretations of race, ethnicity, class, gender, religion, and sexual identity. Because they can also be analyzed with cultural studies approaches, they will be discussed later in the chapter. Because television is representational, these aspects are also discussed in Chapter 7, "Representation and Its Audience."

Television Rhetoric

Television informs, persuades, and represents the real and fictional worlds to its audience. Television utilizes conventional organization both in its scheduling and within the structure of programs. Both fiction and nonfiction television have the capability to elicit identification from viewers. Television relies on viewer memory to keep up with the plots and characters from day to day on soap operas and from week to week on prime-time series. Television has specific stylistic features that use both visual and aural symbols, and television tends to be thematic. The most rhetorical aspect of television is that viewers participate while they watch it and afterwards. They perceive, interpret, and accept or reject images as real or imaginary; they respond with laughter, shock, concern, relaxation, and reassurance; they talk about favorite shows with friends, fellow students, and coworkers. When my oldest son was a teenager, he and my mother would discuss at length the episodes of *All My Children*. Nancy Franklin wrote in *The New Yorker* that people she knew talked about *24,* the series about counterterrorism agent Jack Bauer (Kiefer Sutherland), in which events unfolded in real time over the course of one day. Franklin said that one woman called her friend at the end of each show to discuss it; couples made dates to watch and discuss it together (Franklin, 2006). People of all ages talk about *Jersey Shore*—at school and around the water cooler at work. Television influences our language and what issues we consider important (the **agenda-setting** function of media).

Agenda-setting is about the gatekeeping function of media news, whereby journalists tell viewers what issues are important. Research has shown that the news media have not told people what to think, but they have told them what to think about. Framing analysis, another form of rhetorical criticism, examines the presentation of issues, especially in the news or in documentaries. Jim A. Kuypers said that "frames are powerful rhetorical entities that induce us to filter our perceptions of the world in particular ways, essentially making some aspects of our multi-dimensional reality more noticeable than other aspects" (2010, p. 1) Frames define problems, diagnose causes, make moral judgments, and suggest remedies.

Television also influences our perception of politicians and celebrities, fashion, hairstyles, fitness, and even what breed of dog to acquire. The outcome of the televised Westminster Kennel Club's annual dog show and the selection of "best in show" often results in an increase of popularity in certain breeds of dogs.

Some examples of popular language expressions that were used on television programs are the following: "Awright, I'll tell ya what I'm gonna do!" *(Texaco Star Theater)*, "Beam me up, Scotty" *(Star Trek)*, "Meathead" and "dingbat" *(All in the Family)*, "The Devil made me do it" *(The Flip Wilson Show)*, "yada yada" *(Seinfeld)*, "Wild and crazy guys" *(Saturday Night Live)*, "Don't have a cow, man" and "D'oh!" *(The Simpsons)*, "How you doin'?" *(Friends)*, "Hey, Dummy!" *(My Name is Earl)*, *"Cowabunga!"* (Cookie Monster on *Sesame Street)*, "Respect my authority" *(South Park)* and advertising slogans: "Kodak moment," "Pepsi generation," "Where's the beef?," and "I can't believe I ate the whole thing."

While the sender's intent may be to entertain, there is always the possibility of influence, whether it is direct or indirect. The intention of the sender is to capture a large share of the audience as measured by ratings, or it may be to get an audience to believe that what they see is really there, as in news reporting or documentaries. Television commentators may influence our thinking by interpreting television speeches and events. Other examples of persuasion may be television's attempt to educate the public about a health hazard, to uphold law and order, to strengthen attitudes about diversity, to cherish family values, to foster competition, and so on. Verbal, visual, and aural symbols are chosen, arranged, and delivered to the audience. Which message symbols are attended to by an audience and how they are received is dependent upon a variety of factors—the perceptions, experiences, needs, and uses that an audience makes of television. Just as the senders may choose to treat television programming as messages, audiences also choose to treat television as a message.

Television rhetoric attempts to shape viewer expectations by conspicuously promoting programs and attempting to direct viewer perceptions. Media television critics tell viewers what they will and will not like on television. Internet blogs, sometimes written by television writers, tell viewers what to anticipate. What an audience attends to on television is, however, determined by many factors and individual preferences.

Rhetoric and Values

Television embodies the values of a culture, the values of the people who produce television programs, and the values of the people who watch them. Values are important to understanding the rhetoric of television because they are a crucial part of our belief systems. The accepted and affirmed cultural values of the mass audience are echoed in television situation comedies and dramas' resolutions of conflict as well as in the news and other nonfiction programming. A **value** is defined as an enduring belief that a specific mode of conduct or end-state of existence is personally or socially preferable. Specifically, a value is a prescriptive belief that judges whether or not a means or an end is desirable or undesirable. Conventional values are familiar standards of conduct as the rhetorician Karl Wallace pointed out in his essay "The Substance of Rhetoric: Good Reasons": "Some of them [the values] are compressed in concepts with which all of us are familiar: good and evil, pleasant-unpleasant, duty, obligation, self-interest, altruism, truth-telling, promise-keeping, honesty, fairness, courage, law-observance, utility, right and wrong, and the like. They appear typically in general statements called rules of conduct, regulations, laws, codes, principles, and moral maxims" (Wallace, 1971, p. 363). Values may, of course, be very personal and private, but they are public as well, for they are shared with and taught to others. Because values are important, they operate as measuring sticks against which behavior is measured and goals are obtained.

Television's fictional characters and their stories reinforce audience values, teach values to the audience, and use values as reasons for supporting resolutions of conflict. Television narratives frequently reflect values such as the work ethic, fair play, optimism, sensibility, justice, happiness, and good humor. Television stars such as Oprah Winfrey, Ray Romano, Mariska Hargitay, LL Cool J, Mark Harmon, Katie Couric, and Jay Leno represent honesty, strength, goodness, fair-mindedness, and the vulnerability of the ideal American culture. News anchors like Walter Cronkite, Tom Brokaw, and Peter Jennings represented integrity and compassion. The creators of television programs are more likely to produce programs that reinforce values that relate to the nation's strengths and virtues. Television programs such as *Sesame Street* tend to be morality shapers, touching on themes of love, honesty, tolerance, and altruism. Family situation comedies tend to conclude each program with a mini-moral that reinforces family togetherness and parental authority. Values are inherent in reality shows that emphasize competition, victory, and rewards.

> Every episode of *Frasier* illustrated strong values with which the audience could identify. The values were close family relationships, friendship, decency, compassion, and kindness. For example, in one episode, Frasier, pretentious as usual, wants to buy an educational toy for his son, Frederick, for Christmas, but he cannot decide whether to get a Junior Astronomer set or a Living Brain. Frasier's father, Martin, tells him that he should find out what Frederick really wants for Christmas. On Christmas morning, Frederick tells Frasier that he really wants an Outlaw Laser Robo-Geek. Martin has bought this toy to give to his grandson, but he gives it to Frasier to wrap and give to Frederick, thereby kindly teaching his son a lesson for living.

Values are also explicit in television news. Sociologist Herbert J. Gans analyzed values in network television news over 20 years. His findings were categorized into six types of values: (1) ethnocentrism—American news values its own nation above all, and foreign news is interpreted by the extent to which other nations live up to or imitate American values; (2) altruistic democracy—democracy is presented as superior to other forms of government; (3) responsible capitalism—competition is valued along with optimism and economic growth; (4) small-town pastoralism—small towns are perceived as friendly, cohesive, and slow-paced, all of which are desirable; (5) individualism—rugged individuals and self-made men and women are valued as heroes; and (6) moderatism—groups that behave moderately are valued as opposed to extremists. Gans concluded that most news stories are about the violation of values, although the values themselves may not be explicitly articulated. He also noted that the values perceived by viewers tend to be the values that the viewers themselves believe in. He said that value-laden language reveals values: for example, a politician "arrives" in a city but a troublemaker "turns up" there. Rhetorical analysis of values attempts to uncover what Arnold and Bowers called "attributed intentions" because, as Gans wrote, the values underlying the news stories are implicit and subject to viewer recognition and interpretation (Gans, 1979, 2005).

Values are highly personal and enduring, therefore we defend them with great passion. This is what makes values effective as anchors for persuasion. A value is used as an anchor when audience belief is used as a foundation to create another belief. For example, if the audience believes in national security, then a related belief in support of full-body scans at airports can be derived from the first belief. As a consensus-building exercise in one of my classes, I asked the students to bring to class a list of values that were most important to them. The goal was to eventually compile a list of values that everyone in the class agreed upon in order to construct arguments such as "If you believe in good health, then you should stop smoking," or "If you value the environment, then you should recycle newspapers, plastic, and glass." The students put their values on the board for all to see. After we condensed duplicates—and there were many—I asked the students individually to walk up and erase any values that were not important to them. They erased "competition," "beauty," and "power," but much to my surprise, one person erased "equality." Then a student who is Hispanic American walked to the board and erased everything. He said, "If you do not value equality, then I do not support *any* of your values." Needless to say, we had a strong class discussion that day, but the point of including this incident in this chapter is to remind us that not only are values extremely important to individuals, they are also not universally agreed upon.

Because television addresses a mass audience, the values that are inherent in its programs are collectively dominant in the culture. Values represent patterns of life in a culture, but marginalized people, whose life patterns differ from those of the mainstream, may or may not accept them. How, then, do they gain enjoyment from watching television? To answer that, we turn to cultural studies.

CULTURAL STUDIES

Because television is a major form of communication, a source of social understanding, and a connection to lifestyles other than our own, it is of major concern in cultural studies. Jeff Lewis (2008), whose book *Cultural Studies: The Basics* is a helpful guide to the subject, maintained that there are many forms of culture, for example, national culture, family culture, and television culture. Add to this list religious culture, community culture, and global culture. He defined culture as: "an assemblage of imaginings and meanings that are generated by a given social group. These meanings may be consonant, disjunctive, overlapping, contentious, continuous, or discontinuous. The given social group may be formed around a broad gradient of human communities, activities and purposes. Communication is the central force which binds social groups to culture; in contemporary culture these communicational processes are dominated by various modes of global networked media"

(p. 18). My definition is similar: "**Culture** is made up of actual practices and customs, languages, beliefs, forms of representation, and a system of formal and informal rules that tell people how to behave most of the time and enable people to make sense of their world through a certain amount of shared meanings and recognition of different meanings" (Jowett & O'Donnell, 2007, p. 149). Note that both definitions focus on shared meanings.

Meaning is a key concept in cultural studies, for meaning, as noted earlier, does not reside in a symbol, visual or verbal, but is in the relationship between a viewer of television and what is viewed. Meaning lies in the power of a symbol to signify something and in the viewer's potential to derive meaning from the symbol. In television, the viewer is the necessary other to be provoked into making meaning possible. The relationship between the viewer and the symbol is a complex one in which various elements interact and lead to an outcome that is dependent on culture and the cultural practices. Consequently, the possibility of multiple meanings, ***polysemy,*** exists because various viewers incorporate their own experiences, lifestyles, values, and other cultural practices into their interpretations. The multiple meanings of various viewers cannot be reduced to a common mean or median, nor can derived meanings be fixed or stable across time.

Although the television series *ER* is no longer on prime-time, this example from an episode of the television drama about a Chicago hospital emergency room illustrates polysemy very well. Two African American surgeons, Dr. Peter Benton and Dr. Cleo Finch, are seen attending to a patient while nearby on the other side of the room, a group of five medical students, four men and one woman, are getting a tour of the emergency facilities. Dr. Finch, who is very light in color, says, "What is wrong with this picture?" Dr. Benton, who has much darker skin, is focusing on his patient and says, "Hmm?" Dr. Finch then says, "Those medical students—not a black face in the bunch." Getting no response from him, Dr. Finch says, "That doesn't concern you?" Dr. Benton looks up at the students and replies, "I see five. Not exactly a representative sample." She responds with, "I'm glad you take such an interest." He chuckles and nothing else is said, but the look that is exchanged between these two doctors, who are also lovers, is probably meant to imply that Dr. Benton is not going to make an issue of racial diversity and that he could be quite patronizing when it comes to logic. This is consistent with how his character was portrayed on the series, for he was a brilliant, competent, and ambitious but arrogant surgeon.

A cultural studies critic would ask what meanings viewers could make of this brief scene. One viewer might agree with Dr. Finch that there should be better racial representation. Another might agree with Dr. Benton's logic, concluding that you cannot generalize from a small sample. Another might conclude that practicing good medicine is a doctor's only concern. Someone else might say that both positions are fairly represented and that is acceptable. There could be other meanings. For example, one could dispute the untypical representation of race in an elitist profession that requires years of study at great financial cost because such circumstances are unavailable to those without opportunity. Although Dr. Benton, professionally acted by Eriq La Salle, is an extremely competent surgeon, he is also very arrogant and moody, thus another viewer might say that he is "uppity" and erudite and no longer in touch with people of his race. Michael Michele, who played Dr. Finch, is tall, model-thin, and beautiful. Another viewer might see her as unrepresentative of women in general and therefore be unable to identify with her or her attitude at all. For others, she could be a role model of what other women want to become. Someone else could observe that Dr. Finch did not say anything about the disproportionate ratio of men to women in the group of five medical students. Still another might note that because the chief of staff, Dr. Romano, and the chief attending emergency room doctor, Dr. Green, are White males, they represent White male dominance over the African American doctors.

These various meanings are some of the possible responses of several viewers upon seeing a brief scene on television; therefore, the scene has the potential to be polysemous. Cultural studies critics understand that many meanings can be made from a single scene because viewers observe and interpret images and supporting dialogue through the lens of their own cultural experiences.

There are many ways to conduct a cultural studies critique, for there are many theoretical foundations ranging from writings by Karl Marx, Antonio Gramsci, Louis Althusser, Michel Foucault, Roland Barthes, Jacques Derrida, Raymond Williams, Stuart Hall, Lawrence Grossberg, and others. Also, as historical and political conditions change, cultural studies practitioners respond with relevant analyses. This chapter will not recount the history and various theories behind cultural studies, but rather it offers a selection of some of the most influential ideas in contemporary cultural studies that can be constituted to develop critical approaches. (See Suggested Readings in Cultural Studies at the end of this chapter.)

British Cultural Studies

Although cultural studies can be traced back to the 17th century, certain British academics were the first in the English-speaking world to address the making of meaning within culture. Thus, cultural studies, as we know it, grew out of the British Cultural Studies movement, primarily from the vision of Raymond Williams, a professor at Cambridge University, who said that there was no academic subject that enabled him to ask how culture and society and democracy and the individual voice could relate to one another. Williams believed that culture concerns everyone, for it is about the symbolic life of people. Williams was especially concerned with the customs of the working class. For example, in one of the programs that he made for the British Broadcasting Company, he talked about 18th-century paintings that depicted beautiful land and domestic animals. One painting had a very young girl, obviously of the upper class, dressed up in shepherd's clothes watching the sheep grazing on a meadow. Williams asked, "Where are the real shepherds?" His point was that the workers upon whom the running of the estate depended were invisible. Williams insisted on thinking about a painting or a novel or a television program from a much broader range of cultural practice. His writings encourage us to try to formulate meanings other than our own: "In judging a culture, it is not enough to concentrate on habits which coincide with those of the observer" (Higgins, 1999, p. 59). Williams wrote that "cultural texts should never be seen as isolated but always as part of a shared practice of making meaning involving everyone in a particular culture" (Couldry, 2000, p. 24). Williams asked how a work—any work—relates to the shared conditions of its time and what meanings a work has when it is absorbed into the lives of its audience. He believed that every person has the right to be seen and heard. This is the basic tenet of cultural studies.

Nick Couldry, whose book is a very helpful guide to cultural studies methodology as well as a critique of it, made the point that culture as it is actually practiced is a concentration of voices but not a dispersal of them. This prevents people from speaking in their own voices because they are represented by others (Couldry, 2000).

Williams also articulated his theory of "flow" on television as timed, sequential units that form a montage with confusing, overall meaning. For example, parts of television programs are melded to commercials, promotions, and public service announcements that flow into the news, and a talk show and then to a movie. These disparate items are assembled and placed within the same viewing experience.

Stuart Hall, cultural theorist and professor emeritus at the Open University in the United Kingdom, is probably the most influential and prominent British cultural studies scholar. Whereas Williams was concerned with the laboring classes, Hall has used many examples of race and immigration in the United Kingdom in his writings and videos. (See Hall's entries in the References.) Hall's contributions are many, but his model of the encoding and decoding of meaning is the most famous.

Power, Ideology, and Hegemony

First, however, it is necessary to explain Hall's view of power, a premise with which all cultural studies critics agree. Hall said that symbols are always associated with power relations, driven by economics, politics, or social discrimination, which determine who is represented and who is not, whose voice is heard and whose is not, what issues are important and what issues are not. Lewis refers to **power** as that which enables one person or group to exert his or her will and interest over others. Lewis wrote that cultural studies theory views power as attached to social structures such as class, ethnicity, and gender, or power is concerned with personal manifestations and experiences. He also maintained that power can be mobilized when a viewer chooses to watch a program or not and may also be activated when a person discusses a program with friends or partners.

> Power is derived from the dominant ideology of a culture. *Ideology* is defined as: A set of beliefs, values, attitudes, and behaviors, as well as ways of perceiving and thinking that are agreed on to the point that they constitute a set of norms for a society that dictate what is desirable and what should be done. . . . Ideology contains concepts about what the society in which it exists is actually like. It states or denies, for example, that there are classes and that certain conditions are desirable or more desirable than others. An ideology is also a form of consent to a particular kind of social order and conformity to the rules within a specific set of social, economic, and political structures. It often assigns roles of dominance or subordination to gender, race, sexuality, religion, age, and social groups. (Jowett & O'Donnell, 2007, p. 291)

Related to power is **hegemony,** defined as a way of life and thought that is dominant in society to the point that it seems natural. Williams wrote that hegemony "is lived at such a depth, which saturates the society to such an extent, and which . . . even constitutes the substance and limits of common sense for most people under its sway" (in Higgins, 1999, p. 113). Hegemony gives closure to meaning, for the meaning is intended to be a dominant one. Hegemony can give power or dominance to one group over another. People in the dominated group consent to be dominated, but the consent is negotiated with ongoing renegotiation and redefinition. The consensus may be broken when the ideologies of the subordinate groups cannot be accommodated.

For the producers of television, consumer satisfaction is important, thus focus groups are used in market research to determine what programs are likely to be successful based on ratings and thus economics. Victoria J. Gallagher wrote that hegemony occurs when "dominant groups control the flow of a cultural projection" (Gallagher, 2004, p. 152). Ideologies in place are presented on television as natural, especially since most creators of television come from a similar economic, social, and educational background. Yet, ideologies are subject to change as shown in television's growing openness to racial, ethnic, and sexual diversity. Hegemony is a fluid concept compared to coercion and control. Subordinate groups struggle for recognition and to have their voices heard. Some groups have a greater opportunity to do so than other groups. How groups are represented on television is constantly being redefined and understood. Explaining counterhegemony, Gallagher said that it occurs when "subordinates and their allies convert dominants to subordinate versions of the world. The result of counterhegemony is that many dominants gradually become more accepting of subordinates" (Gallagher, 2004, p. 153). Meanings perceived by viewers of a television program cannot always be predicted. Some may see a program as a reflection of the status quo, while others may perceive it as mockery and satire. Hall recognized that audience members are not passive but rather active consumers who decode symbols and representations and make their own meanings. Hall, in his encoding/decoding model, explains how viewers construct meanings.

Hall's Encoding/Decoding Model

Fundamental to Hall's work is the encoding process or message formulation in television, together with the social and economic conditions that explain why and how viewers decode or find meaning in a variety of ways. Hall's model of encoding/decoding is based on the premise that there is a correlation between a person's social situation and the meanings that person decodes from an encoded symbol (an image/discourse). In other words, there is no single meaning in the image/discourse. If the meaning that the viewer decodes is the same as or similar to the meaning that the television image/discourse encodes, then there would be perfect hegemony. However, if the image/discourse is representative of the dominant ideology and the viewer's social situation is not, then there is tension resulting in a negotiation between the viewer and image/discourse. In other words, the viewer does not necessarily passively accept the dominant meaning unless it is preferred by the viewer. By preferring a certain meaning, the viewer exercises power in interpreting the image/discourse.

For example, the female forensic scientists on the *CSI* series are very slender and beautiful, have perfect hairstyles, and wear tight slacks and low-cut camisoles to work. There are a few African American and Hispanic women who work in the laboratories, but all the main female characters are White. If the viewer resists these images because their appearances are unrealistic and not very pragmatic in a work situation or because of the lack of diversity, then the viewer experiences a certain power in complaining about them. On the other hand, if the viewer believes these glamorous images are desirable, the viewer expresses a preference for them and the ideology that reinforces the image of idealized female bodies.

> Emily Proctor, who plays a forensic scientist on *CSI: Miami,* said, "You don't actually think we dress ourselves, do you? Costume decisions lie with the producers and wardrobe staff, who seem to follow the philosophy 'the deeper the cleavage, the higher the ratings.'" *(Parade,* 2007, December 30, p. 2)

Hall believed that the image/discourse **"hails"** a person as if it were hailing a taxi. In other words, it calls to the person. To answer the call, the person must recognize that it is she or he, not someone else, who is being hailed. By responding to the call or hail, a viewer recognizes the social position that has been constructed in encoding the image/discourse, and if the viewer's response is cooperative, the intended meaning is adopted, and the viewer has constituted herself or himself as a *subject.* A **subject** is a social construction wherein the viewer recognizes that she or he is being addressed or summoned by the hail and decodes the image/discourse accordingly. Thus, television viewers may be hailed as conformists or sexists or patriots or concerned citizens.

Hall named three social positions—dominant, oppositional, and negotiated—although he speculated that there could be multiple positions. The dominant position is decoded by the viewer who accepts the dominant or intended meaning. On the other hand, the oppositional position is in direct opposition to the dominant meaning, and an opposite point of view is decoded. The negotiated position is a completely open category for viewers who primarily fit into the dominant ideology but need to resist certain elements of it. Negotiated positions are popular with various social groups who tend to question their relationship to the dominant ideology. Negotiated meanings are what most people get out of television images/discourses most of the time. For example, *American Idol* consistently gets high ratings, but even faithful viewers question some aspects of the show, especially when a favorite performer gets eliminated. Cultural studies critics can interpret possible decoding positions from their own experience or derive multiple meanings by analysis. Hall said that we decode by interpreting "from the family in which you were brought up, the places of work, the institutions you belong to, the other practices you do" (Cruz & Lewis, 1999, p. 270). Another cultural studies practice is to interview viewers, often over time, to determine how people actively make sense of television images and discourses, social experience, and themselves.

Hall said that we can discover and play with identifications of ourselves, perhaps discovering something of ourselves for the first time. What is important to Hall is openness to understanding that what a person thinks one week may change the next. External events like new social movements and cultural differences can change the cultural context and thus both encoding and decoding processes (Morley & Chen, 1996). John Fiske, professor emeritus at the University of Wisconsin, praised Hall for making us aware that "people are neither cultural dupes nor silenced victims, but are vital, resilient, varied, contradictory, and as a source of constant contestations of dominance, are a vital social resource, the only one that can fuel social change" (Fiske, 1996, p. 220). Fiske has elaborated on Hall's model by breaking down the elements of the encoding process, specifically in television production, in his book *Television Culture* (2011), thus giving the television critic another set of categories to examine.

The Codes of Television Production

The term *code* comes from the study of semiotics. A **code** is a system of signs that is able to communicate meanings. Codes may be simple, as in the case of a STOP sign, or complex as in the case of a language. There are verbal, nonverbal, and representational codes, all of which can operate separately or together to encode meaning. In television studies, code refers to a range of audiovisual systems that have the capability to construct meaning (Casey, Casey, Calvert, French, & Lewis, 2002, p. 27). Fiske regards television as the bearer, provoker, and circulator of meanings and pleasure; echoing Hall, he believes that television is replete with potential meanings. Because a preferred meaning is intended in television production, the conventional codes of culture link the programs and the audience. Fiske defined code as "a rule-governed system of signs, whose rules and conventions are shared amongst members of a culture, and which is used to generate and circulate meanings in and for that culture. Codes are links between producers, texts, and audiences" (Fiske, 2011, p. 4). Fiske organized categories of codes into three levels: reality, representation, and ideology.

Reality

Reality is encoded by certain **social codes** that relate to appearance, behavior, speech, sound, and setting. Appearance includes skin color, clothing, hair, makeup, speech, facial expressions, and gestures. Speech includes spoken language, accent, dialect, formal or vernacular style, and paralanguage, such as pitch, rate, and inarticulate utterances. Sound includes natural sounds, such as wind or rain, and artificial sounds, such as sirens or music. Indoor settings may denote place, such as a living room or a hospital. Objects in the place may denote taste or social class, and could promote certain feelings such as comfort or tension. Outdoor settings may suggest peace and tranquility or fear and danger.

Much depends on other codes to encode certain preferred meanings. Some physical behaviors, such as dancing, kissing, shaking hands, playing sports, fighting, and so on, may be easily recognized as such. Others require more contextual information and supplemental codes to provoke meaning. Clothing can reveal certain personality characteristics such as formality, casualness, and sexuality. Once again, much depends on the other codes as they are put together to form a whole. Obviously, more information is necessary before one can draw conclusions about social codes, and furthermore, different people will interpret these codes in different ways. Social codes, once chosen for a television program, are encoded by representation.

Representation

Representation on television is encoded by technical codes with the camera, lighting, sound, music, and editing in order to transmit conventional representational codes, to convey the narrative, conflict, character, action, dialogue, setting, casting, and so forth. The following technical codes, as indicated by Fiske, have been discussed in Chapter 3, "Television Style." They are vital to representation on television and are suggested here as types of technical codes that function to encode meaning.

Camera use (placement angle, distance, movement, framing, and focus) like other technical codes can be specified by the director in order to achieve desired effects. A close-up, for example, may be used to represent intimacy on one hand or to reveal anxiety by emphasizing a person's furrowed brow or tears. *Lighting* changes the way we look at people by the way it is placed, for example, to create shadows across a person's face or to provide a certain color for special effect. *Editing* is a powerful way to provide continuity when none exists or to transform time, interaction, and other elements and rhythms. For example, I once appeared on a public television forum about television violence and children with eight other panelists. The moderator spoke at the beginning and then not again for 2 hours during which the nine panelists discussed the topic while being videotaped. When we finished, the moderator was videotaped, speaking into the camera for about 10 minutes. The final program was edited to appear as if the moderator would ask a question and two or three of the panelists would respond to it. The moderator appeared to be chairing a panel discussion. The responses had been carefully edited to fit the moderator's questions.

Sound and *music* create mood, attitude, and other various emotions. Music is also thematic and can suggest a program and various characters. Songs with lyrics have become an important part of television shows to provide a subtext to the action and dialogue. It is important to recognize the role that technical codes play in encoding meaning.

Representational codes have to work together to encode a preferred meaning and to appear natural at the same time. A script provides the setting, narrative, conflict, action, dialogue, and characters, but the actors who are cast in various roles bring the characters and the plot to life. Casting of characters is complex because actors are real people whom viewers may know in other contexts, for example from films, talk shows, magazines, and so on. Certain actors bring with them other intertextual meanings from their very public lives.

The social codes (in *Reality*) play a large part in conveying conventional representational codes. Appearance, speech, sound, facial expressions, and gestures in a contemporary setting have to be consistent with what viewers know in their own culture. Narratives set in other cultures or time periods also have to convey a sense of naturalness, but even in these instances social codes are usually adapted to the culture of the present. For example, on American television, a program set in France will most likely have the dialogue spoken in English. The most striking example of adaptation to the present was on *M*A*S*H,* which had a narrative based on the Korean War, but because the show was on from 1972 to 1983, it had more to do with the Vietnam War than the Korean War. Other cultural codes may be more deeply embedded in representation. Fiske refers to these in level 3 as *Ideology.*

Ideology

Representational codes are organized into coherence and social acceptability by **ideological codes,** such as individualism, patriarchy, class, materialism, capitalism, and so on. All the codes come together to encode a preferred meaning that supports a certain **ideology.** Fiske maintains that a patriarchal code is embedded in the dialogue when a woman asks questions and a man answers them, seemingly because the man is supposed to be more knowledgeable than the woman. More broadly, on crime series when the criminal is caught and imprisoned, the ideology of law and order is coded. On the news, the stock market report is a code for the ideology of capitalism. Gans wrote that the daily reports of the Dow Jones Industrial Average are an indicator of the primacy of business, but there is no daily report of fluctuations in the prices of basic foods, and no one reports news about wages and salaries of workers (Gans, 2003). There is no guarantee that a different cultural analyst will make the same meanings or even find ideology at all. Viewers who occupy different social positions may interpret the representation as something altogether different. The process of interpretation and finding meaning gives the viewer a certain kind of **pleasure** in decoding.

Decoding and Pleasure

Fiske said that a viewer not only decodes meanings but also derives pleasure from the process. Pleasure allows viewers to make meanings that are pertinent to them. Pleasure can be derived from opposing the preferred meaning or negotiating an individual meaning or accepting the preferred or dominant meaning. Experiencing pleasure in one of these ways frees the viewers from ideological dominance and gives them a sense of control over the production of meanings. Fiske wrote:

> Pleasure for the subordinate is produced by the assertion of one's social identity in resistance to, in independence of, or in negotiation with, the structure of domination. There is . . . real pleasure to be found in, for example, soap operas that assert the legitimacy of feminine meanings and identities within and against patriarchy. Pleasure results from the production of meanings of the world and of self that are felt to serve the interests of the viewer rather than those of the dominant. . . . Pleasure requires a sense of control over meanings and an active participation in the cultural process. (Fiske, 2011, p. 19)

A viewer may experience pleasure in the validation of his or her social identity from accepting the dominant meaning. There may also be a form of pleasure in negotiating meaning in a person's own terms. Pleasure can even be derived from resisting the dominant meaning; as Fiske wrote, "By maintaining one's social identity in opposition to that proposed by the dominant ideology, there is a power in asserting one's own subcultural values against the dominant ones" (Fiske, 2011, p. 19).

The concept of pleasure is another indicator that viewers make active choices regarding the meanings they decode. People make their own sense out of what they see, and the sense they make is related to a pattern of choices about their own social identities. This is one of the reasons for television's popularity, said Fiske, because it offers "such a variety of pleasures to such a heterogeneity of viewers" (Fiske, 2011, p.19). This enables the viewers to actively participate in culture, which has a social system that can be held in place only by the meanings that people make of it.

To paraphrase Fiske regarding the pleasure of watching television, viewers play a text the way a musician plays a score, by interpreting it, activating it, and giving it a living presence. A television critic can do the same, and that gives much pleasure, too.

SUMMARY

Both rhetoric and culture are interdisciplinary subjects based on various and complex ideas. This chapter has introduced some of the well-known aspects of both. Each of these subjects is worthy of an entire book or several books, and it would be unworthy reductionism to combine them. Rhetoric and cultural studies both have methodological fluidity and can be used in different forms to criticize television discourse. Rhetoric examines the available means of persuasion and information and how they work; cultural studies analyzes the production and exchange of strands of meanings and how they relate to social practices. There are areas where rhetoric and cultural studies intersect:

1. Rhetoric examines attributed intention; cultural studies analyzes the preferred meaning. These may not always be the same, but the preferred meaning can be an intentional one.

2. Rhetoric, as Rosteck has said, analyzes how discourse is produced, what it is, and what it does; cultural studies examines the codes of television involved in its production and generation of ideology.

3. Rhetoric is about the choices that the developer of discourse makes and the choices that a viewer makes in treating the discourse as a message; cultural studies is about the choices made in encoding and decoding meaning.

4. Rhetoric and cultural studies both link discourse to an audience, to society, and especially to context.

5. Cultural studies is about how ideology shapes a work; rhetoric is about how a work stems from and influences ideology.

6. Identification is a key factor in persuasion, and how one's identity is known through the decoding process is a key factor in cultural studies. The substance through which people rhetorically identify may be the same substance that marks identity in cultural studies, for example, nationality, class, gender, race, occupation, beliefs, and values.

7. Cultural studies examines polysemy, the multiple meanings that can be made by viewers from television discourse; rhetoric examines how a sender and receiver co-create meaning.

8. Both subjects focus on symbols and emphasize that meanings do not reside in the symbols themselves but in the people who encode them.

9. Values as foundations for persuasion may be studied in rhetoric; cultural studies analyze the ideology in discourse. Ideology is comprised in part of values.

10. Rhetoric is used to bring about change and enlightenment; cultural studies is about the lives of everyday people and how culture interacts with their lives.

Television rhetoric was defined as the study of technologically enhanced symbol systems and representations through which the senders (television producers, writers, directors, actors, cinematographers, set designers, and so on) attempt to shape perceptions, foster understanding, create identification, and influence the viewing behavior of the receivers (the television audience). Cultural studies has been presented as a way to demystify what attitudes, beliefs, values, preferred forms of conduct, and ideologies are embedded and reinforced in images and supporting discourse. Both approaches are of great value to the television critic and can be adapted as questions to ask when conducting a critique.

EXERCISES

1. Watch an episode of *CSI* and observe how the forensic scientists use evidence and artistic and inartistic proofs to locate the criminal.

2. Find and describe an enthymeme in a television commercial. What did you have to supply to complete the reasoning?

3. Is there anything on television that emphasizes *telos,* the movement toward moral excellence?

4. Find attributed intentionality in a television drama or situation comedy or in the news.

5. Select a television program that you frequently watch and describe the character with whom you identify. Analyze why you identify with this character.

6. Give an example of how a television program engages in courtship with you as a viewer. What desire does it arouse and satisfy?

7. Cite some examples from recent television shows and commercials that use language that has found its way into popular usage.

8. Select a scene from a television drama and analyze its polysemy.

9. Select a soap opera or a nighttime drama and tell how it relates to the shared conditions of our time.

10. Select a television show and examine the codes described by Fiske—reality, representation, and ideology.

11. Listen to the songs and their lyrics in a scene from a drama to find the subtext.

12. Describe an instance in which a television show "hails" you and tell how you answer it.

13. Describe how hegemony has occurred for a disempowered group that has recently been represented on television.

14. By playing with meanings that you make from television, tell what you have learned about yourself in the process.

SUGGESTED READINGS IN RHETORIC

Bormann, Ernest G. (1990). Fantasy and Rhetorical Vision: The Rhetorical Criticism of Social Reality. In B. L. Brock, R. L. Scott, & J. W. Chesebro (Eds.), *Methods of Rhetorical Criticism: A Twentieth-Century Perspective* (3rd ed.). Detroit, MI: Wayne State University Press.

Dorsey, James. (1997). *The Prophetic Tradition and Radical Rhetoric in America.* New York: New York University Press.

Foss, Sonja K. (Ed.). (2004). *Rhetorical Criticism: Exploration and Practice* (3rd ed.). Prospect Heights, IL: Waveland Press.

Hart, Roderick P., & Daughton, Suzanne M. (2004). *Modern Rhetorical Criticism* (3rd ed.). Boston, MA: Allyn & Bacon.

Heath, Robert L. (1986). *Realism and Relativism: A Perspective on Kenneth Burke.* Macon, GA: Mercer University Press.

Kuypers, Jim A. (2010). Framing Analysis From a Rhetorical Perspective. In P. D. Angelo & J. A. Kuypers (Eds.), *Doing News Framing Analysis.* London, England: Routledge.

Lorenzo-Dus, Nuria. (2009). *Television Discourse: Analysing Language in the Media.* New York, NY: Palgrave Macmillan.

O'Donnell, Victoria. (1988). Dreams Can Come True for Little Girls Too. In L. E. Rohler & R. Cook (Eds.), *Great Speeches for Criticism and Analysis* (pp. 43–54). Greenwood, IN: Alistair Press.

Olson, Lester C., Finnegan, Cara A., & Hope, Diane S. (Eds.). (2008). *Visual Rhetoric.* Thousand Oaks, CA: Sage.

Redmond, Sean, & Holmes, Su (2007). *Stardom and Celebrity.* Thousand Oaks, CA: Sage.

Towner, Emil. (2010, May 10). *Apologetic Rhetoric.* Retrieved from http://www.emiltowner.com

SUGGESTED READINGS IN CULTURAL STUDIES

Barker, Chris. (2008). *Cultural Studies: Theory and Practice* (3rd ed.). Thousand Oaks, CA: Sage.

Couldry, Nick. (2000). *Inside Culture: Re-imagining the Method of Cultural Studies.* London, England: Sage.

Evans, Jessica, & Hall, Stuart (Eds.). (1999). *Visual Culture: The Reader.* London, England: Sage.

Fiske, John. (2011). *Television Culture.* London, England: Routledge.

Hall, Stuart. (1997). *Representation: Cultural Representations and Signifying Practices.* Thousand Oaks, CA: Sage.

Higgins, John. (1999). *Raymond Williams: Literature, Marxism, and Cultural Materialism.* London, England: Routledge.

Lewis, Jeff. (2008). *Cultural Studies: The Basics* (2nd ed.). London, England: Sage.

CHAPTER 7

Representation and Its Audience

Illusion holds you captive still.

—Mephistopheles to Faust (Goethe, *Faust*)

INTRODUCTION

In Chapter 6, the concept of representation was presented as a television code, a range of audiovisual systems that has the capability to construct meanings. The concept of representation is central to the study of television. Television provides a continual flow of images and sounds that link viewers to the world. Television production shapes how an event unfolds and limits the meanings of what is seen. Television mediates reality by selecting and interpreting images in order to present them to the viewers. Representation of people and events is encoded by technical codes with the camera, lighting, sound, music, and editing in order to convey the narrative, conflict, character action, dialogue, setting, casting, and so on. Representational codes work together to encode a preferred meaning, yet at the same time to present the illusion of naturalness.

Because it is impossible to show everything on television, selection of images is necessary. The task of news is to represent the realities of daily life from all over the world. What we know about people in places such as Israel, Palestine, Iran, Iraq, China, Japan, Russia, Egypt, Libya, Darfur, the Sudan, and Kenya is very likely to come from television. Television drama and situation comedies have representations of women, men, husbands, wives, parents, grandparents, children, race, ethnic groups, age, rich, poor, class, doctors, lawyers, police, firefighters, religious leaders, people from different parts of America and the world, and so forth. How do we know that what we see resembles the actual people and places? Furthermore, does it matter to us if they do or do not? Which groups are included and which are excluded? By understanding the concept of representation, the television critic can attempt to answer these questions. This chapter is an examination of representation and explains what representation is; how it impacts a viewer; what role it plays in the depiction of gender, ethnicity, race, nationality, and class on television; and how it affects a society's **collective memory**.

WHAT IS REPRESENTATION?

Visual representation means to re-present, to project an image of someone or something. Even though the image will seldom be realistic in size because it depends upon the dimensions of the television screen, the viewer is expected to accept the image as realistic even though it is framed by a camera. As we saw in Chapter 6, verbal representation means that language stands in the place of someone or something, requiring that meaning to be learned. Verbal representation varies from language to language. Visual representation also means that images stand in the place of someone or something, and it requires learning and interpreting the meanings as well.

A common definition of **representation** is "a given which the act of representation duplicates in one way or another" (Iser in Krieger, 1987, p. 217). Stuart Hall, in his book *Representation: Cultural Representations and Signifying Practices,* emphasized meaning in the "language" of words, sounds, and images in his definition of representation: "The production of meaning through language. . . . Any sound, word, image, or object which functions as a sign, and is organized with other signs into a system which is capable of carrying and expressing meaning is, from this point of view 'a language'" (Hall, 1997, pp. 16, 19). Representation was defined by W. J. T. Mitchell in his book *Picture Theory: Essays on Verbal and Visual Representation* as a fabricated stand-in for culture, suggesting the "constructed, artificial character of forms of life, in contrast to the organic biological connotations of 'culture'" (Mitchell, 1995, p. 423). Photographs, paintings, film, television, and computer images are forms of visual representation. They attempt to duplicate objects, places, or persons, but they are truly not duplicates. Rather, they are substitutes that resemble what they attempt to duplicate or imitate. Skill in duplication, such as perspective in art to give a two-dimensional canvas the sense of a real three-dimensional view or knowledge of light and shadow to harness realism in photography and film, is as important to a sense of accuracy as it is to illusion in these media. Jen Webb, in her book *Understanding Representation*, explained, "representation is *made* to happen . . . to construct meaning" (2009, pp. 8, 30).

If the representation is a surrogate for the original, then it could be used as the original might function. This suggests that representation, although it is not the original, presents an illusion of the original and its function. Thus, a representative image *imitates* the real. It is an attempt to *substitute* a *resemblance* in order that a viewer may recognize it as real. An image is *constructed* to *re-present* someone or something. If it resembles the real, it has *verisimilitude,* an appearance of truth. In other words, it has to have credibility.

TELEVISION REPRESENTATION

Television images are complex because they are based on visual representation. Television images are mediated images—three-dimensional places, people, and objects viewed on a two-dimensional plane—not life-size, and produced by technical means controlled by camera angles and movement, lighting, and computer manipulation. High-definition TV has the capability of giving the illusion of three dimensions. (3-D television will attempt to present three dimensions if it is successful.) Acting, directing, camera work, lighting, and editing create a sense of intimacy, emotion, excitement, and other feelings. As we saw in Chapter 3, television employs art directors and set dressers to create realistic-appearing places, such as living rooms, restaurants, offices, hospitals, and other settings. When we see them in the frame of a television set at home, these images are reduced to the size of the screen—20 inches up to 54 inches, depending on the screen's dimensions. Huge television screens at concerts or in open-air locales increase the actual size of people and objects, but residential television sets do not show sets that are as large as the actual studio sets. The actual sets in the television studio often have three walls with the **fourth wall** open to the cameras, directors, producers, writers, and, in the case of situation comedies, an audience. Because the person who watches a program on television cannot see the entire studio or stage, one could say that representation conceals as well as reveals. If a scene is outdoors, set in wintertime snow, for example, the material used to create the illusion of snow is artificial. Projections on green screens create illusions of the real. Yet, the viewer can accept the image as a duplication of a given reality although what is real is represented by an imitation of it. Thus, that which is represented is *re-presented* by a substitute, an imitation. Its effectiveness is dependent on the viewer's recognizing and accepting it. In order to achieve this kind of viewer response, the image must *resemble* that which is real. In other words, the image to be accepted as real has to correspond to the viewer's experience of three-dimensional space. On the other hand, fantasy images such as monsters, dinosaurs, aliens, and space ships lack real referents in viewers' experiences.

INTERPRETING REPRESENTATION

Ultimately, the viewer decides if an image resembles reality. As Kenneth Burke wrote, "A way of seeing is also a way of not seeing" (Burke, 1935/1984, p. 49). The old adage "seeing is believing" can also be construed as "believing is seeing." How we perceive is influenced by our values, beliefs, and experiences, thus a representation on television is constructed via the perceptual filters of the television producers and seen through the perceptual lens of the viewer.

A television situation comedy uses a representation of a funny situation to provoke audience laughter, but the audience must be able to relate it to familiar experiences in order to comprehend the humor. David Marc wrote that the situation comedy is a representational form of American culture: "It dramatizes national types, styles, customs, issues, and language" (Marc, 1984, p. 13).

Television viewers may derive meaning from representations, and, because reality has multiple meanings to people, representations also constitute multiple meanings (polysemy). It is also quite possible that a representation may have no meaning to a viewer, or it may have a large range of meanings. The viewer interprets what is represented within a cultural context and locates meaning according to beliefs, values, and experience, thus an image does not have a fixed meaning. Images can touch levels of experience, according to Hall,

> beyond the purely rational level of awareness, and which disturb by the very way in which they exceed meaning. The cultural practices of looking and seeing, then, . . . rest on complex conditions of existence, some of which have psychic and unconscious dimensions of which the behavioral definition of meaning's "effects" has only a very reductionist understanding. (Hall, 1999, pp. 311–312)

RECEPTION OF TELEVISUAL IMAGES

Television and its viewers comprise a communication system of senders and receivers, messages, the transmission of the messages through a medium, and reception by viewers. The sender encodes through technologically enhanced representations and symbol systems comprised of words, sounds, and images. The receiver decodes meanings by selecting and interpreting images, sounds, and words, and assigning meanings to them. Viewers have certain expectations of established program conventions (as described in Chapter 5, "Television Genres") that color their responses. Producers of television have certain goals that they want to achieve, for example, to have viewers perceive images as credible, to provoke laughter, or to gain a faithful following for a series or a network, but because there is no immediate feedback from viewers, the producers' primary goal is to gain a large percentage of audience shares. Some television programs, mostly the competitive reality shows such as *American Idol* and *Dancing With the Stars,* give viewers feedback opportunities to text, call, or use the online website to vote for contestants, and the Internet offers many opportunities for viewers to give their opinions of television programs. Program websites solicit responses from viewers, displaying them in their "community" links and offering prizes such as free trips to see that particular show being made. There are invitations to Facebook sites where viewers are asked to make comments and even rate the shows. Yet, for the most part, the ratings system is still the primary means for television producers to gauge viewer responses in terms of numbers of people watching.

Viewer reception is dependent upon **perception** of mediated images. Perception is the process of extracting information from outside ourselves as well as from within ourselves. How we perceive is based on "complex psychological, philosophical, and practical habitual thought patterns that we carry over from past experiences" (Hayward, 1997, p. 73). Each individual has a perceptual field that is unique to that person and formed by the influences of values, roles, self-image, and cultural norms. Each of these shapes how a person perceives. The connection between perception and cognition leads to the cultural formation of meanings related to what is seen. Recognition of most meanings tends to be automatic because people have learned them. As Hall wrote, "all sorts of objects, people, and events are correlated with a set of concepts or *mental representations* which we carry around in our heads. Without them, we could not interpret the world meaningfully at all" (Hall, 1997, p. 17). The concepts Hall referred to are organized, arranged, and classified into complex relations with one another. "Meaning," he wrote, "depends upon the relationship between things in the world—people, objects, and events, real or fictional—and the conceptual system, which can operate as *mental representations* of them" (Hall, 1997, p. 18). Because people broadly share conceptual systems and thus make sense of the world in roughly the same way, they can communicate with one another. "That," said Hall, "is indeed what it means when we say we 'belong to the same culture.' Because we interpret the world in roughly similar ways, we are able to build up a shared culture of meanings and thus construct a social world which we inhabit together. That is why 'culture' is sometimes defined in terms of 'shared meanings or shared conceptual maps'" (Hall, 1997, p. 18).

When a thing is different from the usual mental representation, confusion results in the attempt to recognize it. Harvard psychologist Jerome Bruner conducted experiments on perception wherein he had college students recognize playing cards. In one group he switched the colors, so the hearts and diamonds were black instead of red, and the spades and clubs were red instead of black. The students had difficulty recognizing the color-reversed cards. They tried to regularize what they saw by saying the red six of clubs was really a black six of clubs (Bruner, 1973). In extreme cases, if people have no familiarity with a thing, they may not perceive it at all. As we saw in the previous chapter, a wide variety of meanings (polysemy) can be made depending upon the viewer and the context.

SYMBOLS

A **symbol** differs from an imitative representation, for it stands for something else but does not attempt to accurately duplicate it. A Valentine's Day card in the shape of a heart may symbolize love, or the empty boots in the stirrups of a saddle on a riderless horse may symbolize the death of a hero or heroine. Although both symbols and representations rely upon relationships or connections between the image and the receiver of the image, they are connections that are achieved in different ways. A connection between a symbol and its referent is not necessarily causal as is a visual representation of, for example, a living room on television. The heart-shaped symbol "♥" stands for the word "love" in our culture, but the connection between the symbol and its meaning had to be learned. In a culture where the heart-shaped symbol has no known meaning, it is unlikely to get a response, or it may get a different response. On the other hand, an anatomical drawing of a human heart should be a representation of a real human heart to anyone anywhere in the world who has adequate knowledge of human anatomy. In other words, a symbol is understood only because there are shared conventional meanings (Webb, 2009, p. 148). We have learned to attach certain meanings to words, and when they are familiar enough, their presence stimulates a kind of recognition of something similar in our experience. We learn to attach meanings to visual symbols in the same manner that we have learned the meanings of words in our language. Michelle King, co-creator of *The Good Wife,* deliberately had butterfly designs incorporated into the living room coasters, on a bathroom shelf, and a framed exhibit of butterfly wings in the show's set because they symbolize fragility and freedom, just like Alicia, the show's star, who is testing her wings. In one scene, at her husband's celebration on being elected to office, Alicia learned that he had slept with her best friend. She wore a bright red dress to symbolize her rage (Hoffman, 2011, p. 1). To appreciate the symbolism, we have to understand the meaning of the butterflies and the red dress. They are important subtexts in the narrative.

THE ILLUSION OF REALITY

Television images are both symbolic and representational. The camera records and/or transmits both live and filmed moving images that represent people, places, and events that symbolize ideas, values, activities, and other concepts. Although people may respond to television as if they are seeing something firsthand, they are not. What they see is an image of something that someone else has selected, created, or recorded. Images are constructed to perpetuate the illusion that what we see is natural and believable. Representation in television has come to be regarded, for the most part, as a realistic appropriation of the world. What viewers see on television are images demanding to be recognized as real.

Seeing something through a moving image camera is never the same as seeing it with the naked eye. All the facets inherent in the technology come into play to create a unique view. In addition to the production techniques used to transmit images, sound in the form of dialogue, music, and background elements is also important, for it assists in the interpretation of the image and has representative capability. A harsh musical chord in the context of a frightening event, for example, can represent danger. The dialogue that the actors speak conveys not just interaction but also attitude and intentions. Computer technology enables technicians to create elaborate illusions that appear to be real, but, in fact, are so far from reality that viewers can no longer assume that what they perceive was ever real. Computer technology can turn a group of 5 people into a crowd of 500 or place a deceased person like Frank Sinatra in a television commercial that appears to have him talking to a live actor about a product.

THE NEED FOR IMAGES

Often a viewer responds to an image because there is a need for it. William Wordsworth, the early 19th-century poet, said that people *need* images because people want a sense of who their fellow human beings are in order to have a sense of identity. Raymond Williams agreed with Wordsworth, adding that we need representations of what life is like both in our own culture and in others. This is why we watch the National Geographic and Discovery channels in addition to programming that is set in our own country. That is why we are glued to television sets when revolution occurs in countries like Egypt or when natural disasters occur such as tsunamis and earthquakes like the one that struck in Japan. Millions of Americans watched the royal wedding of Prince William and Kate Middleton as the images of the couple were repeatedly shown on television and on websites. Williams said that our society "has been dramatized by the inclusion of constant dramatic representation as a daily habit and need" (Williams, 1989, p. 7).

French psychiatrist Octave Mannoni claimed that people have "a persisting need to posit 'an other scene' of absolute, untroubled faith, whether that 'other scene' be primitive cultures, an epoch's own past, an individual's childhood" (Ray, 1985, p. 36). Further, Mannoni maintained that although people know that what they see is an illusion, they also want to believe it. Translated from the French, Mannoni's premise was "I know very well that this illusion is only an illusion, but nevertheless, some part of me still believes in it" (in Ray, 1985, p. 36). This double system of belief enables audience members who know that what they see on fictional television is not real to become absorbed in it as if it were real.

Thus, the impact of representation is that a need is fulfilled. Individuals may have specific needs that are satisfied from various kinds of representations of characters, plots, and action in television, but all television viewers have some kind of a need for representation.

REPRESENTATION OF THE "OTHER"

The concept of **the "Other"** stems from George Herbert Mead's (1934) social psychology and symbolic interaction. Initially it was defined as a symbolic unity located outside of the self and associated with one or more other individuals, real or fictional people (O'Sullivan et al., 1994). Cultural, queer, and feminist studies have appropriated the concept of the other to mean "a person, persons, group, social class, community, race or nation who are not 'us' and who are defined by their difference from us; yet who by that difference contribute to our concept of self, as individuals, members of groups, etc." (Watson & Hill, 2003, p. 209). There is a generalized "other" as in "*Some people* watch reality shows on television, but I prefer drama." The "other" can also be a positive role model, a real or fictional person, someone who is respected and sets a good example to follow. In television studies, the "other" usually represents a group that people fear, dislike, or feel superior to, resulting in a "them and us" attitude. Dominant groups who have power over representation on television may endow subordinate groups with certain characteristics and habits, turning them into the "other." When a group is the "other," individual differences tend to be lost, for the members of the group are homogenized into a collective "them." Such categories of identity are contrived to appear natural as if determined by biology or psychology. These categories also result in stereotypes that completely ignore individual personalities.

Film, radio, and television in the past were notorious for stereotyping gender, race, and ethnicity. Today one has to look carefully for notions of the "other" on television. Shows such as *Lost* and *Grey's Anatomy* feature diversity in their characters. The characters on *Lost* were African American, Korean, Iraqi, Hispanic, and Whites from America and Australia. Daniel Dae Kim, a Korean-born actor who grew up in New York and Philadelphia, who played Jin on *Lost,* said,

> Nobody wants tokenism, and that's one of the reasons I'm so proud of this show. It shows America and television executives and movie producers that you don't have to have a lily-white cast of twentysomethings to have a successful project. The story lines speak to America regardless of color and can even be enhanced by mixtures of race and gender. (Fernandez, 2005, February 13, p. E30)

John Wells, whose company produced *The West Wing, Southland,* and *ER,* said that producers have a duty to develop interesting characters, not racial types:

> If racial identity is the only thing that's interesting about a character, that's extremely limiting and also insulting to how society works now. Sometimes in an attempt to diversify shows, the characters become stereotypical because they're there for the purpose of providing diversity and you're trying to write to that instead of trying to write human beings. (Fernandez, 2005, February 13, p. E30)

When Michael Crichton wrote the pilot for *ER,* he did not specify gender or race for any of the doctor characters on the show. The *ER* doctors were male, female, African American, Puerto Rican, East Indian, Croatian, White, and disabled. The diverse results came from good casting. Presently, several sit-coms feature East Indians in the cast, for example, Kunal Nayyar in *The Big Bang Theory* and Mindy Kaling in *The Office. Outsourced,* of course, has a large East Indian cast.

Yet, there are many observers who insist that racial, ethnic, and gender "otherness" persists on television news reporting—where members of minority groups are frequently linked to crime and drugs—and that there is a small number of diverse characters on fiction television. Asian Americans have been particularly underrepresented in fiction television; however, the numbers are increasing. Tim Kang, a Korean American, has a major role on *The Mentalist.* A growing Hispanic population in America has subsequently influenced the representation of Hispanic Americans in leading roles on television. Actors such as Eva Longoria and Ricardo Antonio Chavira on *Desperate Housewives,* Sara Ramirez on *Grey's Anatomy,* America Ferrera on *Ugly Betty,* Alana de la Garza on *Law & Order: Los Angeles,* George Lopez on *The George Lopez Show,* and Puerto Rican American Esai Morales on Syfy's *Caprica* have major roles. Fox announced that Jorge Garcia, who was in *Lost,* will have the lead in its new show, *Alcatraz,* in the 2011–2012 season (B. Carter & Stelter, 2011, p. 2).

It was not until *The Cosby Show* (1984–1992) came on the air that Donald Bogle, author of books about the representation of African Americans on television and in film, wrote that he saw on television families such as the ones he knew growing up in the suburbs. Bogle attributed the unique perspective of *The Cosby Show* to having an African American (Cosby) in control of the material (Bogle, 2001). When there is an absence of programs about African Americans, Bogle wrote, "Black viewers felt that television was not fully and fairly representing them, not saying who they were and what their lives were like" (Bogle, 2001, p. 3). White viewers loved Cosby then as they now do Oprah, who has become an American icon. As Beretta Smith-Shomade wrote in her book *Shaded Lives: African-American Women and Television,* Oprah Winfrey had "the potential to unite [the audience] across the [racial] difference" (Smith-Shomade, 2002, p. 176).

From 1999 to 2000, the National Association for the Advancement of Colored People (NAACP) urged the major television networks to improve their racial diversity or face a nationwide boycott. Network executives signed pledges to put more minorities on camera and behind it. Paul Farhi of *The Washington Post* claimed that

> television today is largely a paradise of racial equality and minority progress. . . . African Americans . . . anchor the evening news, pitch products, announce and coach sports events, and are shown as doctors, surgeons, lawyers, business executives, military officers, teachers, reporters. Indeed, television has helped change the social norm in America by denouncing racism and bigotry as morally intolerable. Undoubtedly, exposure to people different than oneself, if only through TV, helps shatter stereotypes and creates a foundation for understanding. (Farhi, 2000, p. 23)

Sexuality as portrayed on television also has changed with gay and lesbian characters in recurring roles. *Ellen* had the first openly gay lead when Ellen DeGeneres's character Ellen Morgan announced that she was gay on her show 3 years after the show began in 1994. The gay characters Mitchell and Cameron play a married couple who adopted a daughter on

Photo 7.1   Doctors Miranda Bailey and Callie Torres in *Grey's Anatomy*.

Modern Family; lesbians Callie and Arizona got married on *Grey's Anatomy; Glee* features a teenage gay boy; and even Homer Simpson grappled with homophobia only to reject bigotry and embrace sexual pluralism and equality in "Homer's Phobia" on *The Simpsons*. Fred Fejes pointed out that gays and lesbians are attractive to advertisers because of their consumption habits. Although gay and lesbian income is not greater than that of the general population, a 1994 study found that gays and lesbians were seen as far more likely to spend their money on new products. "To advertisers," said Fejes, "they were a very desirable group of innovative consumers" (Fejes, 2003, pp. 215–216).

Women's roles on television have progressed from the homemakers of the 1950s shows such as *Father Knows Best* and *Leave It to Beaver,* where women characters such as Margaret Anderson and June Cleaver represented idealized and happy submersions into domestic life where they served others and deferred to their husbands. Today, women are featured protagonists in television narratives as detectives, doctors, executives, lawyers, judges, and action heroines. It would seem that there has been much progress given women's absence in such roles in the past. However, as mentioned earlier in this book, most actresses who play women characters and women in nonfiction roles such as news anchors and entertainment hosts are young, very beautiful, and have slender and firm bodies that are considered perfect. Youthful, male bodies that are buff and perfect are often featured on dramatic television shows, but this is not always the case. Leading men do not necessarily have ideal bodies. Men in nonfiction such as the news and magazine shows are often older with less-than-idealized bodies, while their female costars are very attractive. Although there are exceptions, there is still a double standard for women and men on television as far as age and appearance are concerned.

What about the representation of middle-aged and senior citizen characters? Commercial television is sponsored by advertising that appeals to 18- to 49-year-olds but courts 18- to 34-year-olds more aggressively. That is why most of the lead characters in a comedy or drama tend to be 20 to 30 years old. Parents on television are often positively represented, but, according to Earl Pomerantz, former executive producer of *The Cosby Show* and writer for *The Mary Tyler Moore Show* and *Cheers,* parents on television today are represented as "monsters, maniacs, and morons" (Pomerantz, 2006, p. 42). Pomerantz cited the example of the "ego-crushing mother of *Two and a Half Men."* He suggested that this may be because advertising discounts older consumers over 50 and that television writers tend to be young and may be getting revenge on their own parents by representing parents in a negative way. Yet, this, too, appears to be changing. Marketers like Kellogg's, Skechers, and 5-Hour Energy Drink have announced that they will broaden their focus in the television commercials to appeal to viewers 55 years old and up. NBC's 2011–2012 line-up includes *Harry's Law* that stars 62-year-old Kathy Bates and two new shows set in the 1960s (B. Carter & Vega, 2011, pp. 1–2).

What about the representation of class? Most television dramas feature middle- and upper-class groups. When lower classes are represented on situation comedies, they are often portrayed as unintelligent buffoons, especially lower-class men. What about the disabled? How often are people represented as wheelchair-bound or physically or mentally impaired? *Glee* has Artie, who sings for the glee club in a wheelchair, and episodes with a deaf choir and a woman with Down syndrome; *Private Practice* has a genetics researcher, Dr. Gabriel Fife, who works in a state-of-the-art wheelchair and is played by Michael Thornton, who is paralyzed from the waist down; David Hall, a double amputee, has played the role of coroner on *CSI: Crime Scene Investigation* for 11 years; Marlee Matlin, who is deaf and communicates with sign language, has frequent guest roles on television; Constance Marie uses sign language on *Switched at Birth,* an ABC Family show that merges the hearing and deaf worlds; and *South Park* and *Family Guy* have Timmy in a wheelchair, Jimmy who stutters, and Peter, also in a wheelchair. It appears that disabled characters on television appear more frequently than before, although the wheelchair, perhaps because of its visibility, seems to be used most often to indicate a disability.

ADVICE FOR TELEVISION CRITICS

When we ask questions about representation of gender, sexuality, age, ethnicity, race, and class, we have to be careful that we are not representing these various groups as the "other." African American is a category used to describe people in America who are descendents of Africans, but what term do we use for people from Haiti or the Caribbean who have dark skin? Asian American is a large and meaningless compilation to represent Koreans, Chinese, Vietnamese, Cambodians, and so on. Darnell M. Hunt, in his book *Channeling Blackness: Studies on Television and Race in America,* explains that race does not exist in nature, but rather the idea of race was historically developed; it is social representation, a mental framework that works to order the way we see the world before us. We notice otherwise arbitrary differences on the surface of the human body and imbue these differences with social meaning. . . . Key cultural forums like television today play a crucial role in this ongoing meaning-making process. . . . Much of this meaning-making activity is wrapped up in our own ongoing efforts to establish who we are, who we are not, and who we hope to be. (Hunt, 2005, p. 3)

As a television critic, pay attention to individual casting, the character's personality, and the narrative. Race, gender, age, and so on may not be the most important factors. For example, *Grey's Anatomy* features an interracial couple with the doctors Owen Hunt, who is White and Cristina Yang, a Korean American, but there is nothing in the show that addresses their racial backgrounds. Crosby and Jasmine, are an on-again, off-again White/African American couple on *Parenthood* who have a mixed-race son, but again nothing refers to race in the narrative about them. Another African American on *Parenthood* is Alex, who dates a White girl named Haddie. When Haddie's father objected to their dating, Alex asked, "Is it because I'm Black?" The father answers, "No, it's because you are older and a recovering alcoholic."

As a television critic, you will do more than count categories, although it is important to ask who is represented and who is not. Who is invisible? For example, how often are Native Americans represented on television? How are Muslims represented?

It is important to see how a person is represented and scrutinize whether that representation is stereotypical, fixing the meanings that are given to groups. Are professional people in business and government represented as suspicious? Are Middle Easterners represented as terrorists? Even when groups are represented in quantity on television, such as women

Photo 7.2   Crosby and Jasmine, a racially mixed couple, discuss their occupations for their son Jabbar's school class in *Parenthood*.

are today, many are cast in specific roles that visually focus attention upon their sexual attractiveness. Many female actresses playing professional women wear low-cut tank tops and tight slacks that accentuate their model-thinness. Male actors often have to work out in strenuous fitness exercise to have toned bodies. Medical and empirical evidence indicates that the media play a strong role in conditioning women and men to adopt these idealized body shapes with possible harmful consequences (Wykes & Gunter, 2005).

As a television critic, you look for the visual encoding of men and women on television, whether they are in fiction or nonfiction roles. Also, you will examine the discourse to determine elements of power between and among group representations. As a critic of television, you will ask: What is at stake in a representation? How are we limited in our ways of seeing? Is there meaning that is different from what we expected to find in a representation?

Representation is a construction with a preferred meaning on the part of the encoder (the production staff), but, as we saw in Chapter 6, audience members can derive different meanings by negotiating or resisting the dominant meaning. As a television critic, you can play with meanings and discover what possibilities are there. It is important to remember that television production and distribution is a business, thus the representations may reinforce the identities of the consumer market. This is why representation is so complex. It has both artistic and economic goals.

REPRESENTATION AND COLLECTIVE MEMORY

As anthropologist Gregory Bateson said, human memory is a social and cultural process: "We take image production to be the locus of heightened interplay of mnemonic process and cultural formation" (Kuchler & Mellion, 1991, p. 4). If memory is culturally constructed, then memory operates through representation. Certainly, our memory comes from our own nonmediated and mediated experiences, but there is also a continuum of representations and dramatic conventions that are included in our memories. Jefferson A. Singer and Peter Salovey, writing about how a person remembers the past, related past memories to present representations:

> Representative images crystallize characteristic interests, motives, or concerns of
> an individual into a shorthand moment. . . . [Memories] have collapsed a sequence
> of associated experiences into a single one. By focusing on the one representative
> memory, one gains access, whether implicitly or explicitly, to an extensive series
> of related memories. Individuals may open a memory bank with a snapshot, a
> song, a story, or a film. (Singer & Salovey, 1993, p. 63)

Collective memory is a memory that different persons, unknown to one another, remember of the same event. Societies share collective or public memories with ceremonies, rituals, and television images. Television delivers and creates history through representation in news and drama. Television is an external vessel of recollection, for it delivers and creates history as news. This creates a collective memory whereby we have shared representations of, for example, the Civil Rights Movement, Martin Luther King, Jr.'s "I Have a Dream" speech, the astronauts' walk on the moon, the assassination of John F. Kennedy, the Holocaust, the mushroom cloud of the atomic bomb, the dismantling of the Berlin Wall, the war in Vietnam (the first television war), the collapse of the Federal Building in Oklahoma City, the *Challenger* explosion, the Persian Gulf War, and the fall of the Twin Towers of the World Trade Center in New York City. This is a major means for new generations to "know" history. George Lipsitz wrote, "Time, history, and memory become qualitatively different concepts in a world where electronic mass communication is possible" (Lipsitz, 1990, p. 21). Television also creates history with docudramas, delivering historical events and persons through fictional representations of them. What if the docudrama distorts history? A television critic can reveal such distortions in order that people may realize that what they have seen is not necessarily the way it was. On the other hand, the television critic should also ask what are the limits of fictionalized history and artistic license.

People may have a memory but be unsure of its source. They may know it was not from direct experience but are unsure if it was from television news, a newspaper, magazine, or from another person. David Marc spoke of a shadow memory of "a continuing electronic paratext to experience [that] interacts with individual memory" (Marc, 1984, p. 135). Anthropologist Edmund Carpenter wrote that "television gives us a sense of reliving the past, of knowing the outcome even when we haven't seen the movie" (Carpenter, 1974, p. 16). Representation in its many forms provides us with memory, but it is important to remember that representation is dependent upon individual interpretation and assigned meaning to form memory.

SUMMARY

This chapter has explored the meaning of the concept of representation. Representation cannot duplicate reality, only imitate it, attempt to substitute, or to provoke other stored representations that already reside in a person's memory. Recognition of this enables us to understand that representation is an imitation, never the real thing. Further, there are varying reasons why we need representation. Representations provide us with access to the past, satisfy our need to know what life is like for other people, enable us to live vicariously, fulfill a daily habit, and remind us that life may have been more or less complicated in another time. Finally, they are included in our individual and collective memories. These explanations help us understand the connections between encoded representations and the decoded reception of them. Sorting out these matters is important to you as a television critic, but it is also important for public consumers of representations to know what it is they are consuming, how it is that they are consumed, and how representations intermix with personal memories to create illusions that are a "real" part of our lives. Representation is not just about who is represented, but it is also about who is not represented. Representation is about how people, places, and objects are represented on television and the meaning that is endowed in them. Representation of people may be emblematic of a dominant meaning, but it is important to ask what is at stake in the representation. The more we understand about representations, their rationale, and their interpretations, the more we can effectively assess how they work and learn what their impact is on us.

EXERCISES

1. Select a television representation of a person from a country you have never visited or know little about. What is your impression of the person regarding national characteristics? Do you generalize that the person represents other citizens of the same country?

2. How might a representational image on television function as the real thing? Are you willing to accept the image as the real thing? If so, what function does it perform for you?

3. Watch a situation comedy and try to imagine the fourth wall. Describe what you think is there. In the same situation comedy, select a scene (indoors or outdoors) and ask if you accept it as a given reality. If so, why? If not, why?

4. Select your favorite situation comedy and ask if you relate it to your own familiar experiences. If not the entire situation comedy, how do you relate to a part of the narrative or to a character?

5. The term *polysemy* denotes many meanings. Watch a television show with a friend who has a different background and beliefs than your own. Afterward, discuss the meanings your friend made from the program and compare them with your own.

6. Select a favorite and familiar television show. Is it relevant to your culture as you know it? Does it project shared meanings for other people in your culture? Make a list of the shared meanings that you perceive.

7. Find an example of a visual symbol on television. Describe what it stands for and how you learned its meaning.

8. Select an example of background music, a song's lyrics, or sound in a drama. Within the context of the narrative, describe what you think it means.

9. As an individual television viewer, do you *need* images? If so, what show satisfies that need and why?

10. What does the term *other* mean to you? Find and describe an example of an "other" in a television show.

11. Describe some stereotypes that you observe on television. What shows do they appear on and what purpose do they serve?

12. Watch four hours of prime-time television on a weeknight (or daytime soap operas and talk shows) and identify the following:

    a. Who are the African American characters and what are their roles or positions?

    b. Who are the Hispanic Americans and what are their roles or positions?

    c. Who are the Asian Americans and what are their roles or positions?

    d. Who are the Middle Easterners and what are their roles or positions? Are any of the characters identified as Muslim?

Next, ask if their country of origin is identified (for example, Korea in the case of Asian Americans or Mexico in the case of Hispanic Americans). Are there ways that their race or ethnicity is important to the narrative? If so, describe the ways.

What racial and ethnic group do you belong to? How is your group represented on television? Does it affect you and your sense of identity?

13. Examine the roles of women on fiction and nonfiction television. Are any of the women represented as subordinate in ability to men? Are any of the men represented as subordinate in ability to women? Describe those who are. In work and/or romantic relationships, guess the relative ages of the women and the men. Describe the physical characteristics of the women and the men. Are there any differences in terms of cultural standards of attractiveness?

14. Look for the following groups as represented on television and ask (a) if the representation is positive or negative; and (b) if they are represented at all:

- Italian Americans
- Working-class people
- Middle Easterners—be specific if you can (Arab, Israeli, Iranian, Egyptian, etc.)
- Disabled people
- Russians
- Lawyers
- Irish
- Business professionals
- Middle-aged men and women
- Teachers
- Senior citizens
- Politicians

15. Select any other ethnic, age, or occupational group (farmers, musicians, children, and so on) that is represented that you wish to examine.

16. Select one of your collective memories that was represented on television before you were born. Do you have an image of it? If so, where did it come from?

SUGGESTED READINGS

Bogle, Donald. (2001). *Prime Time Blues: African Americans on Network Television.* New York, NY: Farrar, Straus and Giroux.

Dines, Gail, & Humez, Jean M. (Eds.). (2011). *Gender, Race, and Class in the Media* (3rd ed.). Los Angeles, CA: Sage.

Hall, Stuart. (1997). *Representation: Cultural Representations and Signifying Practices.* Thousand Oaks, CA: Sage.

Hunt, Darnell M. (2005). *Channeling Blackness: Studies on Television and Race in America.* New York, NY: Oxford University Press.

Lipsitz, George. (1990). *Time Passages: Collective Memory and American Popular Culture.* Minneapolis: University of Minnesota Press.

Webb, Jen. (2009). *Understanding Representation.* Los Angeles, CA: Sage.

Wykes, Maggie, & Gunter, Barrie. (2005). *The Media and Body Image: If Looks Could Kill.* Thousand Oaks, CA: Sage.

CHAPTER 8

Postmodernism

It's PoMo! . . . Post modern. . . . All right, weird for the sake of being weird.

—Moe Szyslak *(The Simpsons)*

INTRODUCTION

You sit down in front of your television set to watch an episode of *The Office* in which the characters look into the camera to comment on a situation. You have your laptop computer on your lap, for you are writing a paper, and you are also texting a friend on your cell phone. Then you go online and talk to friends on Google Chat while looking at Facebook to see what is new, and then you decide to look at some clips of television shows on websites and download some music too. All the while, *The Office* is on the television set. How much of the show have you absorbed? You are multitasking, of course, and you can do it because technology enables you to do so. You can watch every television program, news report, listen to music, and communicate with "friends" on Facebook wherever you are. We live in an age of a continuous flow of images, instantaneous communication, and information saturation. It seems as if everything is "here and now." It seems as if there is an acceleration of the pace of living and a great deal of uncertainty in life. Emerging systems of communication have created virtual communities, new identities and interactions, and new vocabulary, for example *tweet* or *blog*. Some would say that this is the **postmodern** age. What does that mean?

Postmodernism is a controversial term that is often used to describe the style and aesthetics of contemporary television as well as architecture, the arts, and fashion. Postmodernism suggests that culture has undergone a transformation due in part to the proliferation of virtual reality–type images and discourses generated by technological developments—satellite and cable television, satellite radio, digital video recording devices, digital electronics, advances in computer use, and the Internet. These technologies have produced a surplus of images and discourses that demand our attention. Postmodern theorists claim that consumers of images and discourses on television have developed "strategies of absorption as they are worked over by popular texts [that] involves the manipulation of the array by an increasingly sophisticated knowledge of the conditions of their production, circulation, and eventual reception" (Collins, 1992, p. 332).

Television critics argue over what postmodernism is and whether it is as prevalent as many writers contend. As a television critic, you will find it helpful to be acquainted with the term and to recognize the postmodern style if it exists in certain types of television programming. This chapter will define postmodernism, examine its roots and theories, and examine how it is manifested in television.

Postmodern theorists believe that the inundation of new technologies has influenced a postmodern society. Lili Berko wrote, "We find ourselves confronted with an image of a postmodern terrain whose geographic boundaries are less determined by physical structures than they are by the scope of the electronic signals emitted via the confluence of video and computational technologies" (Berko, 1994, p. 228). French theorists Jean Baudrillard and Jean-François Lyotard have claimed that the new media created by technology have produced a new social formation with an overload of information and images that have changed how we experience space and time. Certainly, new technologies have enlarged our world. Postmodern theorists describe contemporary life as permeated with consumerism, materialism, and multinationalism. Lyotard wrote, "One listens to reggae, watches a western [movie], eats McDonald's for lunch and local cuisine for dinner, wears Paris perfume in Tokyo, and 'retro' clothes in Hong Kong" (Gitlin, 1998, p. 60). Lyotard and other postmodern theorists are discussed later in this chapter. The new social formation that these critics describe is encapsulated in the term *postmodern* that must now be defined, even though a common definition is almost impossible.

POSTMODERNISM DEFINED

Post means after or beyond, thus postmodernism means beyond modernism. Therefore, let us first look at the definition of modernism. Modernism is characterized as a rejection of realist representation and was thus "a move away from the 19th century's 'objective' depiction of the world to various forms of abstraction and symbolism that emphasized subjective inward consciousness" (Collins, 1992, p. 329). Modernism can be traced back to the Middle Ages, according to philosophers Steven Best and Douglas Kellner, when philosophers such as René Descartes stated his preference for reason and thought as sources of knowledge and progress. Modernism was also associated with industrialization, with the "world view . . . that reality is ordered according to laws that the human intelligence can grasp" (Best & Kellner, 1991, p. 9).

> A postmodern joke: Descartes is on an airplane and the flight attendant asks if he would like something to drink. Descartes says, "I think not" and he disappears.

The *post* prefix, according to Best and Kellner:

signifies an active rupture with what preceded it . . . this rupture can be interpreted positively as a liberation from old constraining and oppressive conditions and as an affirmation of new developments, a moving into new terrains, a forging of new discourses and ideas. . . . On the other hand, the "post" in postmodern also signifies a dependence on, a continuity with, that which it follows, leading some critics to conceptualize the postmodern as merely an intensification of the modern, . . . a new "face of modernity," or a postmodern development within modernity. . . . The discourses of the postmodern therefore presuppose a sense of an ending, the advent of something new, and the demand that we must develop new categories, theories, and methods to explore and conceptualize this novum, this novel social and cultural situation. (Best & Kellner, 1991, pp. 29–30)

Modernism produced bold, new forms of expression in abstract art; functional, machine-inspired architecture; and stream of consciousness literature, but it was also characterized by feelings of hope and anxiety, skepticism, elitism, and the inevitability of human progress. Modernist values were seriousness, purity, reason, and individuality.

There are many definitions of postmodernism, a characteristic of postmodernism itself, but basically, as it relates to television, it refers to a stylistic and aesthetic change in the arts and culture (Casey et al., 2002). Postmodernism breaks down the traditions of modernism, for it means that a body of work is nonlinear, playful, and assembled from various other forms, including modernism, that construct an eclectic pastiche, composed of parts borrowed from other works to create a medley of various ingredients mixed together. Fredric Jameson described a pastiche as

the imitation of a peculiar or unique style, the wearing of a stylistic mask, speech in a dead language; but it is a neutral practice of such mimicry, without parody's ulterior motive, without the satirical impulse, without laughter, without that still latent feeling that there exists something normal compared to that which is being imitated is rather comic. (Jameson, 1993, p. 16)

Boundaries of style and historical periods are blurred. Postmodernism plays with forms of the past, irony, cynicism, and commercialism, as well as with cultural stereotypes. Words like *ephemeral, ambiguity, multiplicity, discontinuity, contradiction, unfinished, fragmentation, superficial, uncertainty, intertextuality,* and *irony* are used to describe postmodernism. Postmodernism resists authority, defends the Other, emphasizes the global and pluralism, is free from rules, and appears to be hyperreal.

Postmodern architecture scorns traditional forms while copying and combining them. Charles Jencks, an architect whose book *What Is Post-Modernism?* includes some of the clearest explanations, defined postmodernism as "double-coding: the combination of Modern techniques with something else (usually traditional building) in order for architecture to communicate with the public and a concerned minority, usually other architects" (Jencks, 1989, p. 14). Jencks emphasized that postmodern architecture is based on new techniques and old patterns, thus keeping some of the modern sensibility. The double-coding is the continuation of modernism and its transcendence. There is also an inherent intention in the work, such as irony, parody, displacement, complexity, eclecticism, or realism. Prominent examples of postmodern architecture combine steel and glass with curved and asymmetrical façades and mixed materials and often have forms copied from Classical Greek architecture or ancient Egyptian style. The form of the Acropolis, the Pantheon, or a pyramid may be copied but in contemporary materials. My favorite example of postmodern architecture is PPG (Pittsburgh Paint Glass) Place in Pittsburgh, Pennsylvania. It has a glass façade, but its spires mimic the neo-Gothic style. Its outline mirrors the Houses of Parliament in London. It is a blend of the past and present, the old and the new, that can be recognized by the public. A more complete definition has been given by Denis McQuail (2010):

> Postmodernism is a cultural theory "that underwrites the view that the 'age of ideology' is over along with the 'industrial society' and its massive forms of social organization and control and dedication to rationality. Instead we are living in an era of unstructured diversity, uncertainty, contradictions, open-ended creativity and individual freedom from imposed rules and social constraint. It has become fashionable to discern the exuberant growth of mass media forms as the essence of popular postmodern culture. Neither the material conditions of contemporary society nor forms of organization of mass media exhibit clear signs of postmodernism. Much as with earlier critical cultural theory, postmodern thinking can support divergent optimistic and pessimistic outlooks." (p. 566)

McQuail's definition makes sense, for although there are many signs of postmodernism in society, it is not altogether clear to what extent it has permeated society. As indicated earlier, there are ample opportunities to engage in postmodern-type activities, but it is up to us to choose. Postmodernism embraces openness, diversity, recognition of cultural differences, and discourse about experiences. Recognition by the public allows participation; thus postmodernism bridges the gap between creator and audience. The postmodern style requires its audience to know what it mimics or parodies. This is also true in television.

POSTMODERN TELEVISION

Quite a few academic scholars believe that postmodernism exists on television. According to Jack Solomon:

> Postmodernism represents a new mode of perception: by radio, cinema, and most importantly, by TV. Viewing the world as a television camera views it, the postmodern eye reduces the length and breadth of experience to a two-dimensional spectacle, to a carnival of arresting images and seductive surfaces. . . . the postmodern experience is best described as a perceptual montage. (Solomon, 1998, p. 50)

Jonathan Bignell wrote that postmodernism is characterized in television as "self-conscious play with the conventions of television. . . . The pleasure of viewing programmes and advertisements . . . derives from the viewer's recognition of this play" (Bignell, 2004, p. 162). Bignell quoted Robin Nelson, who suggested, "Postmodern texts might be summarily characterized by a formal openness, a strategic refusal to close down meaning. They create space for play between discourses, allegedly empowering the reader to negotiate or construct her own meanings" (Bignell, 2004, p. 163).

Television's adaptability and versatility enables borrowing and copying from other media, to create a pastiche of different elements. Postmodern television includes enjoyment derived from mixing up the conventions of various genres and programs. Hybrid genres (see Chapter 5, "Television Genres") such as the docudrama or the dramedy have become commonplace on television. Caren Deming wrote,

> [television] flaunts its fluidity where genre is concerned. Although most individual episodes of any series are formulaic by design, television is determinedly recombinate at the series level. In part, television's generic hybridism is attributable to the paradoxes built into its needs to be familiar and centrist while claiming to cut away at the edges—simultaneously exercising its penchants for recycling and topicality, nostalgia and immediacy. . . . Stars appear as themselves in narratives or in commercials and characters morph into hawkers with ease. Such fluidities combine with other postmodernist characteristics. (Deming, 2005, p. 133)

Intertextuality (references to other texts, genres, discourses, themes, or other media as described in Chapter 4) is part of the play and thus the enjoyment. Intertextuality, which includes allusions to other television programs, films from the past, actors, and news events, is a regular feature in many television programs. Viewer enjoyment of a particular text can be informed by recognition of experience with other texts. It is the interconnection of meanings across different media texts as well as connections between meanings. Intertextuality is symptomatic of self-reflexivity, a characteristic of postmodernism. Television calls attention to itself with an awareness that it is a production, something constructed and consumed. It calls to the viewer to participate in the construction. Intertextual references invite viewers to play with a television program through interactions that give them pleasure from their recognition of the referents.

The openness of postmodern television creates an opportunity for play between and among different texts. This has the potential to give the viewer pleasure, as defined in Chapter 6, and allows the viewer to negotiate or construct various meanings (polysemy) or perhaps no meaning at all. It also provides the viewer with knowledge of his or her own fragmented and fluid identity. Viewers may take a television program at face value, or they may attempt to make sense from the fragments of narrative, characterization, and intertextuality and enjoy the program's irony. *South Park* is known for its parody of cultural stereotypes of race, gender, age, body, and size. Its characters may be racist and sexist, thus it offends everyone while undermining the offense (Barker, 2008, p. 205). *The Simpsons* is characterized by its refusal to accept the norms of situation comedy. Its narrative is often fragmented; the characters defy authority; and, of course, there is an abundance of intertextual reference.

Cable and satellite television enable viewers to watch television programs made over the last six decades, but sometimes they are manipulated in the postmodern style. The Nickelodeon channel broadcasts television shows from the past with campy voice-overs, humorous graphics, and new editing, making new parodies out of old programs. *The Daily Show* parodies the news with commentaries on actual news footage that has been edited for the program. Television circulates "a collage of stitched together images that is core to post-modern style" (Barker, 2008, p. 203). Stars from one show appear on another, for example, Jon Hamm, who plays the moody Don Draper on *Mad Men,* makes guest appearances as a funny doctor who lives in Tina Fey's apartment building in *30 Rock*. Television creates unexpected associations, as viewers also create associations with channel zapping and fast-forwarding. When we watch shows online, we can pick and choose parts of shows through clips and leave out the parts we find uninteresting. The television clips online on the program's website are fragmented into small morsels to suit our attention span.

Not all television is postmodern, for tight programming schedules and time allotted for commercials force timed segments. Situation comedies typically have some narrative resolution as do one-time dramas. However, dramatic series, soap operas, and reality shows that do not have immediate resolution hold the viewer in suspension in a style that could be considered somewhat postmodern. Viewers have to wait until next time—and that could be a different day and time, a lapse of a week or several weeks, or the next television season—to learn the outcome. Season finale cliffhangers make the viewers wait four to five months to find out who got shot or killed, who got elected, and who returned to a relationship. Yet, the viewers are able to resume with the program whenever it returns. Meanwhile, heavy promotions for these upcoming programs tantalize the viewers, urging them to come back to find out what happens next.

Not only do technological innovations bombard viewers with an overabundance of images and discourses, but technological developments also give viewers more control over what they watch on television. The remote control allows them to switch channels at will, creating their own juxtapositions. With digital video recorders, people are no longer bound to television schedules. They can watch what they want, when they want to, and they can zap the commercials, thus compressing the time it takes to watch a television show. If they want to review a scene, they can go back to it, or they can fast-forward through scenes they do not want to watch. DVD sales of entire seasons of television programs enable people to watch television in episodic fashion. Some people will watch an entire season of a television series in a single weekend.

MTV

Any treatment of postmodern television has to include MTV, for it has been the perfect example of visual disorder, exaggeration, and pastiche. John Fiske wrote that MTV is television's "only original art form. . . . MTV at its most typical, most televisual [is a] mosaic of fragments: not sense but sensation. Energy, speed, image, youth, illusion, volume, vision, senses, not sense" (Fiske, 1998, pp. 167 & 171). Initially, MTV consisted of short music videos that sometimes told a story with multiple, flashing images enhanced by special effects and accompanied by a soundtrack. The term "video jockey," a person who conducts a television program of recorded music interspersed with chatter, jokes, and commercials, became a new word in our vocabulary. MTV blurs the boundaries between the videos and the advertising that provides 90% of its financing. The distinction between music video and advertising is broken down on MTV. According to Peter Wollen,

> Music videos are an advertising vehicle, promoting the sale of records. In fact, MTV is often credited with the resurgence of the fortunes of the music industry in the United States. In form, too, music videos have much in common with the more sophisticated ads and there has also been a rapid crossover between the two. (Wollen, 1997, p. 230)

MTV gave advertisers a place to be cool while reaching the desirable youth demographic. According to Beth Broday of Eastman Kodak, "Once MTV legitimized videos as programming with an inherent value, it became a business and an incomparable marketing tool for the record company" ("The Art of the Music Video," 1997, p. 2).

Music video's signature style is compressed storytelling—rapid editing, extreme camera angles, slow motion, freeze-frame, repetition, and emphasis on images in a video style. It relies heavily on the breakdown of objective reality. The shape and clothing of a person or place may change several times within a single video clip. Animation and graphic images morph into shots of real people. It is eclectic and fragmented, appropriating images from old films, commercials, newsreels, modern art, fashion, and animation. It takes these intertextual images and reassembles them in nonlinear fashion with little regard for coherence. Liz Friedlander, a music video director, said that she and her colleagues in the industry are open to new insights and the unexpected. She offered a postmodern description for her work: "People in music video just want to mess things up and make them imperfect" ("The Art of the Music Video," 1997, p. 7).

Jack Solomon said, "In music video, "the look is everything: character, the spirit that lives beneath the skin, is nothing. Images are put on and taken off at will, each new role unencumbered by the need for a coherent plot" (Solomon, 1998, p. 48). Pop celebrities may seem to have no self-identity but instead frequently change their identities, for example, Madonna, who has redefined herself over and over, and Lady Gaga, who changes her hair and make-up so often that she is sometimes unrecognizable. Solomon quoted Pat Aufderheide's essay "Music Videos: The Look of the Sound":

> Music videos have no heroes, because they do not feature individuals in the sense that plot-driven entertainment does. Music video offers unadulterated celebrity. The human beings do not play characters but bold and connotative icons. . . . [Rock-video stars play act as] sailors, thugs, gang members, gangsters, prostitutes, nightclub performers, goddesses, temptresses, and servants. [Their images are] drawn not from life or even myth, but from old movies, ads, and other pop culture clichés. (Solomon, 1998, pp. 48–49)

Kenneth J. Gergen, a professor of psychology, saw MTV as the ultimate breakdown of reason. In his book *The Saturated Self: Dilemmas of Identity in Contemporary Life,* he wrote that MTV

> has carried the postmodern breakdown of narrative rationality to its furthest extreme. It relies heavily on the breakdown of objective reality. The shape or identity of an object or person may change several times within a given video clip, and what appears to be the reality of a photographed world may be revealed to be a drawing. (Gergen, 1991, p. 133)

Ann Kaplan, a prolific author on the subject of MTV, regarded MTV as postmodern because rock videos "abandon the usual binary oppositions on which dominant culture depends . . . the oppositions that are abandoned are between high and low culture, masculine and feminine, past, present, and future, private and public, verbal and visual, realism and anti-realism" (Kaplan, 1998, pp. 35–36). She also wrote that the strategies of MTV must be considered within a profit-making institution. "Its mixture of texts, inclusion of ads, commentaries, displays; the central relationship of programming to the sponsors, whose own texts, the ads, are the real TV texts" (Kaplan, 1998, p. 34).

MTV Reinvented

In true postmodern style, MTV reinvented itself. Music videos are now an Internet-based phenomenon, so MTV changed to scripted television series and reality shows. Tony DiSanto, the network's president of programming, said, "MTV is always evolving for the next generation of youth. We always want to do the unexpected and try new things" (Champagne, 2010, p. 56). David Janollari, MTV's executive vice president of scripted series, said he "jumped onto a moving train" when he joined MTV. "Everytime we read a script or hear a pitch, we think, 'Is this unique enough to be branded MTV? Does this have the attitude, the voice and the relevance that MTV shows have always had?' The litmus test is, if you can see it anywhere else, it's probably not right for us" (Champagne, p. 56).

MTV's reality show *Jersey Shore* has been a tremendous success. Its other reality shows, *Teen Mom* and *16 and Pregnant,* have a scared-straight approach. Its scripted show *Skins,* a racy adaptation of a British series, began in January 2011, attracting 3.3 million viewers with 2.7 of them in the core demographic of 12 to 34 years old. It is about nine suburban teenagers and is filled with risqué scenes of nudity, sexual activity, alcohol, and drug use. It has been accused of being pornography and has lost several of its sponsors. Consequently, MTV executives ordered upcoming episodes to be edited.

Photo 8.1   A scene from MTV's reality show *Jersey Shore.*

MTV'S Influences

The MTV music video model influenced the style of some television dramas that use handheld cameras to produce choppy images, rapid editing, contrasting images, and special effects. Characters in situation comedies sometimes talk into the camera, formerly a taboo in television fiction. Dramatic series often have multiple plots with a half dozen stories running at once and fragmented characters who come and go. Investigative news programs have elements of tabloid newspapers. Docudramas blur fact and fiction. David Letterman throws pencils at the camera, walks around backstage during his show *Late Night With David Letterman,* and on the set, the directors and the camera operators and their equipment are often visible. Songs are used as musical accents and subtexts in *Grey's Anatomy, Rescue Me, Parenthood,* and *CSI.* Many television commercials have postmodern features with multiple images crammed into 15 or 30 seconds, lack of continuity, partial stories, and tangential scenes interspersed and interwoven together. Not all television programs or commercials have postmodern traits, but as a television critic you will recognize them when they are present.

In October 2010 the Cosmopolitan, a hotel in Las Vegas, launched a 60-second postmodern commercial. It opens with a close-up on a man's back holding a large silver tray while quiet, pulsating music plays. The camera moves over his head to a room filled with people in evening clothes around a sumptuous buffet, then to a close-up of a woman licking her plate clean. Next there is a close-up of a woman's high-heeled shoe on the back of another woman in a gown. A young man and a woman dance. Two photographers have their cameras ready. A bellhop goes down the hall in his undershorts. He later walks through water in a pool to deliver food to a woman sitting on a pad. An older couple dances. A large number of white kittens run up the stairs; the elevator door opens to reveal white kittens, puppies, and bunnies. A reclining woman holds baby chicks; more white puppies run up the stairs; a fawn stands in the hallway. There is a close-up of the fawn's head. The photographers look at a line of ducklings walking by. A woman lets a single white rabbit in a room, then turns around to look at the camera while the words "Just the right amount of wrong" appear on the screen. You can watch this commercial online.

POSTMODERN THEORIES

Kaplan regards postmodernism as a theoretical and critical concept (Kaplan,1998, p. 32). She wrote "the postmodern moment is a break initiated by modernism. . . . The break that modernism initiated is at once fulfilled with the development of recent electronic technologies and, at the same time, drastically altered in the process so as to become 'postmodern'" (Kaplan, 1993, p. 1).

Best and Kellner (1991) traced the development of the use of the term *postmodern* to the 1940s and 1950s, when it was used to describe new forms of poetry and architecture. They said that the term was not used to describe that which opposed or came after modernism until the 1960s and 1970s. The 1960s was a time in which new art forms emerged—light shows, mixed media, rock concerts, and Andy Warhol's pop art. (Andy Warhol is best known for painting a Campbell's soup can and multiple images of Marilyn Monroe and Jackie Kennedy. His work reflects the overpowering influence of the many images in society.) The boundaries of low and high culture began to be broken down. In the 1970s, books about the postmodern condition began to appear. Postmodern theorists criticized modernism for its rationalism, causality, and the search for universal themes. These theorists preferred micro or localized theories, fragmentation, multiplicity, and ambiguity. In 1976, sociologist Daniel Bell wrote *The Cultural Contradictions of Capitalism,* in which he developed the theme that the modern era was coming to an end. His view of a postmodern age was:

> the unleashing of instinct, impulse, and will . . . an extension of the rebellious, anti-bourgeois, antinomic and hedonistic impulses. . . . [It] is thus a product of the application of modernist revolts to everyday life, the extension and living out of a rebellious, hyperindividualist, hedonist lifestyle. . . . a radical assault on tradition which is fuelled by an aggressive narcissism that is in profound contradiction with the bureaucratic, technocratic, and organizational imperatives of the capitalist economy and democratic polity. (Best & Kellner, 1991, p. 13)

As rapid changes in social and economic life occurred, they were paralleled by dramatic changes in social theory, especially in France. Political upheavals such as the student strikes in France in 1968, according to Best and Kellner, called for a break from the institutions and politics of the past and brought about developments of postmodern theory. The students in France had called for a change in the university system, its bureaucracy, conformity, and disciplines that they said had no relevance to reality. As a result, Michel Foucault and others generated theories that joined the connections between power and knowledge. Foucault's critique of modernism and humanism made him a major source of postmodern thought. He developed the theme that power and knowledge created new forms of domination. Yet, Foucault was not a postmodernist; rather, his work reflects premodern, modern, and postmodern perspectives (Best & Kellner, 1991). His hostility to modernism is the most obvious postmodern feature of his work. He championed "the amazing efficacy of discontinuous, particular and local criticism" (Best & Kellner, 1991, p. 38).

Other theorists resisted the idea of unified theories, thus many of the postmodern theories that emerged were conflicting and diverse. Because of political upheavals around the world, postmodern theorists were attracted to such political movements as feminism, gay rights, and environmentalism. Their theories tended to

> map in fragments and to ignore the more systemic features and relations of social structure that were the focus of modern social theory. . . . Postmodern theorists do not do social theory *per se,* but rather eclectically combine fragments of sociological analysis, literary and cultural readings, historical theorizations, and philosophical critiques. (Best & Kellner, 1991, p. 259)

Berko wrote that postmodern theories converge around three major philosophical categories: subjectivity, representation, and the transcendental. The subject is seen as unclear, conflicted, and moving about like a nomad. Identity is confused and goes through many changes. Representation, regarded as standing in for reality, has been replaced by simulation and digitizing. Narratives that transcend difficulties and provide culture with a framework for comprehending the world have been rejected. In fact, many postmodern theorists claim there are no narratives anymore. Berko wrote, "The differences among the theorists of the postmodern become manifest in their attitudes toward these philosophical categories; one either celebrates or laments the 'supposed' death of the subject, of representation and/or the transcendental" (Berko, 1994, p. 229). She quoted Hal Foster, who adds another position on postmodernism: "In cultural politics today, a basic opposition exists between a postmodernism which seeks to deconstruct modernism and resist the status quo and a postmodernism which repudiates the former to celebrate the latter: a postmodernism of resistance and a postmodernism of reaction" (Berko, 1994, p. 229).

Lyotard, in an article that he wrote for the *Postmodern Reader,* explained his position on postmodernism as a state that can be recognized only after the event because "being postmodern is a momentary condition that lasts for a short time. The postmodern is not an epoch or period but it is a characteristic of how cultural products are perceived" (Bignell, 2004, pp. 167–168). Lyotard approved of postmodernism, according to Bignell, because "he values things which are hard to categorise and hard to judge. Once something can be explained, judged and categorized Lyotard believes that its creative challenge and artistic interest are lost" (Bignell, 2004, p. 168). Lyotard rejected narrative because it can be controlled and ordered by criteria for judgment. He preferred abstract art because it presents something that is unpresentable.

Jean Baudrillard, a French sociologist, is considered one of the most high-profile postmodern theorists (Best & Kellner, 1991). His work is complex and far-reaching, but essentially Baudrillard claims that modernism, dominated by production, industrial capitalism, and a political economy, is dead and that a new era of postmodernism dominated by simulations and new forms of technology, culture, and society has emerged. The simulations take on a life of their own in this new epoch. Baudrillard wrote about television, in which he said the image of the doctor (the simulated doctor) is sometimes taken for the real doctor, and the image of the lawyer on television is taken for the real lawyer. This he calls "hyperreality," a blurring of distinctions between the real and the unreal. The prefix "hyper" means that it is more real than real. He said that the lifestyle described in magazines has replaced the actual lifestyles of people. In other words, the image becomes that which determines the real. In his postmodern landscape, the boundaries between entertainment and information, between politics and images, implode. This is Baudrillard's theory of implosion—images have replaced reality. (See Best & Kellner, 1991, pp. 111–122.) Yet, Baudrillard described television as a

> pure noise and a black hole where all meaning and messages are absorbed in the whirlpool and kaleidoscope of the incessant dissemination of images and information to the point of total saturation, where meaning is dissolved and only the fascination of discrete images glow and flicker in a mediascape within which no image any longer has any discernible effects. (Kellner, 2005, p. 42)

Kellner summarized,

> On the Baudrillardian view, the proliferating velocity and quantity of images produces a mindscreen where images fly by with such rapidity that they lose any signifying function, referring only to other images ad infinitum, and where eventually the multiplication of images produces such saturation, apathy, and indifference that the tele-spectator is lost forever in a fragmentary fun house of mirrors in the infinite play of superfluous, meaningless images. (Kellner, 2005, p. 42)

After devoting an entire book to postmodern theory, Best and Kellner concluded that postmodern theory is too abstract and lacks concrete, empirical and sociohistorical analysis (Best & Kellner, 1991). They did, however, recognize three different responses to the claim that we are living in a postmodern era: (1) there has been a rupture with modernism, and we are in a totally new era that requires new theories; (2) there is no rupture with modernism, for there are continuities between the modern and the present time; and (3) there is an argument for a dialogue between continuity and discontinuity with theories to explain the breaks between them (Best & Kellner, 1991).

With regard to television, the third option is probably the most acceptable. Television certainly has continuity, but it also has discontinuity. That is why Stuart Cunningham wrote that television is both modern and postmodern.

> Television in its traditional broadcast form achieves effective cross-demographic communication because of its continuing modernist role. It is also a major postmodern form, embodying disjunctive aesthetics, clashes of the superficial and the serious, and pervasive image construction that "threatens" to become constitutive of reality rather than merely reflective of it. Within the accepted understanding of television's role as a provider of information and entertainment, is its postmodern provision of contemporary cultural and DIY [do-it-yourself] citizenship—the construction of selves, semiotic self-determination and functional media literacy. (Cunningham, 2005, pp. 205–206)

Postmodern theories essentially deal with the surface, the immediate, the fragmented, and the abstract. They tend to contradict one another, thus perplexing us as we try to understand them. Yet, they have provided us with different ways of thinking about culture and about television. Although postmodern theorists reject the notion of critiquing television with a set of standards, they have, perhaps inadvertently, given us a set of categories to look for if an instance of television is to be called postmodern.

SUMMARY

There are many "posts" in the literature of culture, for example, post-structuralism, post-colonialism, post-Communism, post-industrialism, post-Marxism, post-humanism, and post-feminism, but the "post" that has been most often applied to television is postmodernism. It has come to mean a sense of rupture, the passing of the old and the advent of the new.

We live in an age of high technology, with multiple digital devices that have enabled us to experience wider communications and alternate realities. The way in which we view and use television has changed accordingly.

Basically, postmodernism is about the stylistic and aesthetic changes in the arts and culture and is notable in some television programs. A television program or commercial that is nonlinear, playful, and assembled from various other forms, including modernism, and constructs an eclectic pastiche can be considered postmodern. These features are especially prevalent in music videos that can be seen online. MTV, once the music video network, has reinvented itself and is now known for scripted and reality shows with questionable taste. The former MTV style has influenced other programming and advertising.

Not only is postmodernism *in* television programs, but it also manifests itself in the way viewers *watch* television using remote controls, recording devices, and online television clips to create their own programming. Yet, it should be recognized that only some television is postmodern. Many programs have linear, straightforward narratives and many viewers watch programs at the time they are scheduled and see all the commercials. It is important, however, that you as a television critic not only recognize the differences between the modern and postmodern on television but also how they overlap.

EXERCISES

1. How many digital devices do you own? In what ways have they changed your life? Do you watch television differently than you did 2 or 3 years ago? Do you think that the programming on television has changed in the past 2 or 3 years? If so, how?

2. Do you multitask? How many things can you do at once? How does it affect your attention span?

3. Do you blog? If so, do you regard your blog as narrative? If you do not blog, then read someone else's blog and determine if it is a narrative.

4. Watch a television situation comedy or a late-night talk show to find self-reflexive instances in which the production itself is revealed.

5. Record some television programs and then construct a postmodern pastiche from parts of the recording. Can you do this without constructing a narrative?

6. To what extent do you rely on reason and universal theories? To what extent have you found reason and general theories prevalent in your education?

7. Other than television, what experiences in your life could be considered postmodern?

8. Watch a television event that has no meaning at all. Describe your reaction to it. Does it give you pleasure? If so, explain.

9. Locate an example of a television program that has an overlap of the modern and the postmodern. Describe it in your own words.

10. Watch a show (reality or scripted) on MTV for an hour. Is it unique from shows on other networks?

11. Look for influences of music videos in another television program or commercial and describe it.

12. How does the remote control or recording device give you control over television?

SUGGESTED READINGS

Berger, Arthur A. (Ed.). (1998). *The Postmodern Presence: Readings on Post-modernism in American Culture and Society.* Walnut Creek, CA: Altamira Press.

Best, Steven, & Kellner, Douglas. (1991). *Postmodern Theory: Critical Interrogations.* New York, NY: Guilford Press.

Brooker, Peter, & Brooker, Will (Eds.). (1997). *Postmodern After-Images: A Reader in Film, Television and Video.* London, England: Arnold.

Jencks, Charles. (1989). *What Is Post-Modernism?* (3rd ed.). London, England: St. Martin's Press.

Kaplan, E. Ann. (1993). *Postmodernism and Its Discontents.* London, England: Verso.

Sim, Stuart. (Ed.). (2011). *The Routledge Companion to Postmodernism* (3rd ed.). London: Routledge.

PART IV

Critical Applications

CHAPTER 9

Guidelines for Television Criticism

INTRODUCTION

Now that you understand the various aspects of television as a business, production proce-dures, television style, narrative, genre, elements of rhetoric and cultural studies, represen-tation, and postmodernism, you are ready to do an in-depth analysis of a television program or an episode from a series. Whether you select fiction or nonfiction program-ming is entirely up to you. Select a program that you can record or watch online and will not mind viewing several times because you will need to examine several aspects of it. Select a program that you want to question or one with which you are familiar. As stated in Chapter 1, it is perfectly acceptable to analyze a favorite program or one that suits your interests and tastes. Your goals are to understand the various elements of a television pro-gram, to analyze it, to interpret possible meanings, to judge the quality of the program, and to communicate your assessment in writing.

This chapter brings together the elements of the previous chapters into eight sections: (1) critical orientation, (2) story and genre, (3) organization, (4) demographics, (5) context, (6) the look of the program and its codes, (7) analysis, and (8) judgment. Each category includes questions that you can ask about a television program. Depending on what you want to know about the program, you can select a few or all of the categories. Not all the questions will be relevant to the program you have selected, so you can choose the ques-tions that are most pertinent. The questions are necessarily general, thus you can tailor them to fit the elements of the program you have chosen and the intent of your criticism.

To use the eight categories of questions in this chapter, the television critic needs to be familiar with the contents of the previous eight chapters of this book. I have used the ideas, theories, and methods of the previous chapters to develop questions for analysis and criti-cism. Rather than repeat unnecessarily, I have assumed that you have read the previous chapters and have participated in the exercises at the end of each chapter.

You will not want to use all the questions in this chapter nor do you need to. I hope that you will pick and choose the questions that will be most useful to you as you conduct your analysis. The more you watch the program you have selected to critique, the more you will see.

CRITICAL ORIENTATION

After you have selected the television program you want to analyze, ask initially what you want to know about it. Assess how you react to it and make a list of those reactions, for example, laughter, fright, shock, anger, empathy, relaxation, boredom, tension, curiosity, and so on. If it is an episodic program, try to be aware of other episodes. You can check the program's website for episode summaries, clips from previous programs, the names of the characters, the cast, the characters' back stories, the production staff, production information, and possibly blogs by the writers, which may give you some insight into the motivation behind the script. The Academy of Television Arts & Sciences has a useful archive of interviews with directors, producers, actors, and other television personnel on its website—http://www.emmystvlegends.org. The easiest way to locate television programs' websites is to use a search engine such as Google or Yahoo. Each of the networks has its own site, for instance, nbc.com. If it is a series or specialty programming, you can check the Nielsen ratings on the Web. You can also read what other viewers say about the program on the website or on Facebook. Music playlists for most shows are available to listen to on the website. You can also purchase the music CDs in most cases. Also, you can purchase or check out available books about the program from the library, bookstore, or online booksellers. Check to see if the book is unauthorized or is the official companion to the show. Unauthorized books may not be accurate, although they may contain useful information. In the authorized books, you are likely to find interviews with the creators, the writers, the producers, the cast, and the consultants. You also may find episode summaries with names of guest actors, writers of particular episodes, and directors. Books such as *Ultimate CSI: Crime Scene Investigation* (Marrinan, 2006) and *House, M.D.: The Official Guide to the Hit Medical Drama* (Jackman, 2010) include glossaries of scientific terms used in the programs.

Here are some questions to ask for critical orientation.

1. What attracted you to this program?
2. Do you identify with any of the characters?
3. Does the program have a personality or an actor whom you enjoy watching?
4. Are there relationships in the program that you find intriguing?
5. What interests you about the story or the contents of the program?
6. Is the program novel in some way, especially in comparison to other television programs?
7. Is this a program that you are willing to take seriously and spend a lot of time with?
8. Do you talk to your friends about the program?

STORY AND GENRE

Now that you have selected a program to analyze, watch it in its entirety and identify its genre. A very important question to ask at this stage is "How is the story told?" For most television narratives, there is deferred gratification and viewer anticipation. The critic asks how these factors occur.

For example, the television series *Monk,* which ran for nine seasons on USA Network, could be considered a hybrid genre, for although it is mostly about solving crime, it also has some comedy in it. (Episodes of *Monk* can be seen on the television channel Sleuth or online at http://www.usanetwork.com/series/monk.) As a crime show, it featured San Francisco police officers and a special detective named Adrian Monk. It was 60 minutes in length and had an ensemble cast. It featured a new crime and its solution each week. As a comedy, it sometimes provoked laughter in a workplace setting. The comedy came mainly from the character of Monk, expertly played by Emmy award–winning Tony Shalhoub, who suffers from the obsessive–compulsive disorder brought on by the murder of his wife. Monk is afraid of germs, crowds, and disorder. He is constantly putting things back in order, in straight lines. Although obsessive–compulsive disorder is a very serious condition, the comedy comes about because Monk constantly gets himself into situations that put him in crowds, get him dirty, and create disorder. The ensemble cast included a detective named Randy who always said and did dumb things. There is also an upbeat, jazzy song *(It's a Jungle Out There)* with the opening credits that suggests lightheartedness. The show, however, centered on Monk's uncanny ability to solve a crime. He is perceptive, very intelligent, and determined to track down the criminals. Thus, as an audience, we could expect to see how the clues come together to solve a crime, but we could also expect to be exposed to humor.

As a narrative, *Monk* followed the disequilibrium (lack)/equilibrium or enigma, delay, and resolution formula in linear fashion in four acts. In the episode "Mr. Monk Can't See," a fireman is killed in the fire station where Monk has brought 30 fire alarms to be tested, which is symptomatic of his obsessiveness–compulsiveness, for he uses all of them in just five rooms. The other firemen have gone to a five-alarm fire, thus the hero Monk is alone with the killer (the villain) who throws a chemical solution in his eyes and escapes. The lack is that Monk cannot see and consequently becomes very depressed. The enigma is twofold: Will the killer be caught? and Will Monk regain his eyesight? The delay is Monk's reluctance to work. To keep him active, the police captain, Leland Stottlemeyer, persuades Monk to help solve the crime. At the fire station, Monk touches the coat rack and discovers that there are five coats—but there were six when he was there earlier. His obsessive-compulsiveness reveals the first clue: the killer stole a fireman's coat so he could go back to the burning house to retrieve something he left there that would identify him. This leads the detectives to connect the five-alarm fire that killed a young woman to the murder of the fireman. In a filthy alley where the coat was thrown in a dumpster, Monk discovers that if he cannot see dirt, he is not afraid of it, and he is elated. This helps him regain his confidence and eventually solve the crime, creating a resolution. However, Monk realizes that the fireman's killer was also hired by another villain, Peter Breen, to kill the woman in the fire—thus another enigma is created with a delay while Monk tries to connect Breen to the killer. He does so and regains his sight in time to shoot Breen who has gone after him with a knife. The murders are solved; Monk's lack is removed; equilibrium is restored. The epilogue depicts a relaxed Monk reading a book in his living room. He looks at the picture of his departed wife and smiles, thus there is closure until the next episode.

As a hero, Monk has superior abilities that he uses to complete his task. Others cannot solve the crime without his help. His obsessive–compulsive disorder gives him insight into things that the other detectives do not have. Because he obsessively counts things, he discovers the missing coat. As an injured hero, he cannot see, but resourcefully uses his intelligence and perceptiveness to track down the villains. Although blinded, Monk is not a mythical prophet like the Greek Tiresias who prophesied the future; Monk is, however, modeled after the archetypal hero who faces obstruction (blindness) but overcomes it to complete a task.

Here are some questions that the critic can ask about the story and genre.

1. What are the conventions that make up the genre?

2. If the program appears to be a hybrid genre, what are the conventions of the genres that have been combined to make it a hybrid?

3. What are audience expectations of that particular genre?

4. What is the narrative progression? Describe the events.

5. How is time presented? Are the events successive? Do they go back and forth in time, or do events occur simultaneously?

6. What is the lack or disequilibrium, and how is the lack removed to restore equilibrium?

7. Is there a hero or heroine and a villain or villainy? How is the hero or villain represented? What are their actions, and how can their personalities be derived from their actions? Does the hero or villain have superior abilities?

8. How does conflict play out? Are there oppositions such as good and evil, legal and illegal, work and home, and/or masculine and feminine?

9. Is there closure or delay until the next episode? How is this presented?

10. Identify the stages of the hermeneutic code—enigma, delay, and resolution—that move the narrative forward. (The enigma engages viewer interest by presenting a riddle such as "who committed the crime?" and teases the viewer to guess what happens next. The delay stalls or postpones the solution to the enigma. A resolution to the enigma is finally found, but it may create another enigma.) Can you identify the enigma, delay, and resolution or several of them in the narrative?

11. Are there elements of older stories that are retold in the narrative?

12. Can you identify myths? Do the myths give lessons for social order?

13. Are there archetypes and rituals in the narrative? If so, how do they relate to the myths?

ORGANIZATION

Examine the parts of the program—the lead-in, the acts, the scenes, and the ending.

Opening Segment

An example from *NCIS* illustrates what you can look for in the opening. "Previously on *NCIS*" appears on the screen, followed by five scenes from the previous week and six opening scenes for the present episode. Director Vance announces that they are on high alert, after which Agents Gibbs and DiNozzo, guns at the ready, break into an apartment where they find two of their agents, one who is dead and the other injured. The third agent was taken, but Gibbs finds her in the trunk of the car. She is alive.

Photo 9.1 The *NCIS* team, agents McGee, Gibbs, David, and DiNozzo.

Then, in very rapid succession, the opening credits are presented in a collage of 35 shots in about 60 seconds. It is so rapid that you can miss some if you blink. The signature opening theme with repetitive beats plays throughout. They are as follows:

1. Gibbs is shown in a medium shot with both hands on a gun with a cityscape in the background. DiNozzo is in the lower right-hand corner.

2. Both Gibbs and DiNozzo point with their guns in front of a fire in the background.

3. A partial skull on the ground.

4. A yellow Mustang automobile swerving away from the flames of a fire.

5. In front of a building reflecting red flames, "NCIS" in white letters is on the screen beside two men with guns.

6. DiNozzo and McGee get out of a car on the left, while Gibbs and Ziva David get out on the right.

7. Two men have their backs to the camera; David in the forefront kicks aggressively at them.

8. Close-up of Gibbs pointing a gun at the camera.

9. Two images of Gibbs—on the left screen, he is grinning slightly; on the right, he is smiling. "Mark Harmon" appears on the lower screen.

10. DiNozzo in sunglasses in front of a light background. "Michael Weatherly" on the lower screen.

11. Two images of DiNozzo—on the left screen he is under water; on the right, a close-up of him smiling.

12. Gibbs looking through a rectangle on the right; a partial image of DiNozzo's face on the left. He is pointing a gun.

13. Two images of David—on the left, she is wearing a glamorous gown and holding a microphone; on the right, she is smiling. "Cote de Pablo" appears on the lower screen.

14. David, hair pulled back, points a gun. She looks as if she rushed through a door. A curtain is askew behind her.

15. Abby, dressed in black, looks at her image in the mirror. "Pauley Perrette" appears on the lower screen.

16. Medium close-up of Abby smiling.

17. Medium close-up of Abby in a black lace dress with a lace parasol.

18. Two images of McGee—on the left, he is in a tuxedo with earphones on his head; on the right, he is pointing a gun. "Sean Murray" appears on the lower screen.

19. McGee in full medium shot; he holds his thumbs in the air and jumps up. The name of the episode, "Pyramid," appears on the screen.

20. Director Vance comes through the door. "Rocky Carroll" appears on the lower screen.

21. Two images of Vance—on the left he has a slight smile; on the right he is on the telephone.

22. Dr. "Ducky" Mallard dressed in scrubs examines a specimen. "David McCallum" appears on the lower screen.

23. Ducky looks through a magnifying glass.

24. Ducky bends over a table and then swings a stick in the air.

25. A checkered orange and white cloth.

26. Flames in the street.

27. Several bones on the ground.

28. More flames.

29. Two large eyes.

30. Someone looking—extreme close-up on one eye. "Executive Producer Floyd Johnson" appears on lower screen.

31. A bulls-eye image.

32. Legs running (upper body cannot be seen).

33. Gibbs fighting with someone; he has a gun.

34. American flag fills the screen.

35. Long shot of road with Capitol Building at the end. It is Washington, D.C. "Created by Donald P. Bellisario and Don McGill" on the lower screen.

Certainly, this collage creates a mood of excitement, danger, and tension. It not only gives the actors' names, but it also reveals the hierarchy of the characters/actors, for it is very clear that Mark Harmon is the star of the series—his image appears eight times, and he appears to be in charge. Michael Weatherly appears six times, while the others appear two or three times. Credits are not given for the minor characters. Shot #6, early in the collage, shows the four agents—Gibbs, DiNozzo, McGee, and David—getting out of a car, guns pointing in unison. This tells us that they are a team. Images of flames and skeletal bones tell us that the team faces danger and death in their work. Because we never see the villains, there is a suggestion that the NCIS team always prevails. The contrast-images of the agents and the medical examiner looking relaxed and smiling in one shot and appearing tense and alert on the other suggests that they not only fight crime, but they also have moments of humor and enjoyment. The shots of the American flag and the United States Capitol building tell us that the value of patriotism and protection of our country is a prominent value. These shots also tell us that the locale is Washington, D.C. The whirlwind 35 shots give us a swift synopsis of the mood and characters of the show, and it is consistent with the narratives of *NCIS* throughout its long-running success as a procedural drama with comedic elements. The six opening scenes of the episode "Pyramid" hook the viewer into wanting to know who killed the NCIS agent and put the other agent in the trunk of the car.

Here are some questions to ask about the opening of the program.

1. Does the program have a collage of scenes from former shows at the beginning? ("Previously on . . .") If so, do they create a sense of tension and curiosity about what will happen next?

2. What happens in the lead-in, the beginning of the narrative that sets the scene? How does it entice the viewer to stay with the program?

3. Look and listen to the opening credits. What mood does the music create? Are there other sounds? Are the characters introduced to you in some context? Are the titles symbolic in their appearance, color, or placement?

4. What mood is evoked by the lead-in and by the credits?

The Structure of the Program

After the opening sequence, look at the structure of the show. If it is a 30-minute show, there should be two acts; if it is a 60-minute show, there should be four acts. Examine the acts and scenes for their structure. If there are commercials, note how the scenes before and after the commercials accommodate them. Here are some questions to ask about structure.

1. How do the scenes build on one another?

2. Does the show have a beginning, a middle, and an end?

3. Are there connectives between the scenes and between the acts?

4. If there are commercial breaks, how does the scene before the commercial end? How does the scene after the commercial begin? What gives the scenes continuity?

5. When the show comes to an end, is there closure or is the plot left open until next time?

6. What happens during the closing credits?

7. How are the previews for the next show presented? Are they immediately after the end of the program or after the commercials?

DEMOGRAPHICS

Demographics—the description of groups of people according to gender, age, race, ethnicity, occupation, income, educational level, and shared values—identify target audiences for television programs, sponsors, and advertisers. There are different ways to determine the demographics for a television program. The story line and the ways in which the contents and characters are incorporated into the program should offer strong hints about the potential audience. The day and time that the program is scheduled reveal general information about the intended audience. Information found on the Internet and in books about the program may include demographics. If there are commercials, the intended audience can be interpreted from them. Product placement within the narrative provides clues about the audience as well. Some of the questions you can ask to interpret demographics follow.

1. Whom does the program "hail"? In order to be a subject of the program, what is the expected social position of the audience?

2. To what demographic group is the subject of the program likely to appeal?

3. Are the characters and the actors who portray them young adults, children, middle-aged, or seniors? Are the characters supposed to be single? Members of families? Lower, middle, or upper class?

4. What are their domestic arrangements? Are the domestic arrangements traditional or nontraditional? What are their domestic surroundings like?

5. If there is product placement embedded in the program, what do the products tell you about the intended audience?

6. If there are commercials between the acts and scenes, at whom are the advertisements aimed?

7. Are the advertised products low, average, or high priced?

8. Are the advertised products for young or older adults, children, or pets?

9. Are the advertisements aimed at singles or couples, male or female, parents or grandparents?

10. Are food advertisements for home cooking, fast foods, or restaurants?

11. To what age groups are medical advertisements targeted?

12. Do the commercials specify certain interests or hobbies?

13. What lifestyles do the advertisements suggest?

CONTEXT

Context refers to what is happening in the world. Context embraces the concept of "ripped from the headlines," television stories that reflect actual events. Events can be serious such as threats of terrorism to places and people or they can be more lighthearted as in situation comedies. An episode of *Law & Order: Los Angeles* that appeared on May 16, 2011, mirrored the January 8, 2011, shooting of Representative Gabrielle Giffords and six others, including a child, at a political gathering outside a grocery store in Tucson, Arizona. The fictionalized account had a female state senator killed, not seriously injured, but the similarity to the real event was completely obvious. It even had a character who played a husband of a victim say, "Some right-wing crazy put a bulls-eye over an ad for the senator." This statement recalled a similar act by Sarah Palin when she put a bull's eye image on her website that targeted Democrat politicians that she wants to defeat. A *New York Times* article noted the similarity of the premise of *The Good Wife*—a political sex scandal—to real-life scandals in the lives of politicians such as Eliot Spitzer and Arnold Schwarzenegger. The same article also mentioned the show's episodes about a political candidate whose hiring of a nanny, an illegal immigrant, brought about her defeat and the use of social media in that political campaign (Bellafante, 2011).

Context also includes cultural values, social issues, trends, and fads. Intertextuality means that the television program contains references to other events, real or imagined, fiction or nonfiction. Here are some questions to ask about context.

1. How do the characters and events in the program reflect real people and events?

2. What societal and cultural values are represented in the television images and discourse?

3. Does the program reinforce or challenge mainstream societal and cultural values?

4. Are contextual and social issues clearly referenced or are they embedded in the plot?

5. What ordinary personal issues and attributes are recognizable?

6. Can viewers recognize their own fallibility in the characters in the program?

7. What evidence of fads and trends can be detected in the images and discourse?

8. Are there intertextual references to other media and/or real events and people?

9. Is it possible to specify an attributed intent or a message to the program?

10. What do you think is the expected reaction from the audience?

THE LOOK OF THE PROGRAM AND ITS CODES

How a program looks contributes to its believability and to the emotions that are conveyed, thus it has to do with the sets, the casting of characters, costumes, makeup, dialogue, physical movement, music, and sound effects. The look of a program is accomplished by camera work, lighting, editing, and direction. Here are some questions to ask about the look of a program and the reality and representation codes.

1. Are the events located in an indoor studio dressed to look like a home, an office, a hospital, coffee shop, bar, restaurant, or another place? Do events take place outdoors in a city, suburb, or rural area?

2. If you are looking at an indoor set, what makes it look realistic and natural? What objects, furniture, and other articles contribute to the look? What symbolism can you detect?

3. Are the colors bright or subdued? How do the colors contribute to the overall look of the set? Do the colors create mood?

4. How do the objects, furniture, and other articles reflect the characters in the set?

5. Are the objects, furniture, and other articles consistent with the time period of the program?

6. What elements provide an authentic look to outdoor scenes? Is there ambient sound?

7. Is there symbolism in the outdoor scenes?

8. Do the actors who were cast for the parts seem right for the characters they play? What personal and physical attributes of the actors contribute to the personalities of their characters on the program?

9. Do the characters have depth or just a few characteristics? Are there repetitive characteristics that reinforce a character's personality? Are any of the characters social types (easily recognizable people such as hippies, hillbillies, yuppies, Southern belles, gangsters, cowboys, maids, and so on)?

10. Do the costumes the actors wear seem realistic? How do the costumes reflect the characters' personalities?

11. Is the makeup natural? Does the makeup convey something about the character?

12. How do the physical actions of the characters reveal their personalities and/or motives?

13. Do the actors express their feelings through facial expressions? Can you observe what the character is feeling but not saying in the subtexts of facial expressions and physical movements? Does sound reinforce the subtext?

14. Does the dialogue sound realistic? What is included and what is left out in the dialogue that could engage the viewer to fill in information or speculation?

15. Is there music in the program other than in the opening credits? If so, what do you think is its intended purpose?

16. If there are sound effects, do they complement the dialogue and action? Can you attach meaning to the sound effects?

17. How does the camera work—the shots (close-up, medium, or long), movement, and angles—convey the characters' emotions, reactions, and personality characteristics? If it is a sports event, how does the camera work present it to the viewers?

18. When there are different shot lengths, how do they move the narrative or the event forward?

19. Do you see "elbows" shots? How do they enhance the story or character?

20. How are reaction shots used to play off characters against one another? Does the silent reaction of a character reveal a subtext?

21. How do the camera work and editing convey continuity or discontinuity in the narrative?

22. Is the lighting bright or dark? What effect does the lighting have on the mood of the program?

23. Are certain actors given special lighting? How can you tell this?

24. If you were the director, would you change any of the shots, lighting, or sound?

25. If you classify the program as postmodern, how would you justify this? In other words, what are the characteristics of the program that make it postmodern?

26. Does the program have a signature look? If so, describe it.

27. How significant is a musical theme?

28. How do the producers of the program get the viewer to believe that what is seen is really there?

ANALYSIS

To analyze means to take something apart; synthesis means to put it back together. As a television critic, you are taking a television program apart in order to understand and evaluate it. Your insights are developed from your knowledge of the critical process. Your interpretation will have given you a deeper understanding of a television program, and your readers will benefit from your work by seeing a television program in a different way. How you approach your analysis of the television program depends upon the questions that you ask of it. Because a television program is made for an audience, questions of analysis focus on audience involvement in the program and how that is accomplished. You will not want to use all the questions for analysis that follow, but they are listed here for your selection.

1. How are ideas developed in the program? How are the ideas adjusted to people and people to ideas?

2. Can you hear laughter from the studio audience? If so, is it likely to provoke laughter from the viewer? Is there any evidence of "canned" laughter from a laugh track?

3. What personal, cultural, and national values are inherent in the program or in certain characters and issues? How are the values communicated?

4. Are there moral lessons? How are they developed? Is the concept of *telos*—a life of moral excellence—evident in the program?

5. Are evidence and reasoning used to support a conclusion? Does the program ask the viewer to participate in the co-creation of reasoning?

6. What emotional appeals are present? How are they conveyed?

7. What shared substances can you detect that may lead the audience to identify with the program's characters, ideas, and lessons?

8. What are the qualities of the characters or real people such as news anchors, game show hosts, and participants on reality shows that are likely to create positive identification for audience members?

9. Can you attribute an intention to the program? If so, is it to persuade or inform?

10. How do you think the program may influence certain types of viewers? Does the program have the capability to influence attitudes, beliefs, values, and behaviors? Could it influence fashion, hairstyles, or body image?

11. How does the program relate to the shared conditions of its time—the culture?

12. Who or what has power or domination over others in the program? Whose voice is heard and whose is not? Who asks questions and who supplies the answers? What issues are given importance and which ones are not?

13. Does the class status play a part in the narrative? Is race, sexual preference, ethnicity, or nationality presented in a positive or negative light, or is it not a factor at all?

14. Is there an ideology that assigns roles to certain people or that advocates a set of norms for all to follow? Is there hegemony, where the subordinates are led to consent to the system that subordinates them? Have the subordinates "consented" to accept the social system as natural? Have the subordinates reversed the power structure causing the subordinates to become powerful and the dominant ones to become weak?

15. What is present and what is absent? How is the viewer limited in ways of seeing?

16. Could the viewer place oneself inside the image, identifying with it? If so, what does the viewer get out of the image through the identification?

17. How does the program position the viewer as a subject? How does the program "hail" the viewer?

18. What meanings are preferred by the program? In other words, what are the dominant meanings? What meanings (polysemy) can different viewers make from the program? What meanings can be derived from resisting the dominant meaning? What meanings can be derived from negotiating with the dominant meaning?

19. How might the decoded meanings give the viewer a sense of power or pleasure? How is this related to the viewer's sense of identity?

20. How could the program help the viewer as subject make sense of social experience?

21. Does the program have the potential to be absorbed into the lives of the viewers? Might they take on new meanings, new identities, and/or new knowledge?

22. As a television critic examining the polysemous meanings, do you discover anything about yourself?

23. Does the representation of characters, places, and events seem natural? Is it possible for the viewer to recognize these characters, places, and events through the representations?

24. How are people represented in categories of gender, race, ethnicity, age, occupation, and physical capabilities?

25. Who is represented and who is not? Is anyone represented as the "other"? Is anyone classified with a loss of individual differences? Are there stereotypes?

26. If there are symbols, how can they be recognized and how do they function? What is the frame of reference for symbolization?

27. Does identification of intertextuality heighten the pleasure derived from the program?

JUDGMENT

While recognizing the limitations of the medium of television, the time allotted, and the business constraints of the television industry, you are ready to evaluate what has been created and how it is presented. Incorporate your answers to the questions you chose to ask in making your judgment. Your judgment is an original contribution and, as such, your conclusions should be substantiated with clear analysis and description. Your evaluation of the program should be based on critical standards such as these:

1. A television program should accomplish what it sets out to do and do it well.

2. A television program should provide entertainment or information.

3. A television program should be well written, engage and respect its audience, and allow for audience involvement and identification.

4. A television program should be professionally produced in such a way that the audience can accept what it sees and hears.

5. You can design your own criteria developed from your questions for analysis.

WRITING TELEVISION CRITICISM

To communicate your evaluation in writing, you will have the following six topic areas in your paper: (1) an introduction with a thesis sentence, a statement of the purpose of your critique, and material that orients the reader to your topic; (2) a description of the television show and a summary of the narrative; (3) production information about the show's creators, cast, and popularity; (4) a description of your critical approach to the program and the questions you chose to ask; (5) your interpretation of the categories you have chosen, with examples from the program that describe and clarify what you found; and (6) your overall evaluation and your contribution to understanding the program. Topic 5, your interpretation, will constitute the bulk of your written evaluation.

When you write television criticism, use the vocabulary of criticism; for example, when you discuss narrative, use specialized terms such as "enigma," "delay," and "resolution," and when you talk about allusions to other media, use the term "intertextuality." It is not sufficient, however, to merely use the vocabulary, for you must explain what it means and how it is presented in the television program. If you reference the critiques or comments of others, be sure to cite them.

Always proofread your writing, and use a dictionary and thesaurus for accuracy and variety. Write to your readers; that is, keep in mind that you have an audience. Remember that your goal is to offer insights to the reader in order to help him or her see television in a new way.

SUMMARY

With guidelines, television criticism can be rewarding and fun to do. Although you are using specific questions for analysis, your work is subjective criticism, dependent on your ability to closely examine the elements of a television program. If you want to check your own objectivity, you can try the same approach on a different program or episode to measure how reliable your interpretations are. It is also possible to work with a coauthor to get different perceptions and points of view.

If at all possible, try to get tickets to a television show in production. It does not matter whether it is a local or national studio; either way, it will enhance your understanding of the creative process to visit a studio and watch either a run-through or a filming of a program.

As a television critic, you will have gained insights that are educational and useful to you. These insights will change the way you watch television, making it more enjoyable. If you plan to produce television, you will have a greater awareness of what television is and what it can accomplish. Overall, you will have become a more discerning consumer of television.

CHAPTER 10

Sample Criticism of a Television Program: *Parenthood*

Season 2, Episode 222, "Hard Times Come Again No More"

INTRODUCTION

Television family dramas are becoming rare. They used to be a strong staple of broadcasting fare, but now families are more likely to be featured on situation comedies. *Parenthood* began in July 2010, and by the end of the 2011 season, it was ranked as the highest-rated drama on NBC. The television drama was inspired by the 1989 film, *Parenthood*, directed by Ron Howard and produced by Brian Grazer, who, along with Jason Katims and Lawrence Trilling, are the executive producers of the television series. The film starred Steve Martin, Mary Steenburgen, Jason Robards, and Dianne Wiest. Like the film, the television drama follows the ups and downs of a large, colorful, and imperfect family of three generations living in northern California. It has a large ensemble cast of 15 actors, most of whom are in each episode. It also features well-known actors as guest stars.

THESIS

Parenthood's basic theme is that the family will stick together no matter what. The parents, their grown children, and their grandchildren tackle serious familial, medical, economic, and social problems, sometimes foolishly and other times sensitively. They deal with moral dilemmas that are not uncommon in today's society and offer a model for effective parenting. Their situations and antics are sad and funny, disappointing and successful, and somber and cheerful. Gender, race, and lifestyles are represented as natural.

PURPOSE

The purpose of this analysis is to critically examine the television program *Parenthood* for its story and substance, the representation of men, women, and children, and the ways that it encourages viewer involvement in the lives of a family. In addition, production information about the show has been included to provide insight into its origins and the producers' motives.

DESCRIPTION OF *PARENTHOOD*

Parenthood is broadcast on Tuesday nights on NBC. *Parenthood* has a low, but acceptable, rating of 2 (about 2.64 million viewers) in the Nielsen ratings, but a 2.9 (about 3.82 million viewers) when its playback (DVR) is included in the ratings (B. Carter, 2011, April 24, p. 2). Season 2 averaged a 2.1 rating in the 18- to 40-year-old demographic, with 5.34 million viewers. Season 3 was picked up for the 2011–2012 season. Fans express positive attitudes toward the show on Facebook. Many viewers say they identify with the characters. *Parenthood* was nominated for the Teen Choice Award, and two of the teenage actors, Mae Whitman and Miles Heizer, were nominated for the Young Artist Award. The first season is scheduled to air on television in the United Kingdom in 2011–2012.

The large ensemble cast that portrays the Braverman family can be viewed as a family tree (see Figure 10.1).

Guest actors have included William Baldwin as Adam Braverman's former boss, Richard Dreyfus as a well-known theatrical producer who is Zeek's old army buddy, John Corbett as Sarah's ex-husband and the father of Amber and Drew, and Michael B. Jordan, who has a recurring role as Alex, Haddie's boyfriend.

Zeek is a Vietnam War veteran who is now retired. He is, of course, the family patriarch who loves his family but sometimes interferes when he should not. He is retired, putters in his garage, and tries to be a father figure to his grandson, Miles. About midway through the series, the family discovers that he had an affair while on the road when he was working. Camille, his artist wife, is hurt and retaliates by having an affair with her art teacher. Over several episodes, they manage to forgive one another and stay together. Camille dresses in bohemian clothing, suggesting that she is a bit of a hippie. She offers quiet strength and understanding to her daughters and granddaughters.

Adam is an upright and serious provider for his family. He works as an office manager for an athletic shoe company, but his new boss is a young, hip guy who aggravates Adam no end. Adam frequently gets angry—at his boss; his brother, Crosby; and his daughter, Haddie—but he displays a great deal of patience and sensitivity with his son, Max, who has Asperger's syndrome, a form of high-functioning autism. Kristina worries a lot—about her children, Adam's siblings, and life in general. She and Adam have a loving relationship and are able to talk things out when they disagree. Haddie is 16 and strong willed. She joined her grandmother Camille as a volunteer at a food bank where she met Alex, an African American who is a recovering alcoholic. When they began to have feelings for each other, Adam and Kristina forbade Haddie to date him. Haddie did not tell Alex this and continued

Figure 10.1 Parenthood Family Tree

Source: Adapted from "*Parenthood* (2010 TV series)." Retrieved from http://en.wikipedia.org/wiki/Parenthood_(2010_TV_series).

to see him. When he dropped in at their home, Adam angrily ordered him out. Alex asked Adam if he objects to him because he is Black, but Adam vigorously denied this. He told him he objected because he is older, has his own apartment, and is an alcoholic. As a consequence, Haddie leaves home and moves in with her grandparents over the dispute, but eventually she and her parents worked out a compromise that enabled her to see Alex as long as she didn't go to his apartment. After the high school prom, however, Alex and Haddie did go to his apartment where they had sex, and Adam and Kristina found out about it. Adam is unhappy about this, but he and Kristina have resigned themselves to their daughter's relationship. Haddie's brother, Max, is obsessive about studying insects, talks loudly, often making untactful remarks, and tends to be self-centered. Children with Asperger's have normal intelligence and language development, but they are lacking in social and communication skills. When Max, who is 10, learns, by overhearing his parents, that he has Asperger's, he struggles to understand his condition.

Julia is a successful attorney, and Joel is a stay-at-home dad. They have an upscale home which Joel keeps up. He cooks and volunteers for the PTA. Julia tends to be a little jealous of the bond between father and daughter, so she overcompensates by planning elaborate mother-daughter activities. Julia would like to have another child, but she cannot. Sydney, their daughter, is a precocious and creative child.

Sarah is a single mother struggling to take care of her two teenage children. She divorced her rock musician husband because he took drugs and was undependable. Because she could not afford to live on her own, she moved home with her parents. She works as a bartender, had an internship at Adam's company, and is a creative writer. She tries hard to be a friend to her children, but she has difficulty with her daughter, Amber, who frequently gets into trouble. Her son, Drew, misses having a father, but Zeek tries to help him. Zeek also introduces Sarah to his old army buddy, a theatrical producer, who encourages Sarah to write a play and helps her get it produced in a community theater.

Crosby is the family's black sheep. He is a successful music promoter and lives in a houseboat. One day a beautiful African American woman, Jasmine, brings her young son to visit him, telling him that he is the boy's father. Eventually, Crosby and Jasmine fall in love; Crosby deeply loves their son, Jabbar, whom he helped care for while Jasmine performed in New York City with the Alvin Ailey dance troupe. They planned to marry, but Crosby's self-esteem plummeted because he felt that he had no say about Jabbar's upbringing, the wedding plans, and domestic chores. He had a one-night stand with Max's therapist, deeply hurting Jasmine, who broke up with him.

These brief sketches of the characters come from watching two seasons of *Parenthood*. The nature of the characters evolved over time until the viewer comes to know them. The character developments are consistent throughout the various narratives. They have flaws, get angry with one another, but each time there is a crisis, the family eventually comes together to help one another.

PRODUCTION INFORMATION

Parenthood was created by Jason Katims, who also created *Friday Night Lights*. Katims has a 14-year-old son with Asperger's. He said, "At first I wasn't sure I wanted to go there, but then I started to remember that everyone is dealing with something, and the goal of great

TV is to reach a universal truth." As a result, Katims has many fans who appreciate the way he has handled the Asperger's theme. Ron Howard, who produces the show along with Brian Grazer, said, *"Parenthood* doesn't play for shock value." "It's about the meaning of life," said Grazer (della Cava, 2011, pp. 1–2). The show is filmed in Berkeley, California, around Mill Valley, and Oakland. Because of the large cast and many sets, the show is expensive to produce. The production companies are Image Television and True Jack Productions. It is also filmed at Universal Media Studios and NBC Universal Network TV. Katims, who answers questions on NBC's website, said, "We shoot with three cameras [Panavision Genesis HD], and we give the actors the freedom to overlap and even improve some of their dialogue to make the show feel as realistic as possible. . . . I encourage our actors to really respond to each other as they would in life, and I encouraged our directors, director of photography, and sound department to work in a way that we could capture the actors honestly reacting to what's happening in the moment. I think this has a dramatic effect on the naturalism we can achieve in the show" (Ask the EP: Inspiration and Influences, 2011). Lauren Graham, who plays Sarah Braverman, said, "There's a controlled looseness on the set that's encouraged, and we all bring something to the party. I think there is reality in what we're creating. But I think (viewers) are out of the habit of being confronted with their own lives on TV" (della Cava, p. 3). Graham, who does such a good job of creating Sarah's character, was not originally cast for the part. Maura Tierney was cast as Sarah, but she had to withdraw when she was diagnosed with breast cancer. Although Tierney is a fine actress, Graham brings so much to the role. She exudes a vulnerability that really defines her character.

Soundtracks are an important part of *Parenthood*'s appeal. There are four to eight songs on each episode by musicians such as Bob Dylan, David Bowie, the Rolling Stones, Lyle Lovett, Paul Simon, Josh Ritter, and many others. These songs can be downloaded from the website or purchased on CDs. There is no "official guide" to *Parenthood* yet, thus this information was gleaned from various websites.

DESCRIPTION OF THE EPISODE

Episode 222, which aired on April 19, 2011, was the finale of Season 2. It is a complex episode with many conflicts and resolutions. Amber has been in a serious automobile accident, and the entire Braverman family is in the waiting room of the hospital. A song, "I'm There," plays in the background. Max acts up because he is hungry, saying that he does not care about Amber, so Adam takes him home. Jasmine comes to the hospital but will not acknowledge Crosby's presence. Alex, accompanying Haddie, brings coffee and juice to everyone. The doctor tells them that Amber is lucky because she is not severely injured. Drew and Sarah wait in Amber's room until she regains consciousness. Meanwhile, Kristina tells Haddie that she made an appointment with a gynecologist to get her birth control pills. At home, Adam tries to tell Max about empathy and why he should apologize to Sarah for what he said about Amber, but Max is unable to understand what is being asked of him. Julia, still at the hospital, meets Sydney's teacher Grace, who is in labor. Grace asks Julia to stay with her. Next, Adam blows up at his boss, Corey, for firing Eddie, who was the head of the design team. Adam protested because Eddie has a family to support. Corey justifies the replacement, Spider, whom he declares is a genius. Adam says he should have consulted him. Also at home, Sarah asks Amber why she got into the car with a drunk driver. Amber is defensive, especially when Drew comes in and says angrily, "What if you had died?" Back at their house, Kristina tells Adam that Max has lost his retainer, which costs $700. Adam is angry and says he will find it. She tells him that Haddie is on the pill, whereupon Adam says, "He (Alex) still needs to wear a condom!"

The next scene is of Julia, Joel, and Sydney having a tea party at home. They are wearing costumes and having a good time. Julia, who cannot have another child, tells Joel that she is happy with just the three of them. The next scene takes place in the community theater where the actors are rehearsing Sarah's play that is based on her family. Sarah keeps interrupting them, causing the director to tell her to be quiet. Sarah walks out, but her father, Zeek, who is one of the actors, catches up with her. She tells him she is terrified because she almost lost Amber, but Amber has not learned anything from the accident. Meanwhile, Crosby bought a house which Joel, Adam, and Sarah have helped fix up. Crosby used a drawing that Jasmine had made indicating the home she wanted in the future, thus Crosby hopes he can win her back. Joel visits Crosby at the house, and the two men sit on the porch step drinking beer. As Crosby tells Joel about it, there is a flashback to Crosby visiting Jasmine, apologizing for cheating on her but telling her that he will no longer pursue her, although he loves her, and that she should feel free to move on. He also says he will always be there for Jabbar. In the next scene, Adam talks to Max about his retainer and gets angry because Max is distracted. Max asks, "Are you mad at me because I have Asperger's?" Adam answers, "No, I am not mad at you because you have Asperger's. Never."

The next scene is pivotal, for Zeek takes Amber to the junk yard to look at the wrecked car in which the accident occurred. He tells her that when he was in Vietnam he dreamed about having a family and grandchildren. As he tells her about his dreams, Amber begins to cry. She was upset because she didn't get into college, but he says that is not important. "If you ever do something like this again, you even think about doing something like this— I will personally kick your little butt all the way from here to the Golden Gate Bridge. You do not have my permission to mess with my dreams." Then he offers to buy her a burger, and they walk away arm in arm.

Back at the office, Adam apologizes to his boss, Corey, for his outburst the previous day, but Corey fires him. Adam is incredulous. The next scene is Sarah's opening night for her play. The various family members come into the theater. Drew and his sister, Amber, sit on the stairs in the lobby of the theater where Amber apologizes to him and asks him to be her friend. He agrees. Then Max apologizes to Sarah for his outburst at the hospital. Adam comes in and greets Kristina, but he does not tell her he has been fired. Alex comes over to tell Adam that he loves Haddie, but Adam's response is "Wear a condom!" Alex says, "Yes, sir." Back stage the actors hug Sarah, telling her how great her play is. When she tells the director how nice the actors are, he tells her that he told them her daughter died. Enthusiastic responses from the audience indicate that the play is a success, but Amber walks out. Sarah follows her. Amber cries and tells her mother how proud she is and that she wants to be like her. Sarah thanks her and goes back into the theater where the audience gives her a standing ovation.

Julia visits Grace in the hospital and holds her baby. Adam goes home to tell Kristina he's been fired. Kristina says, "You've never let this family down. We're in this together." She says she has something to tell him, but instead of telling him what she had planned, she tells him that she found a good price for Max's retainer. In the next scene, Joel brings

Jasmine to Crosby's house. Jasmine and Crosby sit down and discuss the house. This scene suggests that they may reconcile. Next, a brief scene of Sarah and Amber at home laughing happily suggests that all is well between them. Then, in the next scene, Julia tells Joel she wants to adopt a baby. He kisses her. Finally, at the end, Adam is looking in the garbage can outside trying to find Max's retainer. Instead he finds a pregnancy stick with a plus on it. He goes inside in a rage, thinking that Haddie is pregnant. When she gets a word in, Kristina tells him that she is the one who is pregnant. Adams laughs, hugs her, and says, "I'm happy" while Max's voice from upstairs announces, "I found my retainer." The camera pulls back into a long shot as the song "Hard Times Come Again No More" plays. It is a set-up for the next season, with Adam unemployed and a new baby on the way.

QUESTIONS FOR ANALYSIS

I chose the following questions for analysis from the guidelines for television criticism to achieve the purpose stated at the beginning of this chapter. I then clustered the questions into three headings: (1) Story, Substance, and Context; (2) Representation' and (3) Demographics and Viewer Involvement. There are other ways to analyze this episode, but I think these will reveal the most important aspects of *Parenthood*.

1. Story, Substance, and Context

   a. Look and listen to the opening credits. What mood does the music create: Are the characters introduced in some context? What mood is evoked by the lead-in and credits?

   b. What is the narrative progression?

   c. What happens in the lead-in, the beginning of the narrative that sets the scene? How does it entice the viewer to stay with the program?

   d. Identify the stages of the hermeneutic code—enigma, delay, and resolution—that move the narrative forward.

   e. How are ideas developed in the program? How are the ideas adjusted to people and people to ideas?

   f. Can you identify myths?

   g. Are there archetypes and rituals in the narrative?

   h. Are there moral lessons? What cultural values are represented? Is it possible to specify an intent?

   i. Who or what has power or domination over others in the program? Whose voice is heard and whose is not? Who asks questions and who supplies the answers?

   j. Are contextual and social issues clearly referenced?

   k. Is there an ideology that assigns roles to certain people or that advocates a set of norms for all to follow?

   l. What meanings are preferred by the program?

2. Representation

   a. Does the representation of characters, places, and events seem natural?

   b. Do the characters have depth or just a few characteristics? Are the characters and actors who portray them young adults, children, middle-aged, or seniors? Are the characters supposed to be single, members of families, lower, middle, or upper class?

   c. How are people represented in categories of gender, race, ethnicity, age, occupation, and physical capabilities?

3. Demographics and Viewer Involvement

   a. Whom does the program "hail? In order to be a subject of the program, what is the expected social position of the audience?

   b. At whom are the advertisements aimed?

   c. What are the advertised products? To what age groups are they targeted?

   d. What lifestyles do the advertisements suggest?

ANALYSIS AND INTERPRETATION

Story, Substance, and Context

Opening Credits

The signature song that opens the credits is Bob Dylan's *Forever Young,* sung by Dylan. The song and its lyrics are perfect for the substance of this series because they express optimism, youth, and values of truth, courage, and strength. (The chorus and the third verse are omitted during the opening credits.) The lyrics to *Forever Young* can be found at http://www.bobdylan.com/songs/foreveryoung.

The credits open with "Parenthood" on the screen in front of a long shot of the Braverman family sitting around a dinner table in the backyard of a home. Next, there is a collage of still photos and some moving shots of the characters with the actors' names on the screen as they appear—first there is an old photo of a bride and groom, then a baby in a crib. Presumably they are Zeek and Camille and their oldest child, Adam. Next there is a picture of Adam as a boy, then as an adult, and finally Adam and Kristina. A little girl (Sarah) rides a tricycle, then there is a photo of Sarah as a young girl followed by one of her as an adult. A photo of a boy near a haystack, then on a swing, then Crosby as a teenager are followed by a shot of Crosby at the dinner table next to Kristina. There are no photos of Kristina as a child. Julia is next seen as a toddler walking in adult high heels that are much too big for her; this is followed by a picture of a teenage Julia, then Julia as an adult. Joel is seen at the table leaning over his daughter Sydney, followed by a photo of Sydney blowing out candles on a birthday cake. The image fades to a shot of Joel, Sydney, and Julia with two people in furry cat costumes. Haddie is next, shown making a face, then at the table with the family. A little boy is seen with a golden retriever followed by a shot of the same boy, Max. Zeek and Max sit together at the dinner table. Crosby and Jasmine, smiling, are in a photo in which a picture of a happy Jabbar is inserted into the frame. A little boy chasing pigeons fades to a picture of Drew. Then there is a picture of Amber as a little girl, followed by one of her in the present. Next, we see Camille at the table followed by Zeek, who is raising his glass in a toast. The collage ends with a long shot of the entire family at the table, with Dylan's song encouraging them to stay forever young.

The opening credits accomplish two things: (1) Dylan's song and the photo collage introduce the Braverman family and the actors who portray them. The mood is cheerful and the substance is one of unity. They look like a large, joyful family. We see them as happy children and contented adults. They are "forever young"; and (2) The way in which they are introduced tells us the order of importance of the actors as well as the family members. The four Braverman brothers and sisters—Adam, Sarah, Crosby, and Julia—are shown first as children then adults; whereas their spouses are not shown as children. Zeek and Camille, the patriarch and matriarch are depicted at the beginning, the middle, and the end with Zeek at the head of the table. They tie the family together.

Narrative Progression

The episode opens with Sarah awakened by a phone call. There is no dialogue, but her facial expression indicates that something is wrong. The next scene is at the hospital where the entire family waits to learn how Amber is. There are many close-ups on their worried faces. After they learn that Amber will be all right, the episode continues to reveal their various conflicts. The lead-in does not make the viewer wait to find out how Amber is, but the dialogue between Kristina and Haddie about birth control, and Jasmine's evasive treatment of Crosby entice the viewer to see what will happen next.

Photo 10.1   The Braverman family at the dinner table with matriarch Camille at the head of the table in *Parenthood*.

There are *eight* instances of conflict with enigmas, delays, and resolutions in the episode:

1. Amber is hurt in an automobile accident (enigma); she refuses to accept responsibility for her carelessness (delay). After Zeek talks to her at the junk yard, Amber accepts responsibility, then apologizes to Drew and Sarah (resolution). The resolution results in friendship between Amber and Drew, and warmth and happiness between Amber and Sarah.

2. Sarah is traumatized by Amber's accident, causing her to be rude to the actors during the play rehearsal (enigma); when she walks out of the rehearsal, Zeek follows her to hear her say how terrified she is, but he can't comfort her (delay); after Zeek talks with Amber, she apologizes to her mother, telling her she wants to be like her (resolution). The resolution results in a better relationship between mother and daughter.

3. Max has an outburst at the hospital, saying that he does not care about Amber (enigma); Adam tries to explain empathy and familial support to Max, but Max cannot understand (delay); Max apologizes to Sarah (resolution). Sarah understands and invites Max to sit with her during her play.

4. Jasmine has broken up with Crosby (enigma and a lack); Crosby buys a house to win her back, but she tells him he cannot buy his way out of the situation, whereupon Crosby tells her he won't pursue her anymore (delay); Joel brings Jasmine to Crosby's house, and there is a suggestion of a resolution because they sit and talk. There is no dialogue, but the visual image of them sitting side-by-side, looking at the house, suggests that they will reunite in the third season of the series.

5. Julia is unable to have a baby (enigma and a lack); she tells Joel that she is happy with just the three of them (delay that appears to be a resolution); after holding Grace's baby, she tells Joel that she wants to adopt a child (resolution). This also suggests that the narrative of the third season will include their attempt to adopt.

6. Adam gets fired (enigma); he doesn't tell Kristina right away (delay); when he does tell her, she is supportive, telling him that it will be all right (resolution). They have savings and mutual support, but a baby is on the way. This also sets up the narrative for the third season.

7. Adam discovers a pregnancy stick and thinks Haddie is pregnant (enigma); he gets very angry, yelling at Kristina about Alex (delay); Kristina tells him that she is the one who is pregnant. He hugs her and laughs, saying "I'm happy" (resolution).

8. Max lost his expensive retainer (enigma). Adam is angry at Max because he will not help look for the retainer. Max thinks Adam is angry with him because he has Asperger's. Adam reassures Max, but refuses to buy another retainer until he looks for it (delay). At the end, as Adam and Kristina are hugging, Max calls down, "I found my retainer" (resolution). All is well until next season.

Eight conflicts is a lot for a 44-minute episode, but they were presented clearly, with a resolution for each one. It is not altogether clear whether Crosby and Jasmine will reunite, but it was strongly suggested that they were on their way to a reconciliation. The ideas are developed through the conflicts with the conclusion that working things out together with the help of the family is the right way. Within the conflicts, there are oppositions:

- Julia cannot have a baby/Grace has a baby. Julia transcends the opposition by making the decision to adopt.
- Crosby is unfaithful/Jasmine is faithful. Crosby tries to transcend the opposition by apologizing and sacrificing his houseboat and motorcycle in order to buy a house for Jasmine.
- Adam wants his daughter to abstain from having sex/Haddie has sex with Alex. Kristina gets Haddie birth control pills, while Adam insists that Alex use a condom.
- Max's Asperger's causes him to be insensitive/Adam wants him to have empathy. Max transcends his insensitivity by apologizing to Sarah. This is also a good example of rhetorical persuasion, for Adam, using the value of family, explains to Max, "You're part of this family, and when something happens, we have to be there for them."

There are two prominent myths in the narrative. As discussed in Chapter 4, the cosmo-logical myth tells why we are here and where we came from. This is exemplified when Zeek tells Amber about his dreams of family when he was in Vietnam. He tells her that he dreamt about her and his other grandchildren long before they came into existence. "Don't mess with my dreams," he tells her. Zeek is also the archetype of the Wise Old Man, whereas Amber is the modern archetype of the rebellious teenager. Because Sarah is unable to make Amber realize the consequences of her actions, Zeek teaches Amber the lesson that gets through to her. As the patriarch of the family, he sometimes has dominion over the others, perhaps because he is older, has raised his family, and wants to help them succeed. He supplies the answer that leads to a resolution for Amber and Sarah. The other myth, also discussed in Chapter 4, is the eschatological myth that tells where we are going. This myth is exemplified through Sarah who discovers that she can write a play. Her play is successful; now she knows not only where she is going in the future, but Amber tells her that she wants to be just like her. This could be a form of *telos* for both Sarah and Amber, for they seem to be headed for a good life with moral excellence and contempla-tive happiness. Sarah is also the archetype of the Good Mother, who watches over her child. There are three kinds of rituals embedded in the narrative—the healing ritual of Amber, both physically and spiritually, and the ritual of birth when Grace has a baby.

Crosby is an antihero—he deeply hurt Jasmine by having an affair with Max's therapist. This also hurt Adam and Kristina because the therapist quit, leaving Max without her help. Crosby is also the archetype of the unfaithful spouse, but he regrets his action. Crosby can be admired because he loves and cares for Jabbar. He attempts to win Jasmine by selling his beloved houseboat and motorcycle to buy her a house, thus his sacrifice may redeem him. Crosby's behavior opens an opportunity for polysemy, different meanings, for some viewers may condemn him, believing that he does not deserve to have Jasmine's forgive-ness. Others may condemn his action, but negotiate the meaning because he has sacrificed and wants redemption.

There is one social type—Corey, Adam's boss, who is hippie-like in his language and behavior, but because he is Adam's boss, he has dominion over him. Adam criticizes Corey for his actions, saying, "You think you're so cool, and I'm not." Adam treats Corey as the Other, for, even though Corey is the boss, Adam looks down on him. Adam is neither patriarch, although he is a father, nor a hero. His anger gets in his way, causing him to lose his job. He does not reason with his daughter and Alex; instead, he is rude and domineering. Kristina helps him come to grips with his anger, so in that sense she supplies stability.

There are many contextual issues in this series, most of which are embedded in this episode. They are not "ripped from the headlines," but rather they are issues that families cope with in everyday life—loss of job, birth control to prevent teen pregnancy, rebellious teenagers, infertility and adoption, not getting admitted to college, and accidents. The issue of a child with Asperger's syndrome is important because Asperger's and autism are not uncommon.

There are four apologies in this episode: Amber apologizes once to Drew and then to Sarah; Max apologizes to Sarah, explaining, "I have Asperger's"; and Adam apologizes to Corey. Adam's apology is unsuccessful, but the others result in good will. The values exemplified throughout the episode are truthfulness, fairness, loyalty, love, sensitivity, and unity.

Moral lessons (ideology) are prominent in this episode: (1) Take responsibility for your actions; (2) infidelity has its consequences; (3) adoption is a positive alternative, and, above all; (4) love and support your family. These are also the preferred meanings of the program.

Representation

Sarah, Julia, Kristina, Camille, and Jasmine are beautiful women who are slender and have lovely hair and complexions, yet their acting helps us accept them as natural and real. At the hospital, Sarah looks tired and pale, as one would in a similar situation. Amber's face is marked with cuts, but she seems to heal quickly. Adam and Joel are handsome and fit, but their appearances fit their roles. Joel seems natural and easy going, but I question the casting of Peter Krause, for he is stiff and lacks warmth, especially in the scenes where he is supposed to reveal sensitivity. Zeek as the patriarch is quite acceptable, for he not only looks the part, as a character, he has his faults as well as great strengths. Crosby is ordinary in appearance, a bit unkempt, which is natural for his character. The three teenagers and the child Max come across as very realistic. Without knowing much about Asperger's, I accept Max's performance as true to form and find it very credible, especially since Jason Katims, the producer, has a son with Asperger's.

The families appear to be middle class, for they have comfortable homes and dress in ordinary clothing. Zeek and Camille's home looks traditional and well-worn, whereas Adam's and Julia's homes appear to be new and contemporary. All of the families spend a lot of time in their kitchens, however, the focus is on the characters, not their homes. The characters range in age from 6 (Sydney) to 60-something (Zeke). Women and men are represented in an equal fashion. In Julia's case, she is the breadwinner and Joel is a stay-at-home Dad. Joel was a contractor and has skills to help Crosby remodel his house. Crosby and Jasmine and Haddie and Alex are interracial couples. The only time that race was mentioned occurred in an earlier episode when Alex asked Adam if he objected to him because he is Black. The actual objection was due to Adam's fear of his 16-year-old daughter dating a man in his 20s who has his own apartment and is a recovering alcoholic. Adam and Kristina do not condemn alcoholism, but they worry about it. Alex is portrayed as a wonderful man who is working hard to have a decent life. His response to Adam's rudeness

("Wear a condom!") is respectful, and he brings juice and coffee to the family in the hospital waiting room, causing Julia to remark to Kristina about Alex, "He is beautiful." No other ethnic or racial groups were represented, nor is anyone in the episode represented as gay.

Demographics and Viewer Involvement

The social position of the viewer of *Parenthood* is that of a family member, male or female, a parent, grandparent, or child, for all are represented in depth. These are the people who are hailed by the program. Viewers who weigh in on Facebook indicate that is who they are. For example, one user blogged, "We are that target demographic: decent jobs, late-thirties, children, etc." Many viewers write that they identify with the family members, and several people who have children with Asperger's syndrome say how much they appreciate the portrayal of Max. The context, as described above, is about typical family concerns. That Adam loses his job is particularly relevant in today's economy. The adult child, Sarah, returning to live with her parents for financial reasons is also relevant today.

The advertisements are aimed at contemporary middle-class families, for the commercials feature Quaker oatmeal, Reese's Peanut Butter [Easter] Eggs, a "green" laundry detergent, furniture polish, car insurance, wireless phones, iPhones, a computer network, a wireless telephone network, department stores, hair color, mascara, makeup, promotions for NBC television programs, and Home Depot.

Photo 10.2   Adam and Kristina Braverman with their 16-year-old daughter, Haddie, in *Parenthood*.

The Home Depot commercial is unusual, for it features Steven Jordan, the art director for *Parenthood*. He explains how he dresses the set with porch furniture to "create a family feeling," uses soft lighting to achieve a warm glow from the house to the outside, and paints the walls to reveal the characters' personalities, for example, sophisticated pastels for Julia's house and color accents for Sydney's room. Of course, all of the products he speaks of come from Home Depot. The three commercials for hair color, makeup, and mascara suggest that women are a strong demographic group, but the digital products suggest heavy use of social media. The advertised products suggest lifestyles that are comfortable, busy, active, and typical for the middle class.

The music is also multigenerational. There is Bob Dylan and The Rolling Stones for the grandparents, Lyle Lovett and Pearl Jam for the parents, and Junip, Band of Horses, and other groups for the younger generation.

SUMMARY

I think that *Parenthood* fulfills the criteria for a good television show as outlined in Chapter 9. It accomplishes what it sets out to do. It provides entertainment *and* information. It is well written, engages and respects its audience, and certainly allows for audience involvement. It is professionally produced in such a way that the audience can accept what it sees and hears. The look of the show is natural, for the sets look a lot like ordinary homes in our experience. The acting helps bring about a natural feel for the characters. Lauren Graham and Craig T. Nelson are excellent—Graham's facial expressions in reaction shots reveal her emotions very well. Nelson's is more of a poker face, but his spoken dialogue is credible and natural. The young actors are especially good. Mae Whitman, who plays Amber, is very expressive and has a large following on Facebook. I don't think Peter Krause is credible as Adam. He doesn't convey the feelings in the lines he speaks, for he is wooden and stiff. Steve Martin was so good in the movie *Parenthood,* which makes for a difficult comparison to Krause in the television series. Max Burkholder as Max is an incredible child actor. He makes us feel that he really has Asperger's.

Parenthood is melodramatic in its conflicts, but the depicted conflicts are not unusual in today's society. It serves as a good model for family behavior, most of the time. The show is described as a "dramedy," but there is not a lot of comedy in it. There was one episode, "Amazing Andy and His Wonderful World of Bugs" that was very funny, but the episode I analyzed had little humor in it. At the end, when Max calls down, "I found my retainer" is an example of comic relief.

The end of the finale episode had two memorable scenes. When Adam is going through the garbage in the dark, looking for Max's retainer, and finds the pregnancy stick, there is a long shot with him in the foreground looking up at the house. Haddie is framed in a lighted window, thus the viewer can "read" Adam's mind, supplying Adam's conclusion that Haddie is pregnant. (It is a rhetorical enthymeme, for the viewer can co-create meaning with the image and the television character.) The other is at the end after Adam and Kristina hug and Max calls out about finding his retainer. The camera slowly moves away from the interior of the house to the front lawn outside. It is a nice visual moment that says, "Let's leave the Bravermans for now. All is well. See you next season."

Glossary

Action code: Character action in a narrative that makes complex ideas and feelings recognizable to an audience.

Agenda-setting: Gatekeeping in media news, whereby journalists tell viewers what issues are important.

AQRI: An acronym for *arouse quick related interest,* an advertising strategy to relate to audience lives or experiences.

Archetype: Recurrent patterns of actions, character types, or identifiable images whose expression is an unconscious product of the collective experience of the entire human species, an unconscious mental record of such experiences, the collective unconscious. Archetypes depict some eternal quality, some enduring quality of the human race. Examples are the hero, heroine, wise old man, earth mother, temptress, villain, antihero, outcast, scapegoat, initiation, journey, bridge, the fall, fire, light, and water.

Brand identity: When specific television channels appeal to specific target audiences.

Broadcast and cable channel executives: Administrators of the television networks and cable companies, both at the national and local levels.

Close-up shot: A camera shot that shows only a human head.

Code: A system of signs that is able to communicate meanings.

Collective memory: A memory that different persons, unknown to one another, remember of the same event.

Contextual reality: Plots in fiction television that represent actual news events and true-to-life stories.

Convention: Any kind of social or cultural practice used in a narrative that has a meaning that is shared by members of a culture.

Criticism: The practice of informed judgment through which a person understands, evaluates, and communicates to others the what, how, and why something is considered to be of quality.

Cultivation studies: Long-range study of heavy television viewing that concluded that viewers had a heightened sense of danger in a mean and selfish world.

Culture: The actual practices and customs, languages, beliefs, forms of representation, and a system of formal and informal rules that tell people how to behave most of the time and enable people to make sense of their world through a certain amount of shared meanings and recognition of different meanings.

Demographics: The practice of describing groups of people according to gender, age, ethnicity, income, educational level, and other information.

Digital convergence: The coming together of media technologies as the result of digitalization and offering alternative ways of viewing television.

DVR: Digital video recorder.

"Elbows" shot or elbows: A tight medium camera shot that frames a figure so that the lower edge of the screen is roughly the middle point of the person's arms.

Enigma: A question about the narrative's development, such as "Who committed the crime?" or "How might a relationship develop?"

Enthymeme: A process in which the audience supplies meaning by co-creating it interactively and coming to the conclusion that exists in the mind of the communicator.

Ethos: A person's character, integrity, and goodwill; i.e., credibility.

FCC: Federal Communications Commission. U.S. government agency that regulates broadcasting.

Flow: Staying with a channel into the next program. Another similar meaning is a planned stream of television programs from trailers, commercials, and public service announcements to the next program.

Focus groups: Groups of people who represent different demographics and who discuss the appeal of television story lines, characters, and other factors.

Fourth wall: The fourth wall of a set that is left open for camera equipment, lights, microphones, and sometimes a live audience.

Genre: A form of classification of types of programming; tried and true formulae that have certain predictability and familiarity.

Genre bending: Hybrid shows made up of one or more genres.

Green screen: Blank wall used to project images on.

Hail: When an image or a discourse "hails" a person, i.e., it calls to the person and to answer the call, the person must recognize that it is she or he, not someone else, who is being hailed.

"Hammock" strategy: Placing a new or less successful television program before or after a successful series.

HDTV: High definition television.

Hegemony: A way of life and thought that is dominant in society to the point that it seems natural.

Hermeneutic code: Interpretation of a story that includes an enigma, a problem or disruption of some sort that causes an audience to see how it is resolved; a delay that stalls or postpones the solution to an enigma; and a resolution to the enigma is found.

Hybrid genre: One genre blended with elements of another genre.

Hybrid pitch: A description of a television show that is a blend of two or more familiar hit shows from the past.

Identification: When people share a common substance or property that unites them.

Ideological codes: Ideologies such as individualism, patriarchy, class, materialism, and capitalism to encode a preferred meaning.

Ideology: A set of beliefs, values, attitudes, and behaviors, as well as ways of perceiving and thinking that are agreed on to a point that they constitute a set of norms for a society that dictate what is desirable and what should be done.

Intention: A conscious aim to obtain a specific outcome. An attributed intention occurs when it is not possible to know the exact intention of a communicator.

Intertextuality: References to other media, characters, and/or events—an allusion to a "text" outside of the present one.

Journalist television critics: Critics who write about television for newspapers and websites.

Lack: The disruption of equilibrium or harmony by the lack of something or a desire or wish that goes unfulfilled: Resolution occurs when equilibrium is restored, desire is satisfied, or the wish is fulfilled.

Line producer: The detail person who oversees a television show from its concept to its production; supervises the budget, oversees the construction of sets, and keeps costs in line.

Logos: An interactive process in which a communicator and an audience create and share intellectual meaning.

Long shot: A camera shot that includes a human figure from the bottom of the feet to the top of the head, creating a full picture.

Medium shot: A camera shot that is framed on a human figure at or near the waist, so that the torso and head fill the picture while the legs and feet are below the frame line and out of the picture.

Metacritic.com: A website that lists television shows by title with links to television critic reviews where programs are rated by critics and viewers.

"Mobisodes": Customized mini-television programs for cell phones.

Multi-camera production: Several cameras are used simultaneously.

Myth: Fictitious tales, often with primitive or ancient origins, involving supernatural characters embodying timeless virtues and values. Myth offers the young in a society an explanation of why the world is the way it is and why we do as we do. Cosmological myths explain why we are here and where we came from; societal myths teach the proper way to live; identity myths preserve a culture's distinctiveness and provide a sense of collective identity; eschatological myths tell people where they are going and what lies in store for them in both the short and long run.

Narrative or story: A series of events arranged in an order.

Narrowcasting: Reaching for target audiences.

Nielsen ratings: Statistics on television and Internet audiences' exposure to electronic media that are sold to advertisers, advertising agencies, program syndicators, television networks, local stations, websites, and cable and satellite program and system operators. The statistics tell how many people out of a possible total audience are watching media at a time.

The "Other": Person(s), group(s), social class, community, race, or nation who are not "us" and who are defined by their difference from us, yet who by that difference contribute to our concept of self, as individuals, members of groups, etc.

Pathos: Appeals to the emotions of the audience and the situation.

Perception: The process of extracting information from the world outside us as well as from within ourselves.

Pickups: When the networks announce their fall schedules which are being picked up.

Pitch: A description of the concept of a prospective show or series. It is a brief story line presented to a television executive.

Pleasure: Pleasure is derived from making meaning that is pertinent to oneself. Experiencing pleasure by accepting, opposing, or negotiating the preferred meaning frees viewers from ideological dominance and gives them a sense of control over the production of meanings.

Polysemy: Multiple meanings are possible because various people incorporate their own lifestyles, values, and other cultural practices into their interpretations.

Postmodern: A stylistic and aesthetic change in the arts and culture that breaks down or alters traditions of modernism. A body of work that is nonlinear, playful, and assembled from various other forms, including modernism, that construct an eclectic pastiche composed of parts borrowed from other works.

Power: That which enables one person or a group to exert his or her will and interest over others.

Prime time: The hours between 8 and 11 p.m. EST.

Procedurals: These are usually crime shows where a crime is committed; the officials (police, detectives, military agents) investigate the scene, interview witnesses and suspects, investigate evidence, follow leads, and solve the crime.

Producer: The person who puts a television show together. The producer is usually the creator or co-creator and head writer: Executive producers are also known as showrunners.

Product placement: Brand names and products purposely placed within the context of a television program.

Reaction shot: A facial expression or gesture of a person who is not talking in a scene is revealed in reaction to somebody or something.

Social codes: Codes that relate to appearance, behavior, speech, sound, and editing to encode reality.

Reality shows: Scripted or unscripted situations in which ordinary people vie for prizes or rewards. They include talent, make-over, and adventure competitions. They also include voyeurism into the lives of other people.

Representation: A given that the act of representation duplicates in one way or another. It is a surrogate for the original, an attempt to imitate or substitute the real through a resemblance. An image is constructed to re-present someone or something it represents.

Representation code: Technical codes through camera, lighting, sound, music, and editing that convey conventional representation.

Rhetoric: The study of symbols and how they are used to influence. Aristotle, the Greek philosopher, famously defined rhetoric as the faculty of discovering in the particular case what are the available means of persuasion.

Rhetorical criticism: Focuses on the conception, composition, presentation, and reception of messages that tend to be persuasive and informative in nature.

Science fiction: Action usually takes place in the future, often in space, with utopian or dystopian societies that may threaten human life.

Share: A mathematical formula that calculates the percentage of the nationwide audience with sets turned on and tuned into a particular program during a given time.

Showrunners: The producer who oversees a television program; negotiates with television executives, counsels actors, and defines the creative vision of a television series.

Situation comedy: Escapist fare that provokes laughter through jokes, humorous dialogue, situations, and sometimes slapstick. Usually 30-minute television shows located in domestic or workplace settings.

Social types: Collections of real people who resemble one another; popular ideal types of people and folk generalizations (rednecks, hillbillies, hippies, cowboys, bullies, etc.).

Steadicam: A television camera strapped to the camera operator's body for movement shots.

Subject: Recognition and cooperative response by a television viewer to the social position that has been constructed in encoding the image/discourse.

Subtext: When a character's inner feelings are seen visually but not necessarily spoken about.

Surfing: Rapid television channel switching, also known as grazing.

Sweeps: The practice of sweeping all local markets four times a year in month-long periods in January, May, September, and November during which ratings set the advertising rates for the next three months for local stations.

Swish pan: When a television camera lurches in one direction or another, usually left to right, to create a transition within a sequence.

Symbol: It stands for something else but does not necessarily attempt to duplicate it. The meaning of a symbol must be learned.

Table reading: Writers, actors, and producers (perhaps some television executives) sit around a table to determine what in the script works for the characters in a television show and what does not work.

Talk shows: Nighttime and daytime comedy, music, guest appearances, and talk. Often scripted but open to improvisation. Daytime talk shows lend themselves to psychological disclosures.

TCA: Television Critics Association, represents more than 200 journalists who write about television for print and online outlets. See http://tvcritics.org.

Telos: End or completion by experiencing moral excellence and contemplative happiness so that others bestow virtue upon the person.

"Tent-pole" strategy: Scheduling a successful television program between two less successful ones or a new program.

Time-shifting: Watching recorded television at a time after a program was aired.

Treatment: Also known as the writer's treatment. An overview of the plot of a television show with details of the chronological rundown of the scenes of a prospective script with information about the setting and characters: It may have examples of dialogue and camera shots.

Value: An enduring belief that a specific mode of conduct or end-state of existence is personally or socially desirable or undesirable.

Variety comedy: A host, ensemble cast, music, and humorous skits make up an adult show telecast before a live audience.

"Webisodes": Programs specifically designed to be seen on the Internet.

References

Akass, K., & McCabe, J. (Eds.). (2004). *Reading* Sex and the City. London, England: I. B. Tauris.

Allen, R. C. (Ed.). (1992). *Channels of discourse, reassembled* (2nd ed.). Chapel Hill: University of North Carolina Press.

American Playhouse. (1992, December 16). [Seminar on videotape]. Beverly Hills, CA: Museum of Television and Radio.

An evening with *The Good Wife*. (2011, January 31). Retrieved from http://www.emmys.tv

Ang, I. (1990). Melodramatic identifications: Television fiction and women's fantasy. In M. E. Brown (Ed.), *Television and women's culture*. Newbury Park, CA: Sage.

Archive of American Television: Lynn Stalmaster. (n.d.). A program of the Television Academy Foundation. Retrieved from http://emmytvlegends.org/interviews/people/lynn-stalmaster

Aristotle. (1932). *The rhetoric of Aristotle* (L. Cooper, Trans.). New York, NY: Appleton-Century-Crofts. (Original work published 333 BCE)

Arnold, C. C., & Bowers, J. W. (1984). *Handbook of rhetorical and communication theory*. Boston, MA: Allyn & Bacon.

The art of the music video. (1997). Rochester, NY: Eastman Kodak Company.

Ask the EP: Inspiration and influences. (2011, March 29). Retrieved from http://www.nbc.com

Associated Press (AP). (2001, November 23). Morning TV shows busy promoting parent companies. *Bozeman Daily Chronicle,* p. C3.

Associated Press (AP). (2003, August 31). Tuning into television. *Bozeman Daily Chronicle,* p. A7.

Associated Press (AP). (2004, February 1). Super Bowl ads. *Bozeman Daily Chronicle,* p. C4.

Associated Press (AP). (2005, July 22). 'Stealth ads' infiltrate TV programming. *Bozeman Daily Chronicle,* p. TW21.

Auto pilot, it's not, as fall season nears (1998). *USA Today,* 30 June (p. D3).

Avins, M. (2005, May 25). The high life without airs. *Los Angeles Times,* pp. F1, 10.

Barker, C. (2008). *Cultural studies: Theory and practice* (3rd ed.). Thousand Oaks, CA: Sage.

Barnouw, E. (1978). *Sponsor: Note on a modern potentate*. Oxford, UK: Oxford University Press.

Barthes, R. (1974). *S/Z: An essay* (R. Miller, Trans.). New York, NY: Hill and Wang.

Bellafante, G. (2011, May 18). Dirty politics: From halls of power to hotel suites. *The New York Times*. Retrieved May 18, 2011, from http://nytimes.com

Bellamy, R. V., Jr., & Walker, J. R. (1996). *Television and the remote control: Grazing on a vast wasteland*. New York, NY: Guilford Press.

Berger, A. A. (Ed.). (1998). *The postmodern presence: Readings on postmodernism in American culture and society*. Walnut Creek, CA: Altamira Press.

Berko, L. (1994). Surveilled: Video, space, and subjectivity. In N. Browne (Ed.), *American television: New directions in history and theory* (pp. 223–254). Langhorne, PA: Harwood.

Best, S., & Kellner, D. (1991). *Postmodern theory: Critical interrogations*. New York, NY: Guilford Press.

Bignell, J. (2004). *An introduction to television studies*. London, England: Routledge.

Block, A. B. (2007). The ratings ruckus. *Emmy, 29*(3), 182–185.

Bloom, P. (2010). *How pleasure works: The new science of why we like what we like.* New York, NY: W. W. Norton.

Bogle, D. (2001). *Prime time blues: African Americans on network television.* New York, NY: Farrar, Straus and Giroux.

Bormann, E. G. (1990). Fantasy and rhetorical vision: The rhetorical criticism of social reality. In B. L. Brock, R. L. Scott, & J. W. Chesebro (Eds.), *Methods of rhetorical criticism: A twentieth-century perspective* (3rd ed.). Detroit, MI: Wayne State University Press.

Brooker, P., & Brooker, W. (Eds.). (1997). *Postmodern after-images: A reader in film, television and video.* London, England: Arnold.

Brown, J. A. (1997). Television criticism (journalistic). In H. Newcomb (Ed.), *Encyclopedia of television* (Vol. 3, pp. 1643–1644). Chicago, IL: Fitzroy Dearborn.

Browne, N. (1994). *American television: New directions in history and theory.* Langhorne, PA: Harwood.

Bruner, J. (1973). The course of cognitive growth. In J. Angin (Ed.), *Beyond the information given: Studies in the psychology of knowing.* New York, NY: W. W. Norton.

Bryant, D. C. (1953). Rhetoric: Its function and scope. *Quarterly Journal of Speech, 39,* 401–424.

Burke, K. (1931/1957). *Counter-statement.* Chicago, IL: University of Chicago Press.

Burke, K. (1935/1984). *Permanence and change: An anatomy of purpose.* Berkeley: University of California Press.

Burke, K. (1950/1969). *A rhetoric of motives* (reprint). Berkeley: University of California Press.

Buzzard, K. S. (1990). *Chains of gold: Marketing the ratings and rating the markets* (p. 137). Metuchen, NJ: Scarecrow Press.

Campbell, J. (1988). *The power of myth.* New York, NY: Anchor Books.

Carpenter, E. (1974). *Oh, what a blow the phantom gave me.* New York, NY: Bantam.

Carter, B. (2004). 'Friends' finale's audience is fourth biggest ever. *The New York Times.* Retrieved May 8, 2004, from http://www.nytimes.com

Carter, B. (2008, November 17). No mystery: Ratings heat up for 'NCIS.' *The New York Times.* Retrieved November 17, 2008, from http://www.nytimes.com

Carter, B. (2011, March 23). CNN leads in cable news as MSNBC loses ground. *The New York Times.* Retrieved April 5, 2011, from http://www.nytimes.com

Carter, B. (2011, April 24). DVRs give more shows a lifeline. *The New York Times.* Retrieved April 27, 2011, from http://www.nytimes.com

Carter, B., & Stelter, B. (2011, May 16). After weak season, networks strive for fresh ideas. *The New York Times.* Retrieved May 16, 2011, from http://www.nytimes.com

Carter B., & Vega, T. (2011, May 14). In shift, ads try to entice over-55 set. *The New York Times.* Retrieved May 14, 2011, from http://www.nytimes.com

Carter, C. (2001, April 23). Lecture at Montana State University, Bozeman.

Casey, B., Casey, N., Calvert, B., French, L., & Lewis, J. (2002). *Television studies: The key concepts.* London, England: Routledge.

Cavanaugh, T. (2006, August/September). Happy 40th birthday Star Trek. *Reason,* 57–64.

Champagne, C. (2010). Another round of reinvention at MTV. *Emmy, 32*(3), 56.

Chocano, C. (2004, June 4). Heartless hit. *Los Angeles Times,* pp. E1 & E25.

Ciesielski, D. (1999). Secular pragmatism: Kenneth Burke and the [Re]socialization of literature and theory. In B. L. Brock (Ed.), *Kenneth Burke and the 21st century* (pp. 243–267). Albany: State University of New York Press.

Collins, J. (1992). Postmodernism and television. In R. C. Allen (Ed.), *Channels of discourse* (pp. 327–353). Chapel Hill: The University of North Carolina Press.

comScore Releases March 2011 U.S. Search Engine Rankings. (2011, April 13). Retrieved April 13, 2011, from http://www.comscore.com

Couldry, N. (2000). *Inside culture: Re-imagining the method of cultural studies.* London, England: Sage.

Creating prime-time drama: *Law & Order* (1997, November 11). [University satellite seminar]. Beverly Hills, CA: Museum of Television and Radio.

Creating prime-time comedy: *The Simpsons* (2003, February 12). [Brochure]. Beverly Hills, CA: Museum of Television and Radio.

Creeber, G. (Ed.). (2008). *The television genre book* (2nd ed.). London, England: British Film Institute.

Cruz, J., & Lewis, J. (Eds.). (1999). *Viewing, reading, listening: Audiences and cultural reception.* Boulder, CO: Westview Press.

Cunningham, S. (2005). Culture, services, knowledge: Television between policy regimes. In J. Wasko (Ed.), *A companion to television* (pp. 199–215). Malden, MA: Blackwell.

Darcy, J. (1997). *The prophetic tradition and radical rhetoric in America.* New York: New York University Press.

Dawes, A. (2010). Only 2 will do. *Emmy, 32*(3), 191.

della Cava, M. R. (2011, March 29). Like its characters, TV's 'Parenthood' struggles. *USAToday.* Retrieved from http://www.usatoday.com

Della Femina, J. (2001, January 26). The final score: Beer 21, dot coms 0. *The Wall Street Journal,* p. A14.

Deming, C. J. (1990). For television-centered television criticism: Lessons from feminism. In M. E. Brown (Ed.), *Television and women's culture.* Newbury Park, CA: Sage.

Deming, C. (2005). Locating the televisual in Golden Age television. In J. Wasko (Ed.), *A companion to television.* Malden, MA: Blackwell.

Dines, G., & Humez, J. M. (Eds.). (2011). *Gender, race, and class in media* (3rd ed.). Thousand Oaks, CA: Sage.

Dow, B. J. (2001, June). Television and the politics of gay and lesbian visibility. *Critical Studies in Media Communication, 18,* 123–140.

Edgerton, G. R., & Rose, B. G. (2008). *Thinking outside the box: A contemporary genre reader.* Lexington: University Press of Kentucky.

Evans, J., & Hall, S. (Eds.). (1999). *Visual culture: The reader.* London, England: Sage.

Farhi, P. (1997, May 12). The eye that never blinks. *The Washington Post National Weekly Edition,* p. 21.

Farhi, P. (1998, June 22). TV violence: It's not all on the same wavelength. *The Washington Post National Weekly Edition,* p. 21.

Farhi, P. (2000, February 21). TV's skin-deep approach to race. *The Washington Post National Weekly Edition,* p. 23.

Federal Communications Commission (FCC). (2011, March 1). Regulation of obscenity, indecency, and profanity. Retrieved April 16, 2011, from http://fcc.gov/eb/oip

Fejes, F. (2003). Advertising and the political economy of lesbian/gay identity. In G. Dines & J. M. Humez (Eds.), *Gender, race, and class in media* (pp. 212–222). Thousand Oaks, CA: Sage.

Fernandez, M. E. (2005, February 13). *Lost* takes an odd path to diversity. *Los Angeles Times,* pp. E1, E30.

Fernandez, M. E. (2005, May 11). *Raymond*'s writers get ideas from their families. *Los Angeles Times,* p. E7.

Fisher, W. R. (1989). *Human communication as narration: Toward a philosophy of reason, value, and action.* Columbia: University of South Carolina Press.

Fiske, J. (1996). Opening the hallway: Some remarks on the fertility of Stuart Hall's contribution to critical theory. In D. Morley & K. Chen (Eds.), *Stuart Hall: Critical dialogues in cultural studies* (pp. 212–220). London, England: Routledge.

Fiske, J. (1998). MTV: Post-structural, post-modern. In A. A. Berger (Ed.), *The postmodern presence: Readings on postmodernism in American culture and society* (pp. 166–179). Walnut Creek, CA: Altamira Press.

Fiske, J. (2011). *Television culture* (2nd ed.). London, England: Methuen.

Flaherty, M. (2011). It's a Guido world. *Emmy, 33,* 1.

Foote, J. S. (Ed.). (1998). *Live from the trenches: The changing role of the television news correspondent.* Carbondale: Southern Illinois University Press.

Foss, S. K. (2004). *Rhetorical criticism: Exploration and practice* (3rd ed.). Long Grove, IL: Waveland.

Franklin, N. (2006, February 20). Bauer power: A new day dawns on 24. *The New Yorker,* p. 174.

From pitch to polish: The collaborative process. (1996, January 16). [Seminar on videotape]. Beverly Hills, CA: Museum of Television and Radio.

The future [3rd of three seminars with Joshua Brand and John Falsey]. (1993, February 11). [Seminar on videotape]. Beverly Hills, CA: Museum of Television and Radio.

Gallagher, V. (2004). Memory as social action: Cultural projection and generic form in civil rights memorials. In P. A. Sullivan & S. R. Goldzwig (Eds.), *New approaches to rhetoric* (pp. 149–172). Thousand Oaks, CA: Sage.

Gans, H. J. (1979). *Deciding what's news: A study of CBS Evening News, NBC Nightly News, Newsweek, and Time.* New York, NY: Random House.

Gans, H. J. (2003). *Democracy and the news.* New York, NY: Oxford University Press.

Gans, H. J. (2005, 1979). *Deciding what's news: A study of CBS Evening News, NBC Nightly News, Newsweek, and Time.* Evanston, IL: Northwestern University Press.

Garron, B. (2008). Pass the remote and the bifocals. *Emmy, 30*(5).

Garron, B. (2011). Boomer bonanza. *Emmy, 33*(1), 19.

Geraghty, L., & Jancovich, M. (2008). *The shifting definitions of genre.* Jefferson, NC: McFarland.

Gerbner, G., Gross, L., Signorelli, N., Morgan, M., & Jackson-Beeck, M. (1979, Summer). The demonstration of power: Violence profile No. 10. *Journal of Communication, 29,* 177–196.

Gergen, K. J. (1991). *The saturated self: Dilemmas of identity in contemporary life.* New York, NY: Basic Books.

Gitlin, T. (1983). *Inside prime time.* New York, NY: Pantheon Books.

Gitlin, T. (1998). Postmodernism: What are they talking about? In A. A. Berger (Ed.), *The postmodern presence: Readings on postmodernism in American culture and society* (pp. 58–73). Walnut Creek, CA: Altamira Press.

Gliatto, T. (2002, October 14). The dead zone. *People,* 113–115.

Golden, J. L., & Corbett, P. J. (1968). *The rhetoric of Blair, Campbell, and Whately.* New York, NY: Holt, Rinehart and Winston.

Government demand soap opera end. (2011, January 15). *Bozeman Daily Chronicle,* p. A4.

Grossberg, L. (1996). On postmodernism and articulation: An interview with Stuart Hall. In D. Morley & K. Chen (Eds.), *Stuart Hall: Critical dialogues in cultural studies* (pp. 131–150). London, England: Routledge.

Grover, R. (1997, June 2). The art of the TV deal. *Business Week,* p. 121.

Haigh, R. W., Gerbner, G., & Byrne, R. B. (1981). *Communications in the 21st century.* New York, NY: John Wiley.

Hall, S. (1997). *Representation: Cultural representations and signifying practices.* Thousand Oaks, CA: Sage.

Hall, S. (1999). Introduction to looking and subjectivity. In J. Evans & S. Hall (Eds.), *Visual culture: The reader.* London, England: Sage.

Hart, R. P. (1989). *Modern rhetorical criticism.* Glenview, IL: Scott, Foresman/Little Brown.

Hart, R. P. (1990). *Modern rhetorical criticism.* Glenview, IL: Scott, Foresman/Little Brown.

Haynes Johnson delivers the Annenberg lecture (1994). *Newslink, 4*(1), 5.

Hayward, J. W. (1997). *Letters to Vanessa: On love, science, and awareness in an enchanted world.* Boston, MA: Shambhala.

Heath, R. L. (1986). *Realism and relativism: A perspective on Kenneth Burke.* Macon, GA: Mercer.

Hendrickson, P. (2010). Pumping up out-of-home ads. *Emmy, 32*(3), 28.

Higgins, J. (1999). *Raymond Williams: Literature, Marxism, and cultural materialism.* London, England: Routledge.

Hilliard, R. L. (2008). *Writing for television, radio, and new media*. Boston, MA: Thomson Wadsworth.

Hirsch, E. (1999). *How to read a poem and fall in love with poetry*. New York, NY: Harcourt Brace.

Hoffman, J. (2011, April 29). 'The Good Wife' and Its Women. *The New York Times*. Retrieved May 1, 2011, from http://nytimes.com

Honan, E. (2010, April 11). 'Army Wives' offers military spouses an outlet for their daily stress. *The Washington Post*. Retrieved April 11, 2010, from http://www.washingtonpost.com

How Roy Wagner reveals the souls of characters on *House*. (2005, October 3). *In Camera*.

Hunt, D. M. (2005). *Channeling blackness: Studies on television and race in America*. New York, NY: Oxford University Press.

Jackman, I. (2010). *House, M.D.: The official guide to the hit medical drama*. New York, NY: Harper Collins.

Jameson, F. (1993). Postmodernism and the consumer society. In E. A. Kaplan (Ed.), *Postmodernism and its discontents: Theories, practices* (pp. 13–29). New York, NY: Verso.

Jasinski, J. (2001). *Sourcebook on rhetoric: Key concepts in contemporary rhetorical studies*. Thousand Oaks, CA: Sage.

Jencks, C. (1989). *What is post-modernism?* (3rd ed.). London, England: St. Martin's Press.

'Jeopardy!' star Jennings gives show a boost (2004, July 25). *Bozeman Daily Chronicle*, p. A2.

Jones, L. (1996). "Last week we had an omen": The mythological X-Files. In D. Lavery, A. Hague, & M. Cartwright (Eds.), *Deny all knowledge: Reading The X-Files*. Syracuse, NY: Syracuse University Press.

Jowett, G. S., & O'Donnell, V. (2007). *Propaganda and persuasion*. Thousand Oaks, CA: Sage.

Jung, C. G. (1969). *Four archetypes: Mother/rebirth/spirit/trickster*. Princeton, NJ: Princeton University Press.

Jung, C. G. (1971). *The portable Jung* (R. F. C. Hull, Trans.). New York, NY: Viking Press.

Kaminsky, S. M., & Mahan, J. (1985). *American television genres*. Chicago, IL: Nelson-Hall.

Kaplan, A. E. (Ed.). (1993). *Postmodernism and its discontents: Theories, practices*. New York, NY: Verso.

Kaplan, A. E. (1998). Feminism/Oedipus/postmodernism: The Case of MTV. In A. A. Berger (Ed.), *The postmodern presence: Readings on postmodernism in American culture and society* (pp. 30–44). Walnut Creek, CA: Altamira Press.

Kellner, D. (2005). Critical perspectives on television from the Frankfurt School to postmodernism. In J. Wasko (Ed.), *A companion to television* (pp. 29–50). Malden, MA: Blackwell.

Kolbert, E. (1994, April 6). Finding the absolutely perfect actor: The high-stress business of casting. *The New York Times*, pp. C13 & C18.

Krieger, M. (Ed.). (1987). *The aims of representation: Subject/text/history*. New York, NY: Columbia University Press.

Kubey, R. (2004). *Creating television: Conversations with the people behind 50 years of American TV*. Mahwah, NJ: Lawrence Erlbaum.

Kubey, R., & Csikszentmihalyi, M. (1990). *Television and the quality of life: How viewing shapes everyday experience*. Mahwah, NJ: Lawrence Erlbaum.

Kuchler, S., & Mellion, W. (1991). *Images of memory: On remembering and representation*. Washington, DC: Smithsonian Institution Press.

Kuypers, J. A. (2010). Framing analysis from a rhetorical perspective. In P. D. Angelo & J. A. Kuypers (Eds.), *Doing news framing analysis*. London, England: Routledge.

Leverette, M., Ott, B. L., & Buckley, C. L. (Eds.). (2008). *It's not TV: Watching HBO in the post-television era*. New York, NY: Routledge.

Lewis, J. (2008). *Cultural studies: The basics* (2nd ed.). London, England: Sage.

Lipsitz, G. (1990). *Time passages: Collective memory and American popular culture*. Minneapolis: University of Minnesota Press.

Lometti, G. E. (1997). Audience research: Industry and market analysis. In H. Newcomb (Ed.), *Encyclopedia of television* (Vol. 1, p. 112). Chicago, IL: Fitzroy Dearborn.

Longworth, J. L., Jr. (2002). *TV creators: Conversations with America's top producers of television drama* (vol. 2). Syracuse, NY: Syracuse University Press.

Lorenzo-Dus, N. (2009). *Television discourse: Analyzing language in the media.* New York, NY: Palgrave Macmillan.

MacNeil/Lehrer News Hour. (1989). [Seminar on videotape] Beverly Hills, CA: Museum of Television and Radio.

The making of a prime-time schedule. (1997, October 15). (University satellite seminar). Beverly Hills, CA: Museum of Television and Radio.

Malinowski, B. (1961). *Sex, culture, and myth.* New York, NY: Harcourt, Brace, and World.

Manly, L. (2010, May 16). The men who made ABC's 'Lost' last. *The New York Times,* pp. 1–8. Retrieved May 16, 2010, from http://www.nytimes.com

Marc, D. (1984). *Demographic vistas: Television in American culture.* Philadelphia: University of Pennsylvania Press.

Marc, D. (1989). *Comic visions: Television comedy and American culture.* Boston: Unwin Hyman.

Marc, D. (1995). *Bonfire of the humanities: Television, subliteracy, and long-term memory* (pp. 53–56). Syracuse, NY: Syracuse University Press.

Marc, D., & Thompson, R. J. (1995). *Prime time, prime movers* (p. 223). Syracuse, NY: Syracuse University Press.

Marrinan, C. (2006). *Ultimate CSI: Crime scene investigation.* New York, NY: DK Adult.

May, R. (1991). *The cry for myth.* New York, NY: W. W. Norton.

McCarthy, M. (2004). Ad buyers bet on what will hit for new TV season. *USA Today,* 27 May, p. 6B.

McDowell, J. (2008). Hate to love 'em, love to hate 'em. *Emmy, 30*(2), 47–49.

McDowell, J., & Ressner, J. (2006, April). Brave new TV land. *Time Bonus Section,* pp. A1–A6.

McQuail, D. (2010). *McQuail's mass communication theory* (6th ed.). Thousand Oaks, CA: Sage.

Mead, G. H. (1934). *Mind, self, and society.* Chicago, IL: University of Chicago Press.

Meehan, E. R. (2005). *Why TV is not our fault.* Lanham, MD: Rowman & Littlefield.

Metzler, K. (1979). *Newsgathering.* Englewood Cliffs, NJ: Prentice-Hall.

Meyrowitz, J. (1985). *No sense of place.* Oxford, UK: Oxford University Press.

Mindlin, A. (2011, April 17). Tracking TV habits by ethnic groups. *The New York Times.* Retrieved April 18, 2011, from http://www.nytimes.com

Mitchell, W. J. T. (1995). *Picture theory: Essays on verbal and visual representation.* Chicago, IL: University of Chicago Press.

Mittell, J. (2004). *Genre and television: From cop shows to cartoons in American culture.* New York, NY: Routledge.

Monaco, P. (1998). *Understanding society, culture, and television.* Westport, CT: Praeger.

Morley, D. (1988). *Family television: Cultural power and domestic leisure.* London, England: Routledge.

Morley, D., & Chen, K. (Eds.). (1996). *Stuart Hall: Critical dialogues in cultural studies.* London, England: Routledge.

Nakashima, R. (2010, October 27). Spats mean fewer TV shows on web. *Bozeman Daily Chronicle,* p. D2.

Nehamas, A. (1990). Serious watching. *South Atlantic Quarterly, 89*(1), 157–180.

Newcomb, H. (Ed.). (1997). *Encyclopedia of television* (3 vols., p. 1482). Chicago, IL: Fitzroy Dearborn.

Newcomb, H. (Ed.). (2000). *Television: The critical view* (6th ed.). New York, NY: Oxford University Press.

Newcomb, H. (2005). Reflections on TV: The most popular art. In G. R. Edgerton & B. G. Rose (Eds.), *Thinking outside the box: A contemporary genre reader* (pp. 17–36). Lexington: University Press of Kentucky.

Newcomb, H., & Alley, R. S. (1983). *The producer's medium: Conversations with creators of American TV.* New York, NY: Oxford University Press.

O'Donnell, V. (1988). Dreams can come true for little girls too. In L. E. Rohler & R. Cook (Eds.), *Great speeches for criticism and analysis.* Greenwood, IN: Alistair Press.

O'Donnell, V. (1996, August 13). Interview with James Burrows. Hollywood, CA.

O'Donnell, V. (2004, May 15). Interview with Jeff Meyer. Los Angeles, CA.

O'Donnell, V., & Kable, J. (1982). *Persuasion: An interactive-dependence approach.* New York, NY: Random House.

Olson, L. C, Finnegan, C. A., & Hope, D. S. (2008). *Visual rhetoric.* Thousand Oaks, CA: Sage.

Ostrow, J. (2001, July 22). Hybrids old but different. *Denver Post,* pp. 1E, 7E.

O'Sullivan, T., Hartley, J., Saunders, D., Montgomery, M., & Fiske, J. (Eds.). (1994). *Key concepts in communication and cultural studies* (2nd ed.). London, England: Routledge.

Ott, B., & Walter, C. (2000). Intertextuality: Interpretative practice and textual strategy. *Critical studies in mass communication, 17*(4), 429–446.

Parade. (2007, December 30). p. 2.

PBS *Masterpiece* viewership. (2011, April 12). Retrieved April 21, 2011, from http://www.pbs.org

Pecora, N. (2005). The changing face of children's television. In G. R. Edgerton & B. G. Rose (Eds.), *Thinking outside the box: A contemporary genre reader* (pp. 91–110). Lexington: University Press of Kentucky.

Pomerantz, E. (2006). Why do advertisers still covet the 18–49s? *Television Quarterly, 36*(3 & 4), 40–44.

Poniewozik, J. (2010, March 22). The world wide living room. *Time,* p. 21.

Porter, M. (1998). The structure of television narratives. In L. R. Vande Berg, L. A. Wenner, & B. E. Gronbeck (Eds.), *Critical approaches to television.* Boston, MA: Houghton Mifflin.

Pourray, J. (1995). *Behind the scenes at ER.* New York: Ballantine Books.

Powers, L. (2010, October 27). *The most watched show among those 18–49.* Retrieved April 1, 2011, from http://www.hollywoodreporter.com

Propp, V. (1968). *Morphology of the folktale* (2nd ed.; L. Scott, Trans.). Austin: University of Texas Press.

Pusheck, C. (2010). *Emmy, 32*(3), 49.

Ray, R. B. (1985). *A certain tendency of the Hollywood cinema: 1930–1980.* Princeton, NJ: Princeton University Press.

Redmond, S., & Holmes, S. (Eds.). (2007). *Stardom and celebrity.* Thousand Oaks, CA: Sage.

Reed, J. S. (1986). *Southern folk, plain & fancy: Native white social types.* Athens: University of Georgia Press.

Reuters, S. G. (2001). School violence replayed in TV dramas. Britannica.com. Retrieved June 1, 2001 from www.britannica....ews/reuters/article?story_id = 163923

Roberts, R. (2007). Color guard. *Emmy, 29*(4), 56–67.

Rose, B. G. (Ed.). (1985). *TV genres: A handbook and reference guide.* Westport, CT: Greenwood Press.

Rosteck, T. (Ed.). (1999). *At the intersection: Cultural studies and rhetorical studies.* New York, NY: Guilford Press.

Rudolph, I. (2010, November 1–7). Three's company. *TV Guide, 58*(44), 22–25.

Samuels, A., Shorter, B., & Plaut, F. (1987). *A critical dictionary of Jungian analysis* (pp. 152–153). New York, NY: Routledge.

Scholes, R., & Kellogg, R. (1966). *The nature of narrative.* London, England: Oxford University Press.

Searle, J. R. (1979). *Expression and meaning: Studies in the theory of speech acts.* Cambridge, UK: Cambridge University Press.

Searle, J. R. (1984). *Minds, brains, and science.* Cambridge, MA: Harvard University Press.

Seiter, E., & Wilson, M. J. (2005). Soap opera survival tactics. In G. R. Edgerton & B. G. Rose (Eds.), *Thinking outside the box: A contemporary genre reader* (pp. 136–155). Lexington: University Press of Kentucky.

Silverstone, R. (1999). *Why study the media?* London, England: Sage.

Simon, R. (2005). The changing definition of reality television. In G. R. Edgerton & B. G. Rose (Eds.), *Thinking outside the box: A contemporary genre reader* (pp. 179–200). Lexington: University Press of Kentucky.

Singer, J. A., & Salovey, P. (1993). *The remembered self: Emotion and memory in personality.* New York, NY: Free Press.

Slate, L. (2011). For *Wife,* character is the key. *Emmy, 33*(2), 66–67.

Smith, R. R. (1976). *Beyond the wasteland: The criticism of broadcasting.* Falls Church, VA: National Communication Association.

Smith-Shomade, B. E. (2002). *Shaded lives: African-American women and television.* New Brunswick, NJ: Rutgers University Press.

Solomon, J. (1998). Our decentered culture: The postmodern world view. In A. A. Berger (Ed.), *The postmodern presence: Readings on postmodernism in American culture and society.* Walnut Creek, CA: Altamira Press.

Spigel, L., & Olsson, J. (Eds.). (2004). *Television after TV: Essays on a medium in transition.* Durham, NC: Duke University Press.

Stanley, A. (2010, August 20). Yes, they're sleazy, but not originals. *The New York Times.* Retrieved August 21, 2010, from http://www.nytimes.com

Stark, S. D. (1997). *Glued to the set: The 60 television shows and events that made us who we are today.* New York, NY: Free Press.

Stein, J. (2003, May 5). TV's top gun. *Time,* pp. 71–72.

Stelter, B. (2011, March 29). Season 5 of 'Mad Men' is delayed until 2012. *The New York Times.* Retrieved August 4, 2011, from http://www.nytimes.com

Stelter, B., & Carter, B. (2010, May 15). One "Law & Order" gets the death sentence, as another joins the force. *The New York Times,* pp. 1–4. Retrieved May 15, 2010, from http://www.nytimes.com

Stempel, T. (1996). *Storytellers to the nation: A history of American television writing* (p. 237). Syracuse, NY: Syracuse University Press.

Television and the mind, the infinite mind. (2002, October 2). New York, NY: Lichtenstein Creative Media. Broadcast on National Public Radio.

The Thursday factor. (2005, June 5). *TV Guide,* p. 10.

Timberg, B. (2000). The unspoken rules of television talk. In H. Newcomb (Ed.), *Television: The critical view* (6th ed.). New York, NY: Oxford University Press.

Toff, B. (2011, May 3). A good night for ABC. *The New York Times.* Retrieved May 4, 2011, http://www.nytimes.com

Tomashoff, C. (2011). Tell it to me one more time. *Emmy, 33*(1), 10.

Towner, E. (2010, May 10). *Apologetic rhetoric.* Retrieved from http://www.emiltowner.com

Turner, C. R. (2002, November 23). Product placement of medical products. Presented at the conference of the National Communication Association, New Orleans, LA.

Unger, A. (1997). It's the writing, stupid. *Television Quarterly, 4,* 10–23.

Vedantam, S. (2001, November 19–25). A hit to our psyche. *The Washington Post National Weekly Edition,* p. 34.

Viewer reaction saves *Cagney & Lacey.* (1984, February 17). *Dallas Morning News,* p. C11.

Wallace, K. (1971). The substance of rhetoric: Good reasons. In R. L. Johannesen (Ed.), *Contemporary theories of rhetoric: Selected readings.* New York, NY: Harper and Row.

Watson, J., & Hill, A. (2003). *Dictionary of media and communication studies* (6th ed.). London, England: Arnold.

Webb, J. (2009). *Understanding representation*. Thousand Oaks, CA: Sage.

Webster, J. G., Phalen, P. F., & Lichty, L. W. (2000). *Ratings analysis: The theory and practice of audience research* (2nd ed). Mahwah, NJ: Lawrence Erlbaum.

Wells, W., Burnett, J., & Moriarty, S. (2002). *Advertising: Principles and practices* (6th ed., p. 271). Upper Saddle River, NJ: Prentice Hall.

Wilkins, L., & Patterson, P. (1987, Summer). Risk analysis and the construction of news. *Journal of Communication, 37*(3), 80–92.

The William S. Paley Television Festival. (2001, March 3). CSI: Crime scene. #63602. [Seminar on videotape]. Beverly Hills, CA: Museum of Television and Radio.

Williams, R. (1974). *Television: Technology and cultural form*. London, England: Fontana.

Williams, R. (1989). Drama in a dramatised society. In A. O'Connor (Ed.), *Raymond Williams on television* (pp. 3–13). London, England: Routledge.

Wollen, P. (1997). Ways of thinking about music video (and postmodernism). In P. Brooker & W. Brooker (Eds.), *Postmodern after-images: A reader in film, television and video* (pp. 229–232). London, England: Arnold.

Writers Guild of the East. (n.d.). *The Late Show With David Letterman*. Museum of Television and Radio, New York, NY.

Wykes, M., & Gunter, B. (2005). *The media and body image: If looks could kill*. Thousand Oaks, CA: Sage.

Index

About the Author

Victoria O'Donnell is Professor Emerita and former director of the University Honors Program and Professor of Communication at Montana State University–Bozeman. She teaches a seminar in television criticism for the School of Film and Photography at Montana State University. Previously she was the chair of the Department of Speech Communication at Oregon State University and chair of the Department of Communication and Public Address at the University of North Texas. In 1988 she taught for the American Institute of Foreign Studies at the University of London. She received her PhD from the Pennsylvania State University. She has published articles and chapters in a wide range of journals and books on topics concerning persuasion, the social effects of media, women in film and television, British politics, Nazi propaganda, collective memory, cultural studies theory, and science fiction films of the 1950s. She is also the author (with June Kable) of *Persuasion: An Interactive-Dependency Approach, Propaganda and Persuasion* (with Garth Jowett), *Readings in Propaganda and Persuasion: New and Classic Essays* (co-edited with Garth Jowett), *Television Criticism,* and *Speech Communication.* She made a film, *Women, War, and Work: Shaping Space for Productivity in the Shipyards During World War II,* for PBS through KUSM Public Television at Montana State University. She has also written television scripts for environmental films and has done voice-overs for several PBS films. She served on editorial boards of several journals. The recipient of numerous research grants, honors, and teaching awards, including being awarded the Honor Professorship at North Texas State University and the Montana State University Alumni Association and Bozeman Chamber of Commerce Award of Excellence, she has been a Danforth Foundation Associate and a Summer Scholar of the National Endowment for the Humanities. She has taught in Germany and has been a visiting lecturer at universities in Denmark, Norway, Sweden, and Wales. She has also served as a private consultant to the U.S. government, a state senator, the tobacco litigation plaintiffs, and many American corporations. She is an active volunteer with Intermountain Therapy Animals, taking her golden retriever, Argus, to the elementary schools where the children read to the dog in the R.E.A.D. program. She writes children's stories about Argus.

$SAGE research methods online

The essential tool for researchers . . .

. . . from the world's leading research methods publisher

Discover SRMO Lists— methods readings suggested by other SRMO users

"I have never really seen anything like this product before, and I think it is really valuable."

John Creswell, University of Nebraska–Lincoln

Find exactly what you are looking for, from basic explanations to advanced discussion

Explore the Methods Map to discover links between methods

Watch video interviews with leading methodologists

Search on a newly designed taxonomy with more than 1,400 qualitative, quantitative, and mixed methods terms

Uncover more than 100,000 pages of book, journal, and reference content to support your learning

find out more at
www.srmo.sagepub.com